Proclaiming Jesus Christ

Evangelicals and Catholics in Dialogue III

PROCLAIMING JESUS CHRIST

Catholic *and* Evangelical Perspectives *on* Evangelization

edited by
Steven Hoskins *and* Christian D. Washburn

SAINT PAUL SEMINARY PRESS

SAINT PAUL, MINNESOTA • 2026

Published 2026 by
Saint Paul Seminary Press
2260 Summit Ave., Saint Paul, Minnesota 55105

Library of Congress Control Number: 2026930263
LC record available at https://lccn.loc.gov/2026930263

ISBN 979-8-218-71695-0 (paperback)
ISBN 979-8-218-71696-7 (e-book)

spspress.com

Dedicated to Fr. Walter Kedjierski

Contents

Foreword

THIS IS THE THIRD VOLUME to be published as the fruit of the ongoing National Evangelical-Catholic Dialogue. In the first book, *Justified in Jesus Christ: Evangelicals and Catholics in Dialogue*, Christians from various faith traditions reflected on the nature of soteriology and justification. Subsequent rounds of conversations gave rise to the second book, *Walking with Jesus Christ: Catholic and Evangelical Visions of the Moral Life*, in which the group wrestled with many contested questions about the nature of the human person and the moral consequences of our life in Christ.

In this third book, *Proclaiming Jesus Christ: Catholic and Evangelical Perspectives on Evangelization*, the group examines various issues that arise from the Great Commission that was given us by Jesus Christ. How can we best proclaim the good news of the love that God has shown us in his incarnate Son, to a world that desperately needs to hear this kerygma, this good news that will thoroughly transform the hearts and minds of all who dare to embrace it? Many of us, Evangelicals and Catholics together, strive to find ways to proclaim the living Christ anew to those whose ears have been deafened by the din of secular ideologies.

As is typical of ecumenical dialogues that are undertaken with honesty and good will, the participants of the National Evangelical-Catholic Dialogue discerned many moments of profound agreement, of shared joy in the Risen Christ, moments that were sometimes surprising and energizing, while still acknowledging, with clarity and charity, those positions that still keep us from perfect unity.

This text is the work of many gifted and dedicated persons. Although the contributors to this volume—pastors, theologians, and other scholars—strive to work as faithful leaders within their respective ecclesial traditions, they speak here for themselves, and not in any official capacity for their affiliated institutions or faith communities. The members of the dialogue hope this book will provide a fruitful starting point for future conversations between Evangelicals and Catholics as we strive together to proclaim Christ to the world.

We would like to thank all those who have made this work possible. We are most grateful for the hospitality extended to us by The Saint Paul Seminary in St. Paul, Minnesota, and for the invaluable support offered by the Rector there, the Reverend Joseph C. Taphorn, JCL. We also wish to thank the following for their invaluable assistance in fostering this ongoing dialogue and for helping to prepare this work for publication: Gretchen K. Washburn, Kathryn Wehr, Erika Zabinski, Sibyl Niemann, and Judy Gilats.

May the Lord bless all of us, writers and readers of this book, as we continue this dialogue and work together toward a deeper unity between us, a unity that will bear witness to the life of Christ within each of us. May the world look upon our work and exclaim: "Behold how these Christians love one another!"

Most Reverend Alfred A. Schlert
Bishop, Allentown, PA
U.S. Conference of Catholic Bishops Committee for Ecumenical and Interreligious Affairs
Catholic Chair

Reverend Bruce N. G. Cromwell, PhD
Superintendent, Central Region Conference
Free Methodist Church–USA
Protestant Chair

Evangelization and Friendship

> "Go therefore and make disciples of all nations, baptizing them in the name of the Father and of the Son and of the Holy Spirit, teaching them to observe all that I have commanded you. And behold, I am with you always, to the end of the age." (Matt 28:19–20).

THIS BOOK, *Proclaiming Jesus Christ: Catholic and Evangelical Visions of Evangelization*, is the fruit of the National Evangelical-Catholic Dialogue's common commitment to Jesus Christ and a desire to fulfill his Great Commission to the church at the end of his earthly ministry. The common statements are indicative of our shared commitment to evangelization, even if we sometimes have understood this commitment and how it is to be achieved differently. As in the last round of the dialogue on the moral life, there was an exciting amount of convergence. That convergence and the shared vision of evangelism among our communions is, in many ways, indicative of where the dialogue has come after many years together and the common commitment we share to the Gospel.

This dialogue began as a regional Evangelical-Catholic dialogue in 1993. For many years this dialogue gathered for annual meetings, discussing a new topic every year. In 2014, the dialogue made the decision to move to the format of having "rounds," i.e., a series of annual meetings focused on a particular topic, and that has helped the dialogue mature in its common work and proven productive in issuing common statements and books that reflect the dialogue's proceedings and the papers given.

In the first round, lasting from 2014 to 2017, the dialogue took up the issue of justification. Each year some aspect of the doctrine of justification was examined. These meetings were held on the campus of the University of Mary in Bismarck, ND. The result was our first volume, *Justified in Jesus Christ: Evangelicals and Catholics in Dialogue*, which was published in 2017, the 500th anniversary of the Protestant Reformation.[1]

In 2017, the dialogue moved back to The Saint Paul Seminary at the University of St. Thomas in St. Paul, MN, the original site of its beginnings. The dialogue decided to discuss the moral life for its second round, which lasted from 2017 to 2021. The topic was chosen because the dialogue members hoped that there would be significant convergences on the issue between Catholics and Evangelicals, and indeed there were. Those many convergences reflected the commitment of Evangelicals and Catholics to faithfully adhere to the word of God and make faithful Christian disciples. The fruit of this dialogue was *Walking with Jesus Christ: Catholic and Evangelical Visions of the Moral Life*, published in 2024.[2]

After the successful completion of that round, the dialogue decided that the topic of the third round would be evangelization. Again, we hoped that there would be significant points of convergence. In three meetings held at The Saint Paul Seminary, the dialogue discussed three aspects of evangelization: evangelization and doctrine (spring 2023), evangelization and salvation (fall 2023), and evangelization and culture (fall 2024). At each of these meetings, both Evangelical and Catholic members presented background papers on that meeting's topic. These formed the basis of that meeting's discussion and served as the starting point for constructing a common statement presenting points of convergence and divergence.

The Catholic essays offered during this round of the dialogue begin with the contributions of Catholic theologians Daniel Keating and Christian D. Washburn, who examine the nature of evangelization and the role of doctrine in it (spring 2023). Michael Sirilla and Mary Healy then examine evangelization and salvation as presented in

1. Steven Hoskins and David Fleischacker, eds., *Justified in Jesus Christ: Evangelicals and Catholics in Dialogue* (University of Mary Press, 2017).

2. Steven Hoskins and Christian D. Washburn, eds., *Walking with Jesus Christ: Catholic and Evangelical Visions of the Moral Life* (Saint Paul Seminary Press, 2024).

Scripture and the doctrine of the Catholic Church (fall 2023). Finally, Daniel Keating and William Stevenson discuss what "culture" is and what it means to evangelize in a particular cultural context (2024).

The Evangelical essays presented to the group begin with the contribution of Evangelical theologians Gregg Allison and M. William Ury, who jointly discuss what evangelization is and the interaction between evangelization and doctrine from their denomination's perspective (2023). Dennis Jowers next discusses the destiny of the unevangelized from a Reformed perspective, and Alex Mayfield provides a Pentecostal perspective on justification and evangelization (2023). Finally, Dean Erickson and Steve Hoskins discuss evangelization and culture from the perspectives of the Christian and Missionary Alliance and the Wesleyan tradition (2024).

The Catholic participants were chaired by the Most Reverend David Kagan, Bishop of the Diocese of Bismarck, North Dakota (2023) and the Most Rev. Alfred A. Schlert, Bishop of Allentown (2024). Reverend Walter F. Kedjierski, Executive Director of the Secretariat of Ecumenical and Interreligious Affairs for the USCCB, was an encouraging and insightful presence. The Evangelicals were chaired by Bruce Cromwell, Superintendent of the Central Region Conference of the Free Methodist Church, with participants coming from a variety of Evangelical churches and communions throughout the United States.

This book is the fruit of the work on the round on evangelization and the many years we have worked together to achieve common understanding. It is composed in the same format as its two predecessors. This book contains the convergence statements drafted at the end of each meeting, followed by the background papers that formed the basis for the discussion that led to the convergence statement. The book also includes a list of those who participated in the dialogue in the three sessions from 2023–2024.

As was noted in our first volume, "Christian dialogue, especially ecumenical dialogue, is a testament to friendship."[3] Our dialogue

3. Steven Hoskins, "A Dialogue in Testament to Friendship," in *Justified in Jesus Christ: Evangelicals and Catholics in Dialogue*, 5.

is not an ecumenism of hate; instead, it springs from the common belief that Christ is Lord and that he desires that "all Christians be one" (John 17:21). This firm conviction leads our members to undertake ecumenical dialogue as a means to this end. Through dialogue and prayer, the members of the dialogue over the years have become friends. The friendship we share in the happiness of ecumenical work has built up the conditions for deeper dialogue and sharing the concerns and commitments among us as we share Christ with the world. As a result, we are able to recognize significant convergences in the arena of evangelization and offer them here in a humble spirit, thankful for the work we are called to in him.

Steven Hoskins, PhD
Trevecca Nazarene University

Christian D. Washburn, PhD
Saint Paul Seminary School of Divinity
University of St. Thomas

Abbreviations

AB	*Anchor Bible*
ANF	Ante-Nicene Fathers, ed. Alexander Roberts, James Donaldson, and A. Cleveland Coxe (Buffalo, NY: Christian Literature Publishing Co., 1885)
CCSL	Corpus Christianorum: Series Latina
CCSS	Catholic Commentary on Sacred Scripture
CDF	Congregation for the Doctrine of the Faith
CSEL	Corpus Scriptorum Ecclesiasticorum Latinorum
DH	Heinrich Denzinger, Peter Hünermann, Helmut Hoping, Robert L. Fastiggi, and Anne Englund Nash, eds., *Compendium of Creeds, Definitions, and Declarations on Matters of Faith and Morals*, 43rd ed. (Ignatius, 2012)
ESV	English Standard Version
LCL	Loeb Classical Library
NIV	New International Version
RSV	Revised Standard Version
USCCB	United States Council of Catholic Bishops
WJW	Thomas Jackson, ed., *The Works of John Wesley*, 14 vols. (Baker Book House, 1978)

SECTION I.
Spring 2023

April 2023
Convergence/Agreement Statement

Topic: Evangelization and Doctrine

PREAMBLE

Catholics and Evangelicals agree that evangelization is a participation in the missions of the Son and Spirit by which God is reconciling the world to himself. Jesus prayed on the night before he died that we may be one (John 17). We also seek Christian unity because our lack of a unified witness is a scandal to the world and a hindrance to evangelization.

CONTENT OF THE MESSAGE

Evangelicals and Catholics agree that the Gospel can be summarized as: the Lord Jesus Christ was crucified for our sins and is now risen from the dead as Lord of all, pours out his Holy Spirit, and gives everlasting life to all who repent and believe.

THE AGENTS

Jesus entrusted the Church's mission of evangelization in a particular way to the apostles. He gives the Holy Spirit to the Church to do the work of evangelization, which is incumbent upon all members of the Church in every age.

For Catholics, the bishops, as successors of the apostles, have a guiding role in the work of evangelization even though the initiative in evangelistic efforts often arises from the laity.

For some Evangelicals, pastors and ecclesiastical leaders have a guiding role in the work of evangelization. For other Evangelicals, parachurch and lay-led movements often guide the work of evangelization.

MOTIVATIONS

Evangelicals and Catholics agree that we evangelize in obedience to Christ's command, out of love for the lost and for the sake of their salvation, all for the glory of God.

We agree that everyone in a state of sin is liable to everlasting condemnation on account of sin and that all unregenerated persons are captives of Satan. Hell and its punishments are everlasting. For this reason, evangelization is urgently necessary.

Catholics understand the state of sin that deserves everlasting condemnation to be either the state of original sin or actual mortal sin. Venial sin is displeasing to God but does not deserve everlasting condemnation.

Evangelicals understand that all sins, whether original or actual, deserve everlasting condemnation.

THE MANNER

Catholics and Evangelicals agree that evangelization is carried out through the verbal proclamation of the Gospel, accompanied by the witness of the fruit of the Spirit in the life of the Church. Catholics and some Evangelicals also hold that signs and wonders have an important role to play in evangelization.

Catholics and Evangelicals stand united against any ideology that undermines evangelization such as universalism, pluralism, syncretism, indifferentism, and latitudinarianism. Such ideologies are contrary to the truth of the Gospel.

We agree that the unevangelized need the grace of Jesus Christ. We also agree that for the unevangelized, the gift of faith is a grace and that an indispensable component of faith is cognitive assent to revealed truth.

Catholics say that faith is primarily an assent of the intellect to revealed truth. Some Evangelicals say that faith is primarily trust in Christ's atoning work. Other Evangelicals say that faith is both intellectual assent to revealed truth and heartfelt trust in Christ.

1.1 What Is Evangelization? What Do Doctrine and Evangelization Have to Do with One Another?

Gregg R. Allison

Introduction

THE THESIS OF THIS PAPER is that evangelization is grounded on and shaped by Christian doctrine. I demonstrate this thesis in three steps. First, I define evangelization from both an Evangelical perspective and a Roman Catholic perspective, relying on classical definitions from both traditions and not offering a new definition (e.g., one that might reflect the outcome of this dialogue on evangelization). Second, I (all too) briefly consider four doctrinal *loci*—theology proper, particularly the doctrine of the Trinity; Christology; pneumatology; and ecclesiology—and how they ground evangelization. Third, I offer a few reflections on how these doctrines related to evangelization could shape our traditions' practice of evangelization.

Definitions of Evangelization

Whereas there are many varieties of definitions of evangelization from an evangelical perspective, I cite the classical definition from the Lausanne Covenant (1974), specifically its article on the nature of evangelism:

> To evangelize is to spread the good news that Jesus Christ died for our sins and was raised from the dead according to the Scriptures,

> and that, as the reigning Lord, he now offers the forgiveness of sins and the liberating gifts of the Spirit to all who repent and believe. Our Christian presence in the world is indispensable to evangelism and so is that kind of dialogue whose purpose is to listen sensitively in order to understand. But evangelism itself is the proclamation of the historical, biblical Christ as Savior and Lord, with a view to persuading people to come to him personally and so be reconciled to God. In issuing the gospel invitation we have no liberty to conceal the cost of discipleship. Jesus still calls all who would follow him to deny themselves, take up their cross, and identify themselves with his new community. The results of evangelism include obedience to Christ, incorporation into his Church and responsible service in the world.[1]

I draw attention to four key points: (1) evangelization is the verbal announcement of the Gospel, (2) which focuses on the death and resurrection of the Lord Jesus Christ as set forth in Scripture and historically/catholicly affirmed and (3) includes the act of persuading/inviting people to repent of their sins and believe in the Savior (4) so that they might be forgiven, receive the gift of the Holy Spirit, and become devoted followers/servants of Christ and identified with his Church.

For the Roman Catholic perspective on evangelization, I weave together a few sections of Pope Paul VI's *Evangelii nuntiandi* (1975). Affirming that "the first means of evangelization is the witness of an authentically Christian life" (§41), the pope underscores,

> This always remains insufficient, because even the finest witness will prove ineffective in the long run if it is not explained, justified—what Peter called always having "your answer ready for people who ask you the reason for the hope that you all have" [1 Pet 3:15]—and made explicit by a clear and unequivocal proclamation of the Lord Jesus. The Good News proclaimed by the witness of life sooner or later has to be proclaimed by the word of life. There is no true evangelization if the name, the teaching, the life, the promises, the kingdom and the mystery of Jesus of Nazareth, the Son of God, are not proclaimed. (§42).

1. Lausanne Covenant (1974), §4, https://lausanne.org/statement/lausanne-covenant#the-nature-of-evangelism.

Indispensably,

> The proclamation only reaches full development when it is listened to, accepted and assimilated, and when it arouses a genuine adherence in the one who has thus received it. An adherence to the truths which the Lord in His mercy has revealed; still more, an adherence to a program of life—a life henceforth transformed—which He proposes. In a word, adherence to the kingdom. (§23).

Of course, this aspect does not come at the expense of catechetical instruction (§44), and evangelization always engages those who receive the Gospel into the Church and its sacramentalization (§47).[2]

I draw attention to four key points: (1) evangelization is the verbal announcement of the Gospel, (2) which focuses on the name, the teaching, the life, the promises, the kingdom, and the mystery of the Son of God and (3) demands on the part of its listeners the reception and understanding of and adherence to the good news, (4) leading to and expressing itself in life transformation as citizens of the kingdom of God and members incorporated into and sacramentalized by the Church.

There is significant overlap between these two definitions of evangelization. But what do doctrine and evangelization have to do with one another?

Doctrinal Loci as Ground for Evangelization

I briefly answer that question by focusing on four doctrinal *loci* as ground for evangelization.

THEOLOGY PROPER (SPECIFICALLY THE DOCTRINE OF THE TRINITY)[3]

According to classical trinitarian theism, there are two eternal processions, or relations of origin, within the Godhead (God *ad intra*).

2. Paul VI, *Evangelii nuntiandi* (December 8, 1975) (Saint Paul Books and Media, 1975), §23, §41, §42, §44, §47.

3. Much of this discussion is taken from Gregg R. Allison and Andreas J. Köstenberger, *The Holy Spirit*, Theology for the People of God (B&H Academic, 2020), 273–94; and Gregg R. Allison, *God, Gift, and Guide: Knowing the Holy Spirit* (B&H, 2023).

The first procession—the eternal generation of the Son—is the relation of origin of the Son with respect to the Father: The First Person eternally generates or begets the Second Person. The second procession—the eternal procession of the Holy Spirit—is the relation of origin of the Holy Spirit with respect to the Father and the Son: The First Person and Second Person eternally spirate the Third Person, or the Holy Spirit proceeds from the Father and the Son. These eternal processions are necessary, eternal, and uncreated.

From these eternal processions flow the temporal missions of the Son and the Holy Spirit sent by the Father (God *ad extra*). Processions and missions are not separate matters; rather, they are intimately connected: a mission is a procession turned outside and in time for the benefit of image bearers who have fallen into sin.[4] The processions "go out" or "come forth" as the two missions, mission 1 of the Son and mission 2 of the Spirit. Both divine persons are "sent to" image bearers and thus have a temporal effect.[5] These missions are contingent, temporal, and created (at least in terms of their effects).

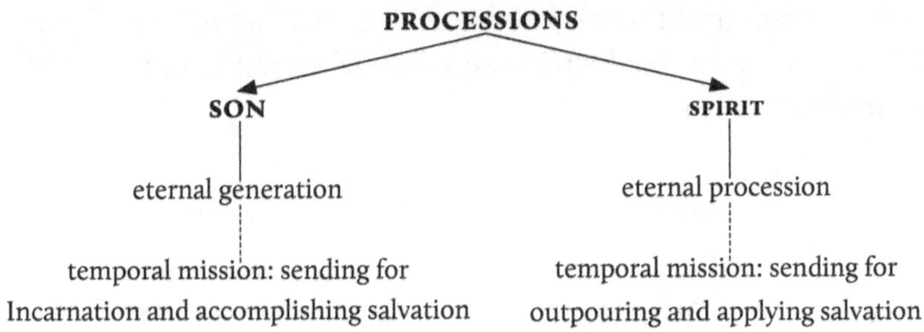

4. Aquinas addresses this relationship in Thomas Aquinas, *Summa Theologiae* I, q. 43, a. 2 (trans. Fathers of the English Dominican Province [Benzinger, 1947]). I follow Matthew Levering's discussion in *Engaging the Doctrine of the Holy Spirit: Love and Gift in the Trinity and in the Church* (Baker Academic, 2016), 189–90.

5. According to Aquinas, "That a divine person may newly exist in anyone, or be possessed by anyone in time, does not come from change of the divine person, but from change in the creature." Aquinas, *Summa Theologiae* I, q. 43, a. 2, ad 2. As explained by Levering, "The change described by a divine 'mission' consists in a creature gaining a new real relation to the Son or Holy Spirit, a relation of intimacy that elevates the creature into a participation in the trinitarian community." Levering, *Engaging the Doctrine of the Holy Spirit*, 189. See also Allison and Köstenberger, *The Holy Spirit*, 275n3.

The temporal missions of the Son and the Spirit express and are reflective of their eternal processions.[6] There is an appropriateness to the Son's becoming incarnate and accomplishing salvation as the particular mission of the Son who is eternally generated by the Father. The Son is eternally *from* the Father, and he is temporally sent *from* the Father on mission 1. And there is an appropriateness to the Holy Spirit's being outpoured and applying salvation as the particular mission of the Holy Spirit who eternally proceeds from the Father and the Son. The Holy Spirit is eternally *from* the Father and the Son, and he is temporally sent *from* the Father and the Son on mission 2.[7] Importantly for the purpose of this chapter, the Son who is eternally generated from the Father and the Spirit who eternally proceeds from the Father and the Son undertake their missions on behalf of fallen image bearers so as to save them and bring them back to the triune God.

This *missio Dei* is made known to fallen image bearers through the enterprise of evangelization; that is, evangelization is grounded on, flows from, and points to these two missions:

> Jesus said to them [his disciples] again, "Peace be with you. As the Father has sent me, even so I am sending you.' And when he had said this, he breathed on them and said to them, 'Receive the Holy Spirit.

6. Again, according to Aquinas, "The mission of a divine person is a fitting thing, as meaning in one way the procession of origin from the sender, and as meaning a new way of existing in another." Aquinas, *Summa Theologiae* I, q. 43, a. 1, s.c.

7. According to Augustine (*De Trinitate*, 4.5.29): "Just as the Father, then, begot and the Son was begotten, so the Father sent and the Son was sent. But just as the begetter and the begotten are one, so are the sender and the sent, because the Father and the Son are one; so too the Holy Spirit is one with them . . . . And just as being born means for the Son his being from the Father, so his being sent means his being known to be from him. And just as for the Holy Spirit his being the gift of God means his proceeding from the Father, so his being sent means his being known to proceed from him. Nor, by the way, can we say that the Holy Spirit does not proceed from the Son as well; it is not without point that the same Spirit is called the Spirit of the Father and of the Son. . . . [Christ's breathing upon the disciples and saying, 'Receive the Holy Spirit' (John 20:22)] was a convenient symbolic demonstration that the Holy Spirit proceeds from the Son as well as from the Father." Augustine, *The Trinity*, trans. Edmund Hill, ed. John E. Rotelle, vol. 5 of *The Works of Saint Augustine: A Translation for the 21st Century*, pt. 1, *Books*, 2nd ed. (New City Press, 2015), 218–19.

> If you forgive the sins of any, they are forgiven them; if you withhold forgiveness from any, it is withheld." (John 20:21–22; ESV).

Jesus commissions his Church (here, in the persons of the apostles—Evangelicals and Roman Catholics disagree on many points), and this mission of evangelization flows from the nearly accomplished mission 1 of the Son[8] and the soon to be inaugurated mission 2 of the Holy Spirit.[9] This *missio Dei* involving the three Persons is similarly found in Jesus' Great Commission, the "marching orders" for evangelization (Matt 28:18–20).

Trinitarian theology grounds evangelization.

CHRISTOLOGY

As the Nicene-Constantinopolitan Creed confesses in regard to the Second Person:

> I believe in one Lord Jesus Christ, the Son of God, the Only-Begotten,
> begotten of the Father before all ages;
> Light of Light; True God of True God; begotten, not made; of one
> essence with the Father, by Whom all things were made;
> Who for us men and for our salvation came down from Heaven, and was
> incarnate of the Holy Spirit and the Virgin Mary, and became man.
> And He was crucified for us under Pontius Pilate, and suffered, and was
> buried.
> And the third day He arose again, according to the Scriptures, and
> ascended into Heaven,
> and sits at the right hand of the Father;
> and He shall come again with glory to judge the living and the dead;
> Whose Kingdom shall have no end.

This creedal Christology of the person and work of God the Son is, of course, reflective of the biblical presentation of both. For example (Phil 2:5–8):

8. According to Jesus' words (John 7:35–37), he has not yet ascended and been seated at the right hand of the Father, from which he will pour out the Holy Spirit and thus launch mission 2.

9. The reason for Jesus' instructions that his disciples remain in Jerusalem until the outpouring of the Holy Spirit on the day of Pentecost (Luke 24:44–48; Acts 1:1–5; 2:1–4).

> Have this mind among yourselves, which is yours in Christ Jesus, who, though he was in the form of God, did not count equality with God a thing to be grasped, but emptied himself, by taking the form of a servant, being born in the likeness of men. And being found in human form, he humbled himself by becoming obedient to the point of death, even death on a cross.

Indeed, the Bible's grand Christological narrative can be summarized as follows:

> Jesus' earthly ministry was launched by a movement that aimed at the restoration of *Israel*. But he himself launched a movement that aimed at the ingathering of the *nations* to the new messianic people of God. The *initial impetus* for his ministry was to call Israel back to their God. The *subsequent impact* of his ministry was a new community that called the nations to faith in the God of Israel.[10]

Theologically, the Incarnation of the eternally existing, fully divine Son of God resulted in the hypostatic union by which the God-man—fully divine and fully human—would enter into the state of humiliation and be crucified for the sake of sinful image bearers. As Christ himself explained this mission (Mark 10:45): "The Son of Man came not to be served but to serve, and to give his life as a ransom for many."[11] Because of the person of the Son—he is the eternally

10. Christopher J. H. Wright, *The Mission of God: Unlocking the Bible's Grand Narrative* (IVP Academic, 2006), 506 (emphasis in original).

11. Paul VI, *Evangelii nuntiandi*, §6: "The witness that the Lord gives of himself and that Saint Luke gathered together in his Gospel—'I must proclaim the Good News of the kingdom of God' [Luke 4:43]—without doubt has enormous consequences, for it sums up the whole mission of Jesus: 'That is what I was sent to do' [Luke 4:43]. These words take on their full significance if one links them with the previous verses, in which Christ has just applied to himself the words of the prophet Isaiah: 'The Spirit of the Lord has been given to me, for he has anointed me. He has sent me to bring the good news to the poor' [Luke 4:18; citing Isa 61:1]. Going from town to town, preaching to the poorest—and frequently the most receptive—the joyful news of the fulfillment of the promises and of the Covenant offered by God is the mission for which Jesus declares that he is sent by the Father. And all the aspects of his mystery—the Incarnation itself, his miracles, his teaching, the gathering together of the disciples, the sending out of the Twelve, the cross and the resurrection, the permanence of his presence in the midst of his own—were components of his evangelizing activity."

generated Son sent on mission 1 by the Father who generates him—and because of the work of the Son—he accomplished the salvation of fallen image bearers for which he was commissioned by the Father—Christians and their churches have been given the task of evangelization (2 Cor 5:18–20):

> All this is from God, who through Christ reconciled us to himself and gave us the ministry of reconciliation; that is, in Christ God was reconciling the world to himself, not counting their trespasses against them, and entrusting to us the message of reconciliation. Therefore, we are ambassadors for Christ, God making his appeal through us. We implore you on behalf of Christ, be reconciled to God.

Christology grounds evangelization.

PNEUMATOLOGY

Significantly expanding on the Creed of Nicaea's sparse confession of the Third Person, the Nicene-Constantinopolitan Creed affirms a specific work of the Holy Spirit: "He spoke by the prophets." This confession summarizes well the fact that according to many passages of Scripture, when the Spirit comes/falls/rushes upon someone, that person engages in some form of speech: prophecy, praise, prayer, and/or proclamation.[12] One example (in the form of a petition by the early Church) connects this speaking by the Holy Spirit with evangelization (Acts 4:29–31):

> "Now, Lord, look upon their threats and grant to your servants to continue to speak your word with all boldness, while you stretch out your hand to heal, and signs and wonders are performed through the name of your holy servant Jesus." And when they had prayed, the place in which they were gathered together was shaken, and they were all filled with the Holy Spirit and continued to speak the word of God with boldness.

According to the promise of Jesus, it was for this very purpose that the Holy Spirit was poured out on the day of Pentecost (Acts 1:8): "You will receive power when the Holy Spirit has come upon you, and

12. For further discussion, see Allison and Köstenberger, *The Holy Spirit*, 286–89.

you will be my witnesses in Jerusalem and in all Judea and Samaria, and to the end of the earth." Andreas Köstenberger summarizes the pneumatology of Acts:

> Throughout the book we see that the Spirit is a Spirit of *mission*. In particular, he provides the power for mission (see esp. Acts 1:8) and boldness for witness (Acts 4:31). Not only does he empower believers' witness; he himself is said to witness to the risen and exalted Jesus (Acts 5:32). He sends Philip to evangelize the Ethiopian eunuch (Acts 8:29). He sends Peter to the Gentile Cornelius (Acts 10:19; cf. 11:12). He sends out the first missionaries, Barnabas and Saul, from Antioch, where believers in Christ are first called Christians (Acts 13:2, 4). He sends Paul to Macedonia by redirecting him twice, then giving him a vision (Acts 16:6–7, 16, 18).[13]

Moving to our contemporary scene, Pope Paul VI affirms (EN, §75):

> It is the Holy Spirit who, today just as at the beginning of the Church, acts in every evangelizer who allows himself to be possessed and led by Him. The Holy Spirit places on his lips the words which he could not find by himself, and at the same time the Holy Spirit predisposes the soul of the hearer to be open and receptive to the Good News and to the kingdom being proclaimed.
>
> Techniques of evangelization are good, but even the most advanced ones could not replace the gentle action of the Spirit. The most perfect preparation of the evangelizer has no effect without the Holy Spirit. . . . It must be said that the Holy Spirit is the principal agent of evangelization: it is He who impels each individual to

13. Allison and Köstenberger, The Holy Spirit, 99–100. Pope Paul VI adds, "Evangelization will never be possible without the action of the Holy Spirit. . . . In fact, it is only after the coming of the Holy Spirit on the day of Pentecost that the apostles depart to all the ends of the earth in order to begin the great work of the Church's evangelization. Peter explains this event as the fulfillment of the prophecy of Joel: 'I will pour out my Spirit' [Acts 2:17]. Peter is filled with the Holy Spirit so that he can speak to the people about Jesus, the Son of God [Acts 4:8]. Paul too is filled with the Holy Spirit [Acts 9:17] before dedicating himself to his apostolic ministry, as is Stephen when he is chosen for the ministry of service and later on for the witness of blood [Acts 6:5, 10; 7:55]. The Spirit, who causes Peter, Paul and the Twelve to speak, and who inspires the words that they are to utter, also comes down 'on those who heard the word' [Acts 10:44]." Paul VI, *Evangelii nuntiandi*, §75.

> proclaim the Gospel, and it is He who in the depths of consciences causes the word of salvation to be accepted and understood. But it can equally be said that He is the goal of evangelization: He alone stirs up the new creation, the new humanity of which evangelization is to be the result, with that unity in variety which evangelization wishes to achieve within the Christian community.

This stirring of the Holy Spirit to effect salvation as the goal of evangelization comes through his various works:[14] conviction of sin, righteousness, and judgment (John 16:8–11); union with Christ (Rom 8:9–10); justification (1 Cor 6:11; Gal 3:2–6); regeneration (John 3:1–8; Titus 3:5–7); conversion—repentance[15] and faith[16]—and confession of Christ (1 Cor 12:3); sealing (Eph 1:13–14; 2 Cor 1:22; 5:5); adoption (Gal 4:4–7; Rom 8:14–15); sanctification (1 Pet 1:2); perseverance (1 Pet 1:5) and assurance (Rom 8:15–17); and glorification/resurrection (Rom 8:11).

Pneumatology grounds evangelization.

ECCLESIOLOGY

Whereas the Evangelical tradition has emphasized the responsibility of each believer to engage in communicating the Gospel, in the last few decades, a concerted effort has been made to move toward seeing evangelization as a corporate matter. This trajectory means that

14. For further discussion, see Allison and Köstenberger, *The Holy Spirit*, 367–414. Commenting on the effectiveness of the Spirit's operation, John Owen offers, "When [the Spirit] exerts his power in and by the word, to the creation of a new heart and the opening of blind eyes, he so removes the principle of resistance, that he is not, cannot be resisted." John Owen, *Pneumatologia: A Discourse Concerning the Holy Spirit*, vol. 3 of *The Works of John Owen*, ed. William H. Gould (Banner of Truth Trust, 1965), 202.

15. As Barth maintains, "Being the Spirit of grace, the Holy Spirit strikes against man's hostility to grace," thereby opposing human opposition to God's call to salvation. Karl Barth, *The Holy Spirit and the Christian Life: The Theological Basis of Ethics* (Westminster John Knox, 1993), 25.

16. As Luther explains in his *Small Catechism*, "I believe that I cannot by my own reason or strength believe in Jesus Christ, my Lord, or come to him; but the Holy Spirit has called me by the gospel, enlightened me with his gifts, sanctified and kept me in the true faith." Martin Luther, *Small Catechism*, II. The Creed; Third Article; Of Sanctification; What Does This Mean?—Answer, trans. *Luther's Small Catechism with Explanation* (Concordia, 2005), p. 205.

Evangelicalism considers missionality as one of the identity markers of the Church.[17] By this affirmation is not meant primarily *the activity of mission* (for example, sharing the good news with a friend, church planting, sending and supporting missionaries—though all of these are essential activities) but *the attribute of mission*: the Church *is* missional. Jürgen Moltmann enjoins us to understand "not that the church 'has' a mission, but the very reverse: that the mission of Christ creates its own church. Mission does not come from the church; it is from mission and in light of mission that the church has to be understood."[18] The reversal is significant: being missional is a matter of identity first, then activity. As George Hunsberger offers,

> A missional ecclesiology stresses that the church's very existence has been sent into the world. . . . The fundamental point is that missions is not peripheral or additional for the church. The fact that it has been sent is of its essential nature, so much so that the sending is implicitly and explicitly formative in all aspects of its life—its worship, its koinonia, its engagements, its witness, its birthing of new communities, its sociopolitical engagements, its compassion and mercy.[19]

This emphasis on communal evangelization seems to be Paul's point in his commendation of the church of the Thessalonians (1 Thess 1:6–8):

> You became imitators of us [Paul, Silvanus, and Timothy] and of the Lord, for you received the word in much affliction, with the joy of the Holy Spirit, so that you became an example to all the believers in Macedonia and in Achaia. For not only has the word of the Lord sounded forth from you in Macedonia and Achaia, but your faith in God has gone forth everywhere, so that we need not say anything.

17. For further discussion, see Gregg R. Allison, *Sojourners and Strangers: The Doctrine of the Church*, Foundations of Evangelical Theology (Crossway, 2012), 140–48.

18. Jürgen Moltmann, *The Church in the Power of the Spirit*, trans. Margaret Kohl (Harper & Row, 1977), 10.

19. George Hunsberger, "Evangelical Conversion toward a Missional Ecclesiology," 105–32 in *Evangelical Ecclesiology: Reality or Illusion?*, ed. John G. Stackhouse, Jr. (Baker Academic, 2003), 110.

The Church itself was a missional community—a witnessing Church. Indeed, John uses the metaphor of a golden lampstand to underscore the Church's responsibility to shine as a light of the Gospel (Rev 1:12).[20]

In terms of implications, Evangelicals envision evangelization as a divinely mandated commission (Matt 28:18–20) and not a responsibility that the Church invents and takes to itself.[21] Moreover, Evangelicals conceive of evangelization as the mission to which church members join themselves, a collective task that is undertaken by all of its members in every phase of their life and work. Additionally, Evangelicals recognize evangelization as a first step in creating a countercultural reality that is distinct from and a challenge to the current context in which the Church exists. Again, Hunsberger explains, "No more is the church the chaplain to an assumed Christian society, nor the moral glue that holds things together, nor the guardian of civility and duty."[22] It is rather a witnessing/evangelizing Church, empowered and moved by the Holy Spirit (Acts 1:8; e.g., 16:6–15), sending out its members as ambassadors for Christ through whom God makes his appeal: "be reconciled to God" (2 Cor 5:20).

Reflections on How These Doctrines Might Shape Our Traditions' Practice of Evangelization

I offer four brief reflections. First, evangelization originates with the Trinity and brings us back to the Trinity. It flows from the mission of the Son and so must be Christocentric, and it flows from the mission of the Holy Spirit and thus must also be pneumadynamic. Evangelization creates and expands the Church—with its co-instituting principles of the Son and the Spirit[23]—by the announcement and embrace of the Gospel.

20. This idea would explain Jesus' warning to the church of Ephesus—the removal of its lampstand for failure to repent (Rev 2:5–6): the church "no longer expressed [its] former zealous love for Jesus *by witnessing to him in the world.*" G. K. Beale, *The Book of Revelation: A Commentary on the Greek Text* (Eerdmans, 1999), 230 (emphasis in the original).

21. For further discussion, see Allison, *Sojourners and Strangers*, 147–48.

22. Hunsberger, "Evangelical Conversion toward a Missional Ecclesiology," 110.

23. Yves Congar, *I Believe in the Holy Spirit*, 3 vols., trans. David Smith (Crossroad/Herder & Herder, 2015), 2:9.

Second, this Gospel-centered, Spirit-empowered Church should constantly preach the good news to its own members. As articulated in *Evangelii nuntiandi*:

> The Church is an evangelizer, but she begins by being evangelized herself. She is the community of believers, the community of hope lived and communicated, the community of brotherly love, and she needs to listen unceasingly to what she must believe, to her reasons for hoping, to the new commandment of love. She is the People of God immersed in the world, and often tempted by idols, and she always needs to hear the proclamation of the "mighty works of God" [Acts 2:11; 1 Pet 2:9] which converted her to the Lord; she always needs to be called together afresh by Him and reunited. In brief, this means that she has a constant need of being evangelized, if she wishes to retain freshness, vigor and strength in order to proclaim the Gospel.[24]

We dare not overlook those in our midst in our evangelizing endeavors.

Third, we should prepare our church members to communicate the Gospel to those around them. After presenting the process of evangelization, Pope Paul VI concludes, "Finally, the person who has been evangelized goes on to evangelize others. Here lies the test of truth, the touchstone of evangelization: it is unthinkable that a person should accept the Word and give himself to the kingdom without becoming a person who bears witness to it and proclaims it in his turn."[25]

As part of the Evangelical tradition, I can attest to the fact that decades ago, churches of which I was a member regularly offered classes and trainings to equip our members to share the Gospel. Sadly, this is rarely the practice today. The Evangelical church either (wrongly) assumes that its members know how to communicate the good news or (more darkly) is embarrassed to have its members engage with others in this endeavor. Importantly, this third reflection is not an encouragement to mass produce Gospel-spewing robots who insensitively shout the message at uninterested hearers,

24. Paul VI, *Evangelii nuntiandi*, §15.
25. Paul VI, *Evangelii nuntiandi*, §24.

employing a cookie-cutter approach. But it does reflect my concern that Evangelical churches and their members have abandoned what is at their heart: the evangel and the ability to communicate it clearly, winsomely, urgently, and compassionately.

Fourth, I am hopeful that our Evangelical-Roman Catholic dialogue can turn the attention of both of our traditions to a revival and renewal of the significant and joyful life and task of evangelization.

Conclusion

This paper has demonstrated that evangelization is grounded on and shaped by Christian doctrine through three steps: citation of two definitions of evangelization, consideration of four doctrinal *loci* that ground evangelization, and reflection on how these doctrines might shape our traditions' practice of evangelization.

1.2 The Relation Between Evangelization and Doctrine in The Salvation Army

M. William Ury

Our mission is saving souls, growing saints and serving suffering humanity.[1]

Introduction

The study of evangelism is a heuristic venture. The biblical concept of sharing the "good news" with the accoutrements of birth announcement, exuberant victory, sudden joy, and kingdom implications bears connection with surrounding cultures historically and etymologically.[2] The key distinction of the Gospel for the earliest

1. Gen. John Gowans, from an address given at the International Millennial Congress, Atlanta, GA, June 28–July 2, 2001. Gowans served as General of The Salvation Army from 1999–2002.

2. John the Baptist proclaims the "good news" of Jesus (Luke 3:17 NIV). In the next chapter Jesus affirms that he has been sent to "proclaim the good news." The content and proclamation of the Gospel are expressed in the noun and the verbal forms related to *euangelion* (54 times) and *euangelizo* (76 times). The role of evangelist (*euangelistes*, 3 times) does not affirm an office per se. Proclamation is an irreducible element in the meaning of "gospel." Its relation to terms such as persuade, witness, teach, speak, or tell expands the styles of communication. David Barrett estimates that the amalgamation of all the synonyms for evangelism would incorporate more than 40 different terms, which include nearly 2,500 references in the New Testament alone. David Barrett, *Evangelize! A Historical Survey of the Concept* (New Hope, 1987), 14. Cited in Darius Salter, *American Evangelism: Its Theology and Practice* (Baker Books, 1996), 21. For an excellent survey of the historical, etymological, and scriptural meaning of "gospel" or

Christians centers on the person and work of Jesus Christ. He is the Gospel.[3] Everyone and everything that pertain to being transformed by him and making him known are secondary. What must be clear for all orthodox believers committed to consensual Christianity are the central theological commitments that form the essence of the Gospel. It is here where a dialogue between Catholics and Evangelicals must be undertaken. The mutuality of shared perspectives and practices is necessary as we together seek to offer Christ to the world.

It will be the contention of this chapter that The Salvation Army has offered the elements of the Gospel in both evangelistic and doctrinal ways which are consonant with its Wesleyan-Arminian grounding as well as being firmly committed to consensual theology. The historical exigencies of the founding of the Army are important to note as the warriors of that day sought to connect all they knew of Christ with their surrounding culture. Though it is normally viewed as a ministry solely focused on practical expression, we will trace the essential nature of doctrine in the evangelism of the Army.

The Salvation Army has a long history of "aggressive" Christianity.[4] Due to the fronts on which the Army continues to fight for a

"good news" / *euangelion*, see Colin Brown, ed., *The New International Dictionary of New Testament Theology* (Zondervan, 1982), 2:107–15. Also, Gerhard Kittel, ed., *Theological Dictionary of the New Testament* (Zondervan, 1964), 2:720–30.

3. Mark 1:1; 8:35; 10:29; 14:9; Acts 2:22–40; 1 Cor 15, esp. vv. 1–28, *passim*. Michael Green offers a thorough analysis in *Evangelism in the Early Church* (Eerdmans, 1970), ch. 2, esp. 52–53. John Piper's doxological theology connected to evangelism in his *God Is the Gospel* (Crossway Books, 2005). He underscores the trinitarian foundations of the Gospel, emphasizing the historical redemption in Christ, but attempts to correct a theology that ends with deliverance and does not find its fulfillment in the glory of God. *God Is the Gospel*, 167–68.

4. Catherine Booth formulated this summation based upon the quasi-militaristic structure of The Salvation Army. She often referred to the "aggressive spirit of primitive Christianity," as in her *The Highway of Our God* (The Salvation Army Supplies and Purchasing Department, repr. 1986), part II, ch. 3, 44. The perspective is always on the spiritual battle both for the soul of every person and constant vigilant opposition to all forms of institutional evil. That orientation is foundational to everything the Army is concerned with as a denomination. See Catherine Booth, *Practical Religion*, where she entitles a whole chapter "Aggression," at https://www.gospeltruth.net/booth/cath_booth/practical_religion/cbooth_prac_rel_pap10.htm (accessed September 9, 2022). One of her most famous works is *Aggressive Christianity*, found at https://www

holistic salvation it has not always given sufficient ongoing attention to a theology of evangelism. The tendency in any movement, which allows an inadequate theological base for outreach, is to emphasize function. If the theology for sharing Christ is not the motivation of service, then "doing" soon determines "being" and the result is a diminishment of calling, ministry, self-understanding and, most of all, of the nature of the very Gospel itself.[5]

The mission statement of The Salvation Army finds prominence often in written and spoken form by its members:

> The Salvation Army, an international movement, is an evangelical part of the universal Christian Church. Its message is based on the Bible. Its ministry is motivated by the love of God. Its mission is to preach the gospel of Jesus Christ and meet human needs in his name without discrimination.[6]

As a member of the Wesleyan Holiness tradition, The Salvation Army continues to draw from that rich theological heritage. Historically, that theological formulation has emphasized a deep connection between evangelism and doctrine. Methodism consistently grounded the revival spawned in the eighteenth century on the Thirty-Nine Articles of the Anglican Church, which reflected consensual Christianity and Protestant theological commitments of the main streams of the Reformation.[7]

.gospeltruth.net/booth/cath_booth/agressive_christianity/cbooth_agress_index.htm (accessed September 9, 2022).

5. The practical nature of Salvationism has been its greatest strength and a consistent place of needed correction. Practicality was easily transmitted to doctrinal issues, and in the case of sanctification the Army was at some points aligned with the more pragmatic expressions of holiness (ex. Phoebe Palmer's "altar theology") rather than the more nuanced and balanced approach of Samuel L. Brengle. David Rightmire, *Sanctified Sanity* (Crest Books, 2009), 150–56.

6. *The Salvation Army Handbook of Doctrine* (Salvation Books, The Salvation Army International Headquarters, 2010), 266. Another summation that reveals similar emphases is in the statement on ecclesiology: "The Salvation Army, under the one Triune God, belongs to and is an expression of the Body of Christ on earth, the Church Universal, and is a Christian denomination in permanent mission to the unconverted, called into and sustained in being by God." *The Handbook of Doctrine*, 310.

7. Thomas C. Oden, *Doctrinal Standards in the Wesleyan Tradition* (Francis Asbury Society [an imprint of Zondervan], 1988), 112–26 .

Wesley was keenly aware of the demise of orthodoxy that had produced a rampant strain of deism accompanied by an attendant antinomianism within Anglicanism. His version of the *via media* incorporated all the major creedal commitments of the Great Tradition, what he referred to as the "root of Christianity," while emphasizing those elements that distinguished Methodism within the larger Protestant framework.[8] Wesley, who never left Anglicanism, understood himself as a Reformed Anglican. According to him, the purpose of the people called Methodists as a reform movement was ensconced within the Church of England, an *ecclesiola in ecclesia*. He was adamantly opposed to schism and insisted that every Methodist attend the Anglican Church as often as possible, especially to receive the sacraments. One might say that a dynamic form of evangelism formed the self-perception of the Wesleyan movement in this statement from an annual conference in 1744.

> Q. What may we reasonably believe to be God's design in raising up the preachers called "Methodists"?
>
> A. To reform the nation, and in particular the Church, [and] to spread scriptural holiness over the land.[9]

Reform, to these itinerant and mostly lay preachers, included every aspect of biblical evangelism. It was a radical term which was taken quite seriously. History reveals that by the grace of God cultural reform did occur through the revitalization of the Spirit in the hearts of Methodists who offered Christ to all.[10]

8. J. Wesley Bready, *England, Before and After Wesley: The Evangelical Revival and Social Reform* (Hodder and Stoughton, 1939), 33–63. There are many places where Wesley decries the demise of true, scriptural Christianity in his lifetime. See his withering assessment of the spiritual state of Anglican clergy and those who made up the theological center of Anglicanism in Oxford in "Scriptural Christianity," in Thomas Jackson, ed., *The Works of John Wesley*, 14 vols. (Baker Book House, 1978), vol. 5, esp. 47–52. Hereafter, *WJW* with volume number and page following. Also, "A Farther Appeal to Men of Reason and Religion," *WJW* 8:46–247.

9. Wesley, "Large Minutes of Several Conversations," *WJW* 8:299.

10. There are many works devoted to this culture-altering ministry. One of them that strives to connect theology and reformation is Leon Hynson's *To Reform the*

Elements of Evangelism

A contextual study of the use and contexts pertaining to *euangelion* in the New Testament and in several traditions reveals three recurring categories which come to the foreground. Each of these is reflected in the ministry of the Army.[11] Much like the earliest days in Whitechapel, the first evangelistic outreach of William and Catherine Booth in East London, many of those to whom the Army ministers are struggling to simply survive. The needy rarely possess sufficient biblical or theological frameworks to place their situation in a Christian worldview. Ordained ministers have to be vigilant in providing a strong scriptural and doctrinal foundation. Given the unending social crises that arise, it is mandatory that strong encouragement for studying the Word and rightly dividing it is a priority. One will find as much emphasis on these three elements pertaining to evangelism in Salvationism as there was in its spiritual parent, Methodism.

TRINITARIAN/THEOLOGICAL ELEMENT

The ground of salvation is found within the life of the Trinity. All conceptions of the essence of holiness and love must find their origin there. It is out of that eternal other-orientation, not solely as a response to human sinfulness, that the "sentness" of Son and Spirit make sense. It is the self-revealing and self-dispensing nature of God in himself out of which evangelism arises. Having the mind of Christ, whose self-giving reveals the heart of God as well as the nature of true humanity, those who have been born from above are likewise "sent" into the world (John 20:21). God's universally extended holy

Nation: Theological Foundations of Wesley's Ethics (Francis Asbury Press [an imprint of Zondervan], 1984).

11. Michael Green's *Evangelism in the Early Church* highlights numerous elements, but he concludes with three: 1) every Christian was expected to witness as if the Gospel was their prime concern, 2) they lived holy lives, and 3) they knew the time was short before the judgment. *Evangelism in the Early Church*, 274–75. A classic within modern Evangelicalism is Robert Coleman's *The Master Plan of Evangelism* (Fleming Revell, 1978). Other excellent sources are: Darius Salter, *American Evangelism: Its Theology and Practice* (Baker Books, 1996); Jerram Barrs, *The Heart of Evangelism* (Crossway Books, 2001).

love forms the theological foundation for evangelism. Triune Love precedes and funds all Spirit-enabled, supernaturally informed seeking to win the lost.[12]

As a reflection of the nature of God, evangelism is a secondary revelation in word and deed offered throughout the world to every person. The mutual, eternal communication of the divine Persons is translated into incarnated words through the apostolic nature of all believers.[13] The witness of the Church is originally the witness of the triune God.

CHRISTOCENTRIC/MISSIONAL ELEMENT

This theological foundation is concentrated in an orthodox Nicene-Constantinopolitan Christology. Jesus Christ reveals the heart of the Father in the power of the Spirit as the one mediator between God and humanity. Overflowing love from persons transformed by the gracious life of God in Christ results in the intentional, other-oriented seeking of unevangelized persons where they live by creative and specific proclamation. The message, or means, of this selfless, humble, yet lovingly insistent offering is imitatively centered on both the example and the power of the exalted Christ. The substance of the Gospel offered pertains to the benefits of the Son of God who became the Son of Man. The exclusive claim that Christ is Lord is presented in culturally sensitive and understandable ways. Evangelism, which points to justification for sins through Christ alone, includes both a miraculous change and a radical initiation into the Kingdom of God. The desire to persuade nonbelievers necessarily includes a volitional confrontation due to the inexorable nature of conviction and repentance of personal sin. New life in Christ is only possible in an intimate and personal relationship with Jesus,

12. Jonathan Raymond, *Social Holiness: The Company We Keep* (Aldersgate Press and Crest Books, 2018) reveals a rich basis of trinitarian thought from a well-trained Salvation Army soldier (member). His work shows the modern trinitarian renaissance that was not a part of the thought life of the early Army, but the major themes are still present, even though in much less articulate forms.

13. This is a recurrent theme in Evangelical theology, which emphasized the relational nature of the Trinity. Royce Gruenler, *The Trinity in the Gospel of John: A Thematic Commentary on the Fourth Gospel* (Baker Books, 1986), 12–13, 63, 114. T. F. Torrance, *Space, Time and Resurrection* (Eerdmans, 1976), 118–22.

incarnate and risen from the dead, the only Savior, in the power of the Holy Spirit through the agency of the Body of Christ. The mission of the Son of God becomes the passion of anyone who has met him in transforming grace.

SALVIFIC/TRANSFORMATIONAL ELEMENT

This encounter with the living God results in a redemption from death and the gift of a "vast inward change."[14] Proclamation is never to be shared without the desire for the recipient to be transformed by grace. The goal of evangelism is spiritual re-creation. This new life touches both the individual and the community in which that person resides. First, there is the

A) *Personal.* Evangelism is an engagement person-to-person with the intention of total transformation, soul and body. The moral image which had been lost is renewed. Being made new creatures in Christ through the regenerating work of the Spirit begins the process of the restoration of the wholeness God intends for all believers. Discipleship in holy love, the active following of Jesus, results in godly character. Which must inescapably influence the

B) *Contextual.* The compassionate goal of evangelistic sharing with individuals is accompanied by a desire for their comprehensive welfare as a whole person within a community. The Gospel is never individualistic or atomistic. It is holistic. It redemptively incorporates the circumstances of the unevangelized. This Gospel is always incorporative of shalom, wholeness, healing, justice, and re-creation that results in social change. It is an active engagement with the surrounding culture seeking the betterment of both the individual and the communal for the eternal glory of God.

14. Salvationist soteriology would be in full consonance with John Wesley's description of regeneration. He describes the new birth as "a change wrought in the soul, by the operation of the Holy Ghost; a change in the whole manner of our existence; for, from the moment we are born of God, we live in quite another manner than we did before; we are, as it were, in another world." "The Great Privilege of Those That Are Born of God," *WJW* 5:224.

Evangelism and the Rise of The Salvation Army

Salvationism has offered each of these elements in a robust theology of evangelism since 1865. In the account of his earliest days of Christian discipleship, William Booth made his commitment to all things Wesleyan when he stated, "Truly, I thought then there was one God, that John Wesley was His prophet, and that the Methodists were His special people."[15] When Booth was forming the outlines of the faith for the neophyte group, later to be called The Salvation Army, he did so with an unmistakable dependence upon Methodism's Articles of Religion.[16] That doctrinal commitment has never waned since the inception of Salvationism.[17] As an expression of the Wesleyan Holiness arm of Protestantism, the Army has always seen itself within the larger ambit of orthodox, consensual Christianity.

Unlike Wesley, the Booths did not form a distinctive theological construct of their own. Due to earlier family pressures, including extreme poverty, William was not able to complete his education. Catherine was homeschooled by a mother who was deathly afraid of ungodly influences in public education. After a surprising two years of being allowed to go to a school nearby, Catherine became bedridden for several months during her teen years and thus, like William, was self-educated on many fronts.[18]

15. George S. Railton, *General Booth* (The Salvation Army Book Department, 1912), 17.

16. Doctrines of the Methodist New Connexion (1838). See Appendix 2 in *The Salvation Army Handbook of Doctrine*, 282–83. The name changes which eventually resulted in The Salvation Army included: The Christian Revival Union, The Christian Revival Union Society, The East London Christian Mission, and subsequently, The Christian Mission (1865). In 1878, Booth corrected an article referring to the mission as a "volunteer army" to a "salvation army." Thus, the origin of the name until today.

17. As a Protestant Evangelical, formed by the Wesleyan tradition, I have never seen anything comparable to the place given to doctrine in the Army. Soldiership (membership) is couched in learning the eleven doctrines. Officership (ordination) is focused on studying each in depth, memorizing all of them, and inculcating them in every aspect of corps (church) life. They are constant elements in worship and in study. The effectiveness of that focus is debated, but the reality of the presence of doctrines, at least in their basic form, is undeniable. The only comparison that I can think of is the place of the Westminster Confession in some Reformed camps.

18. Roger J. Green, *Catherine Booth: A Biography of the Cofounder of The Salvation Army* (Baker Books, 1996), 22–24.

Both of the Founders of the Army were articulate and voluminous communicators. William's theological commonplaces are more difficult to discern due to the various, discrete avenues in which he chose to write.[19] Catherine was inclined to write her theology in a more reflective way.[20] Her essays, books, and sermons offer more specific theological engagement. In the earliest theology of Salvationism the bedrock of scriptural authority is unquestionably laid. There is an unwavering agreement with consensual theology and a grounding in the formative and definitive elements of the Wesleyan tradition.[21] Though early influences through the Holiness movement fed into the Army, there was never a bifurcation from the larger, more theologically honed traditions that formed its theological basis.

Evangelism, the salvation of souls, or persons, has always been the heartbeat of the Army. In large measure, the origin of this movement was a long and painful reaction and removal from institutional Methodism's missional calcification by the early nineteenth century. William and Catherine Booth formed their earliest ministry to the troubled East End of London. In a remarkable replay of the context for the Wesleyan revival of the previous century, evidenced primarily by the waning of the offer of transforming grace to every person, the Booths began their evangelism on the streets. They realized that an entire sector of British culture, beleaguered by the crushing impact of cultural and personal sin, would never enter a physical church. The immediate concern was, where would any of them hear the Gospel of Christ? In much the same way as John Wesley who, under the encouragement of George Whitefield, submitted to be "more vile" by leaving the precincts of customary ordained ministry, the Booths went to the

19.Andrew M. Eason and Roger J. Green, *Boundless Salvation: The Shorter Writings of William Booth* (Peter Lang, 2012). Laura Petri's assessment is that to determine who actually began the Army in any way that divides William from Catherine is comparable to dividing a child from one of two parents: "The Army was started not with one motor but with two." Gen. Frederick Coutts cites Petri in *Essentials of Christian Experience* (Salvationist Supplies, 1969), 24.

20. Andrew M. Eason and Roger J. Green, eds. Settled Views: The Shorter Writings of Catherine Booth (Lexington Books, 2017).

21. Oden states that the pan-Wesleyan world is represented by a variety of denominations that "demonstrate the familiar consensual (and Wesleyan) textual definition." *Doctrinal Standards in the Wesleyan Tradition*, 161–66.

least, the lost, the poorest, and the working classes.[22] When the decision was made to move from itinerant evangelism to a focus on the Mile End Waste in July of 1865, William Booth's first service was held in a dilapidated tent. He came to refer to the open-air meetings that ensued as his "cathedral."[23]

Virtually any written source from the earliest days of the group which was to become The Salvation Army will provide proof of an unrelenting, at times, nearly breathtaking commitment to share the Gospel with every person possible. William's work, *How to Reach the Masses*, emphasized "missioning the streets" by any creative means possible.[24] The open-air meeting, which those ministering recognized required a "rough and ready style," was by far the most effective. The theological background of those who listened was varied, of course.[25] He notes how those who were churched had not been evangelized either in Sunday School or in regular services.[26] This cultural

22. Wesley in his journal entry of April 2, 1739 reflected on what he noticed was the "field preaching" of Jesus: "At four in the afternoon, I submitted to be more vile, and proclaimed in the highways the glad tidings of salvation." His first sermon to the three thousand people who listened was based upon Luke 4:18–19. *WJW* 1:185. Arnold Dallimore is exercised to dispel the "Wesley myth" that John Wesley was more holy in comportment than his mentor in evangelism, Whitefield. Dallimore notes that Wesley's first salvo against the Predestinarians, beginning with the publishing of the sermon *Free Grace*, also began in April 1739. See his *George Whitefield: The Life and Times of the Great Evangelist and the 18th Century Revival*, 2 vols. (Banner of Truth Trust, 1979), 2:9, 19–28. The Booths' remarkable journey, which has been chronicled often, is movingly related in St. John Ervine's *God's Soldier: General William Booth* (Macmillan Press, 1935), 1:282–84.

23. Ervine, *God's Soldier*, 2:285. There were many open-air preachers in the late nineteenth century in London; some say hundreds at the same time. The continual concern of many of the ministries behind that phenomenon was the maintenance of believers in any meaningful way.

24. Many of these early sources are very difficult to find. A website that has gathered an amazing amount of otherwise unavailable resources is the Salvation Factory. While academic bibliographic notes are not found there, it is still a profoundly helpful resource. Find there William Booth, *How to Reach the Masses*, http://www.salvationfactory.org/wp-content/uploads/2015/12/How-to-Reach-the-Masses (accessed September 8, 2022).

25. Booth indicates that many they encountered were aware of the basics of the order of salvation.

26. Booth, *How to Reach the Masses*, ch. 2:1.

loss of theological input was met with simple language drawn from Scripture. Due to the utter lack of catechetical instruction, there was a remarkable dependence upon the Holy Spirit to apply the truth of the Gospel to every heart, especially to children.[27]

The offer of salvation included belief in Christ in both assent and fiducial trust.[28] Basic questions of all proper evangelism were always employed: "Do you believe Jesus saves you?" or "Do you believe his blood washes you from all sin?" What shakes modern sensitivities was the constantly proffered dichotomy of mercy or judgment, happiness or hell.[29] The theology of holy love is seen throughout Salvationist doctrine. That essential view of ultimate reality must be proclaimed with a complete, biblical view of God. It is abundantly clear that the emphasis is on the loving heart of God, grace extended, and Christ as Friend.[30]

The heartfelt desire to engage with the personal background of the hearers is affirmed where the Founder states, "Not a doctrine propounded was beyond the comprehension of those to whom it was addressed."[31] Also, noteworthy is the emphasis on trusting for salvation but also the constant refrain of walking by faith in a continued discipleship.[32] The modern preoccupation with receiving blessings from God was never the focus of this evangelism. Rather, it was a call to radical discipleship. Being a true Salvationist following Jesus automatically eclipsed every individualistic or materialistic leaning within this expression of evangelical theology.

Another unique tool was the use of testimony by recent converts from the same socioeconomic strata as most of the hearers. Booth states, "The crowd may not understand their theology, although

27. Booth, *How to Reach the Masses*, ch. 4:5, ch. 5:11, ch. 2:9.

28. Booth, *How to Reach the Masses*, ch. 4:6.

29. Booth, *How to Reach the Masses*, ch. 5:6. In an 1895 interview, William Booth was asked what motivated his life of sacrificial service for the masses. His answer was indicative of the eschatological emphasis of the Army. He said, "If you take Hell out of our doctrine, the Salvation Army will soon disappear." R. G. Moyles, *William Booth in America: Six Visits 1886–1907* (Crest Books, 2010), 225.

30. Booth, *How to Reach the Masses*, ch. 6:14, *passim*.

31. Booth, *How to Reach the Masses*, ch. 4:7.

32. Booth, *How to Reach the Masses*, ch. 5:6.

that is simple enough; but they can understand and appreciate this [verbal testimony]."[33] In Wesleyan fashion, immediate follow-up was extended to those expressing any level of interest.[34] The offer of small group meetings consonant with the particular needs of respondents was consistently carried out.[35]

All of this was done under constant awareness of negative reaction, which often resulted in insult, loud and disgusting distractions, and the inevitable beating and stoning which accompanied many of these ventures.[36] The fruit of this type of evangelism was staggering in the East End, which was considered by most churchgoers as recalcitrant to the Gospel.

No major differences can be discerned between the cofounders of the Army in their theology of evangelism. Each offered strong, clear statements about the primarily evangelical purpose of the Army. One example of William's pithy and somewhat reductionistic rhetoric states that:

> We are a Salvation people—this is our specialty—getting saved and keeping saved, and then getting somebody else saved, and then getting saved more and more, until full salvation on earth makes heaven within, which is finally perfected by the full salvation without, on the other side of the river.[37]

33. Booth, *How to Reach the Masses*, ch. 8:1 (terms added by author from context).

34. Booth, *How to Reach the Masses*, ch. 2:8.

35. This is another indication of the deep dependence of the Army on Wesleyan soteriology and its inseparable and immediate connection to ecclesiology. Wesley would never preach where he could not follow with some form of small group discipleship. D. Michael Henderson, *John Wesley's Class Meeting: A Model for Making Disciples* (Evangel Publishing House, 1997), 83–126.

36. Booth says that when the shouting overcame the preaching they would immediately begin to either sing or pray for their opponents. Booth, *How to Reach the Masses*, ch. 8:1–2.

37. William Booth, *Salvation Soldiery*, ch. 3, 1, at http://www.salvationfactory.org/wp-content/uploads/2015/12/Our-New-Name.pdf (accessed June 9, 2022). This website offers many of the Army's seminal thinkers' major works that have been difficult to find in one place. Another well-known epithet of Booth's was the summation of the Army's ministry under three heads, "Soup, Soap, and Salvation."

Catherine's unyielding missional heart and theological depth is evident in most of her works. The underappreciation of her contributions to the history of Christian thought is a remarkable loss.[38] Her "system" of theology was more astute, nuanced, and often more engaging than William's. Nonetheless, the intertwining of their minds and hearts in every form of ministry is a remarkable example of shared leadership in a denomination.

Elements of Evangelism Expressed in Salvationist Doctrine and Practice

With a strong foundation in consensual Christianity and its Wesleyan-Arminian trajectory, The Salvation Army expressed a distinctive and holistic theology of evangelism which evidenced all of its major elements as enumerated above. It should be noted that five of the eleven doctrines which form the basis of Salvationist theology are devoted to the doctrine of salvation (see Appendix Three).

TRINITARIAN/THEOLOGICAL

The Booths grounded all reality, and thus, all their ministry in the love of God.[39] That love was the foundation of creation, which cli-

38. As stated above, Catherine was never formally trained, but her homeschooling, training in Methodist and Holiness circles and lifelong self-education, and giftedness placed her at the forefront of theologians in the late Victorian period. Thomas Oden claimed that between Teresa of Avila and Georgia Harkness the premier female theologian was Phoebe Palmer. In my view, Catherine Booth deserves to be considered in that rank. The difference between Catherine Booth and the others mentioned is that she not only wrote theology but raised a large family, was physically weak all of her adult life, inaugurated a culture-altering ministry, preached every Sunday, and both raised funds and sustained friends at the inception of the Army's worldwide ministries. Her influence and fruitfulness are truly among the most remarkable stories in all of Christian history. See Bill Ury, review of Andrew M. Eason and Roger J. Green, eds. Settled Views: The Shorter Writings of Catherine Booth (Lexington Books, 2017), in Word and Deed 22, no. 1 (November 2019): 49–54.

39. Speaking of the source of all Army outreach, William states, "I believe in the very heart of God Himself." *In Darkest England and the Way Out* (International Headquarters of The Salvation Army, 1890), 280. See also an intriguing discussion on the heart of the Father, *Darkest England*, 43.

maxed in communion with persons created in the divine image. Divine love is the ground and grammar of Salvationist theology. A distillation of Wesleyan theology incorporates a consistent and formative balance of two essence statements: holiness and love. That paradigm is quite evident, though not supported by extensive articulation, in the evangelical thought of the Booths. Love, for them, is never saccharine sentimentality. It always involves the dynamic of the unchanging moral law and the restoration of the moral image in all of its Gospel promise.

As with Wesley before them, there was little emphasis on the intricacies of the immanent nature of the triune life. Affirming the creeds and consensual thought on what was considered vibrant but highly contemplative theology, the Army's doctrinal basis focused on how to communicate theology in popular language and tangible service.[40]

CHRISTOCENTRIC/MISSIONAL

When once asked which doctrine was the principal one for the Army, William Booth replied, "The bleeding Lamb."[41] Redemption through the entire incarnate life of the God-Man distilled in the Cross and Resurrection is non-negotiable in the Army's evangelistic doctrine. That one focus on salvation through the incarnate Son's self-giving sacrifice is central to every other facet of doctrine, superseding all else. To be born from above was, for the Booths, to be brought into gracious union with Christ.

> All through the New Testament, and indeed the Bible, no truth is taught with greater force and frequency than this, that without a vital union of the soul with Christ all ceremonies, creeds, beliefs, professions, church ordinances, are sounding brass and tinkling cymbals, and all who trust in them are deceived.[42]

40. *Handbook of Doctrine*, 51–77. A typical assessment of the need for sound doctrine while not rejecting sincere input from continual doctrinal clarification is found in S. L. Brengle's chapter, "What Is Fundamental?," in *Resurrection Life and Power* (Salvation Army Supplies, 1925), 28–38.

41. *Handbook of Doctrine*, 142.

42. Catherine Booth, *The Highway of Our God*, part l, ch. 4, 27.

Mirroring one of Wesley's outlines of salvation, Catherine summarizes the Christian life in three synoptic terms: repentance, faith, and holiness.[43] She is one of the Wesleyan tradition's clearest exponents of the judicial sufficiency of the substitutionary atonement, while adding every time that its concomitant, regeneration, must also be present in order for salvation in Christ to be truly and fully effective. She was quite exercised in the direction of Protestant thought that emphasized the objective work of Christ to the exclusion of regenerative change wrought by the Holy Spirit. Christ has come to conquer sin and to renew his image in us. Grace both redeems and heals from sin's death-producing power. We are "saved from sin, from second purposes, from selfish aims."[44]

TRANSFORMATIONAL

Thoroughly committed to the teachings of total depravity and original sin, the Booths eschewed any criticism of latent Pelagianism in their Wesleyan/Arminian perspective.[45] Due to the rejection of the life of God, an ever-present life-or-death decision had to be offered to every person. But the recurrent refrain was that sin and death were the result of the turning from, the spurning of the offered love of their Creator. One of John Wesley's clarifications for seekers in his day was the constant affirmation that repentance did not save. It was, as Wesley put it, "remotely" necessary. What was "immediately necessary" for salvation was faith.[46] The same pastoral guidance is present in many of the Booths' references to repentance. Very few evangelists (or theologians) are clearer on each aspect of how one is born again.[47]

43. See Wesley's discussion in "Principles of a Methodist Further Explained," *WJW* 8:472–74; Eason and Green, eds., *Settled Views*, 49; also, Catherine Booth, *The Highway of Our God*, pt. II, ch. 1, 32–36.

44. Eason and Green, eds., *Settled Views*, 64.

45. It is fascinating that Wesley's longest theological treatise is on original sin: "The Doctrine of Original Sin According to Scripture, Reason and Experience," *WJW* 9:192–464.

46. Wesley, "The Scripture Way of Salvation," III:1, *WJW* 6:48. Here Wesley discusses the conditions of justification.

47. Catherine Booth, *The Highway of Our God*, pt. I, ch. 1, 9–13, on repentance, ch. 3, 17–24, on saving faith. Both sections are heavy on genuine repentance and the

Their hearers had to be led carefully through all the elements which preceded regeneration.

Ever vigilant against false doctrine and resultant confusion about true conversion, the Booths dwell on the call to see, hate, and renounce all sin.[48] Conviction, conscience, and repentance in relation to faith are heavily defined and emphasized. The meaning of true faith as the crucial element in the new birth is found throughout the corpus. There is a constant refrain against any formalistic or institutional trappings misunderstood as saving in themselves.

The theology preached and written in Salvationist theology keeps in tandem the objective and the subjective elements of the atonement. Like their theological forebears, the Booths consistently communicate the antinomian implications of an overemphasis on the objectivity of the atonement to the exclusion of the full "healing" of the restored, moral image.[49]

PERSONAL

Though the Booths were convinced that most church-connected persons were imbibing an inadequate theological diet which limited their vision of salvific grace, they strove to make all the crucial elements of the Gospel apprehensible. There are never esoteric flights or mere philosophizing on doctrinal matters in Salvation Army theologians. Their distinctive didactic gifts were harnessed to be "exceedingly plain and practical" in countering, with graphic theological prowess, any incomplete conceptions of the power of the love of God in the human heart. The Army pleaded with sinners to "step right into the lifeblood of his broken, bleeding side."

A dynamic and personal pneumatology, evident everywhere in their combined corpus forms a telic orientation, a ubiquitous emphasis on the goal-oriented nature of salvation. At the new birth the love of God is introduced to the soul, and the spiritual eyes of the believer

renunciation of sin as a foundation of true faith. Belief is never mere assent; it is a total reversal of life.

48. Eason and Green, eds., *Settled Views*, 56–59.

49. Catherine refers to the "vermin" of antinomianism. Eason and Green, eds., *Settled Views*, 42.

are opened to the full purpose, the "scheme" of the triune God.[50] The Booths viewed the definition of a Christian as a "miserable sinner" as truncating the fullness offered to all in Christ. In a poignant passage, Catherine imagines if a believer were to bring that epithet into the presence of the Savior and they were then to realistically answer the question: what has grace really produced in my life?[51] Catherine's rejection of the antinomianism inherent in most of the theologies which regarded subjective righteousness as only "filthy rags" is a compelling rebuke against belief in sin as an unremovable reality.[52] She fought that inadequate form of the Gospel with its biblical antidote. For her, the "most glorious top stone" was the reality of the sanctified life. William confirms that focus. By the power of triune grace every Christian can possess something more than a heart that is a "cage of unclean birds."[53]

Here a vital portion of Salvationist soteriology is highlighted. Even though it might have been reasonable to not expect more than an initiatory experience of saving faith for most, the offer was always a "full" salvation. Catherine relates that it was to the "poor Salvation Army" that many wrote or came for counsel on how to deal with the lie of "partial" sanctification. Many Christians came to this upstart Mission, this uncouth group of street evangelists, to find the secret to a clean heart.[54] For her the realization of sanctification resided on four heads: 1) return (self-knowledge), 2) embracing God as the highest good, 3) coming to a "death-point," 4) and lastly, being possessed by divine love. It was that gift, a heart set free from self-will and filled with perfect love, which was the best, in her terms, the "highest good" that could be offered by the Army.[55]

50. Henry H. Knight III, "The Transformation of the Human Heart: The Place of Conversion in Wesley's Theology," 43–55 in *Conversion in the Wesleyan Tradition*, ed. K. Collins and J. Tyson (Abingdon, 2001). Eason and Green, eds., *Settled Views*, 98.

51. Eason and Green, eds., *Settled Views*, 93.

52. Eason and Green, eds., *Settled Views*, 96–97, 111–12.

53. Eason and Green, eds., *Settled Views*, 102, 109.

54. Eason and Green, eds., *Settled Views*, 103.

55. Eason and Green, eds., *Settled Views*, 103, 99–101.

CONTEXTUAL

It is often thought that the ministry to those whom Booth graphically referred to as the "submerged tenth" of English society began out of meeting social needs. Roger Green's assessment regarding the actual beginnings of the Army's social outreach has brought the relationship of evangelism and meeting needs into clearer historical and theological focus.[56] In a remarkable piece, Booth referred to his shift in evangelistic focus as the sole emphasis of the Army as a "War on Two Fronts."[57] Actual evangelism within the evangelical tradition has always borne the potential for conflict of emphasis between conversion and meeting human needs. The Wesleyan tradition, from which the Army drew its life both theologically and practically, was originally able to balance personal and social needs in the offer of a full salvation. Through several influences the Booths became convinced that to separate the spiritual from the crushing physical context of those to whom they ministered was not possible.

Of note, this Gospel ministry to the poor never devolved into mere sympathy or the impersonal dispensing of physical assistance. Every person was viewed as made in the image of God and thus of inestimable valuable. But that created glory was never lost in the necessity to respond as a person. No matter what the state of the needy, there was the unflinching insistence that there should be some responsible work or appropriate engagement that would lift the self-esteem of the recipients.[58]

56. William Booth, *Darkest England*, 31. The "Submerged Tenth" refers to the most destitute of English society. He compared these persons to the slaves emancipated decades before. They were caught in the vice of cruel cultural systems. He was deeply aware of the decimation of much of the culture around him, which most of the Church neglected or treated with disdain. Booth used many graphic terms for the neediest in his time, e.g. "the vilest of the vile" (166) and "human sludge" (81).

57. Title of a sermon preached in 1898 which changed the course of the Army's ministry.

58. Booth, *Darkest England*, 80. He says in a chapter entitled "Chaotic Charity," "There has never been an attempt to treat them as human beings. (The poor) are simply units . . . which dehumanizes. . . . It is well, no doubt, sometimes to administer an anaesthetic, but the Cure of the Patient is worth ever so much more." What follows are numerous ministries to lift the poor out of the "bog" in which they were hopelessly submerged.

The leadership of the Army in its infant stages was aware of how a division of spiritual transformation might be obfuscated by social outreach. One can find numerous indications where they felt the tension and expressed disagreement with the social ministry emphasis as a distinctly possible detraction from ultimate things. This disequilibrating concern can be heard in William Booth as he says:

> I have no intention to depart in the smallest degree from the main principles on which I have acted in the past. My only hope for the permanent deliverance of mankind from misery, either in this world or the next, is the regeneration or remaking of the individual by the power of the Holy Ghost through Jesus Christ. But in providing for the relief of temporal misery I reckon that I am only making it easy where it is now difficult, and possible where it is now all but impossible, for men and women to find their way to the Cross of our Lord Jesus Christ.[59]

Salvationism and the Distinctives of the Wesleyan Holiness Tradition

It is important to place the Army in relation to the roots of its theology, both in connection to some of the major traditions as well as the Wesleyan Holiness heritage of which it is a direct descendant.

A general comparison (see Appendix Two) of the major Christian traditions reveals a fundamental agreement on much of how believers have articulated the Way of Salvation.[60] Though there are major

59. Booth, *Darkest England*, this and many similar comments are found throughout. See *Darkest England*, 43, 53, 54, 93, 295. George Railton and Catherine were extremely concerned about this move from its earliest conception. William was equally wrought about the potential misalignment and loss of God's favor in an overemphasis on the social to the exclusion of the spiritual. Owen Chadwick stated, "Yet in Booth's lonely old age . . . he sometimes wondered whether he had been right to allow the Army to divert its energies from conversion." *The Victorian Church*, 2 vols. (Adam and Charles Black, 1960), 2:297. Quoted in Roger J. Green, "An Historical Salvation Army Perspective," 43–81 in *Creed and Deed: Toward a Christian Theology of Social Services in The Salvation Army*, ed. John Waldron (Triumph Press / The Salvation Army, 1986), 73.

60. Michael Green outlines the evangelistic elements of several Church Fathers, comparing the early Church with contemporary evangelistic themes. Of Macarius he writes, "It would be difficult to say that that man had lost his grip on Christian

differences in relating salvation to the eternality and sovereignty of God, the relationship between an individual's will and the reception of grace and the exact necessity of sacramental and ecclesiological elements for salvation, there remain similar theological commonplaces. Salvation is all of God. Salvation is a trinitarian reality. Nothing a human can do earns or maintains grace. God graciously and lovingly offers new life to those who have rejected him. That grace enables a response from each person, regardless of where the emphasis on that response may lie in a particular order. Repentance, belief, and faith are crucial elements in the relationship God offers.

Within the larger Christian tradition, Wesley's theological prowess is best exemplified in the distinctive order of salvation which found complete affirmation in the ensuing theological formation of the Army. As Appendix One shows, apart from the Articles that pertain to ecclesiology, the major, consensual, and distinctive elements are nearly identical. The only place where there is an unmistakable addition is Doctrine 10 on Entire Sanctification.

The Salvation Army has always borne the telic orientation of the Wesleyan *ordo salutis* (see Diagram One). They saw and agreed fully with what has been referred to as the "second half of salvation." The dynamism of a full appropriation of the Gospel meant that there was a grace-filled expectation of freedom from sins and the source of those sins by grace. It was there that the Army offered the same goal-oriented nature of triune grace that was central to the Wesleyan revival.

The focus is not on divine determinism or sacramentalism but on the trajectory (*telos*) of grace in every person's life. The underlying importance of both being created in the image of God and the restoration of the moral image marks every aspect of the Salvationist concept of being born anew.[61] Even though the more recent discussions

fundamentals, or that no signs of the New Testament doctrines of faith, grace, the atonement, the new birth, and perseverance were to be found in his *Homilies*." *Evangelism in the Early Church*, 138.

61. It is interesting to note the amount of times Booth mentions the individual in *Darkest England*. See *Darkest England*, 53, 80. Chapter 8 reveals a culturally challenging assessment of children as not born into the world but "born into damnation," in a day when they were not valued as persons. Booth deplores that any child be viewed as a "half-person." *Darkest England*, 75.

DIAGRAM ONE

The Wesleyan *Ordo Salutis* in Salvationist Theology

creation in the image of God	**re-creation of the image of God**
original sin (atonement)	**conviction of inward sin**
prevenient grace	**sanctifying grace**
repentance	**evangelical repentance of believers**
saving faith by grace alone	**sanctifying faith by grace alone**
justification/new birth	**true righteousness/restored image**
initial sanctification	**entire sanctification**
assurance	**assurance**
growth	**growth**

on personhood, which arose originally in the creedal discussions surrounding the development of trinitarian and Christological theology, were not overtly articulated, the Army's robust view of human personhood is redolent.

A short assessment of Wesleyan thought as foundational to Salvationist doctrine as communicated in its evangelistic outreach helps to see similarities and articulate their transformative ministries in the historical moments when they were expressed. The careful rearticulation, refinement, and expansive doctrine of prevenient grace found in Wesley's thought is presumed in Salvationist theology.[62] The foundation of prevenient grace, which issues into personal conviction of sin and the opportunity to place oneself in recumbent trust in Christ alone, permeates every aspect of the Army's evangelistic outreach.

62. W. Brian Shelton, *Prevenient Grace: God's Provision for Fallen Humanity* (Francis Asbury Press, Warner Press, 2014) is an excellent recent survey of biblical, historical, and systematic understandings of prevenient grace. His analysis renders Wesley as "the theologian *par excellence* on the doctrine of prevenient grace," 139. He quotes Stanley Ayling's assessment that Wesley's popularization of Arminius's major theological commonplaces made him the "single most influential Protestant leader in the English-speaking world since the Reformation." Shelton, *Prevenient Grace*, 95.

Both traditions offer a rich theology of faith. Faith is always and only seen as a gift of God. The nature of personhood, both divine and human, secures the true meaning of faith. Faith is never imposed against anyone's will. Belief as trust is, in good Wesleyan fashion, a "full reliance . . . a recumbency" of the person through the enablement of the Spirit into the very life of God, as the Son also enters into the life of the believer.[63] There is a ready affirmation of all the "solas" which have been distilled from the Reformation period. So close, a "hair's breadth" as Wesley put it, is this sector of the Wesleyan Holiness tradition to magisterial Calvinism that it might best be delineated as a monergistic synergism.[64]

The One who died upon the Cross offers more than a juridical pardon. He is salvation in his person, whose goal is to recreate persons in his image. That balance of the objective and subjective benefits of the atonement is immediately seen in the insistence that justification is concomitant with initial sanctification. The constant salvific refrain is that both sins and inward sin, any heart idolatry expressing defiant self-will, are both dealt with in biblical salvation. Redemption includes deliverance both from the symptoms of sin as well as their source. The goal of all evangelism is the entire sanctification of, that is, the restoration of the moral image in, every person. Once again, the relationship between doctrine and experience is a constant focus of these two conjoined traditions. The synthesis of nature and grace, atonement and reliance, law and Gospel, pardon and holiness, reveals a dynamic relationship between doctrine and evangelism in the theology of The Salvation Army.

The axiomatic implication of the salvation begun by grace in the heart of every convert is that it must issue in some form of cultural

63. Wesley, Sermon 1, "Salvation by Faith," *WJW* 5:9. It is telling that this recurrent theme, if not always in the same language, is placed at the head of all of Wesley's preached theology.

64. A time-honored summary of Wesleyan emphases is:

All need salvation
All can be saved
All can know that they are saved
All can be saved "to the uttermost" (or, can be made holy).

transformation. Holiness is always teleological rather than deontological. The communal support for those who desired to "flee the wrath to come" was evident in both revivals.[65] That form of interpersonal discipline, maintained by the leadership genius of Wesley and inculcated using a quasi-military structure in the Army, assisted in the production of maturing disciples, as well as being a foundation for training leaders. The "social holiness" of transformed, maturing disciples was expected to offer substantial means of altering the immediately surrounding culture and beyond.

Conclusion

The Salvation Army stands in line with the foundational doctrines of consensual Christianity. The theological nuances of that basis are best seen through the lens of the Wesleyan tradition and its Holiness expression. Ecumenical dialogue, a catholicity of spirit, and a deep desire to share in ministry to the neediest regardless of theological differences have been hallmarks of the approach to essential doctrines in Salvationism.[66]

Meeting the One who is salvation himself is the primary focus of all that is truly the Army's evangelism. While not demanding doctrinal agreement on discrete theological concepts—i.e., the Trinity, the dual natures of Christ, or other deeper issues—there is doctrinal emphasis woven into the fabric of salvation. Salvationist theology bears a foundational doctrinal concern while always emphasizing the transformational reality of all Christian truth.

There are issues which the Army must face in the days to come. 1) Without a strong and ever-deepening doctrinal foundation, in both clergy and laity, the denomination will find itself floundering in a sea of postmodern theology. 2) The lack of robust theological

65. One of three General Rules. See Wesley, "The Nature, Design and General Rules of the United Societies," *WJW* 8:269–71.

66. From 2007–2012 Salvationists and Catholics met each year for theological discussions, found in *Conversations: A Record of the Papers Presented and Recommendations Made during the Informal Conversations between the Catholic Church and The Salvation Army* (Salvation Army, 2014).

engagement in the particular ministry areas that the Army is best suited to offer will result in the same institutionalization as the "dead sects" of the past. 3) Social ministry and the respect that it brings will not be enough to shore up the challenges that already threaten Salvationist orthodoxy. This is not a new concern. Lillian Taiz offers a sobering comparison where she writes:

> During the early twentieth century the Salvation Army ceased to be a working-class-dominated religious organization. . . . Its social institutions offered temporal salvation to the poor while its spiritual work ministered to the upwardly mobile. . . . In contrast to the blood-washed warriors of the nineteenth century, Salvationists of the twentieth century generally regarded themselves as members of a church that sponsored *professionalized* Christian social services to the downtrodden.[67]

Given the theological minefield of present-day engagement with culture, it is crucial that the divine call upon the Army for its over sesquicentennial history not be bartered away. Desire for cultural acceptance will always be a threat to the offer of salvation in distinctly personal, and thus, confrontative ways. But more threatening are the financial implications, if the Army is seen as a church which requires salvation in Christ as a standard that will not be compromised under any cultural norms which stand against historic Christianity. 4) Lastly, the unending pressure of relentless "needs" can also blunt the central theological components of the Army's purpose. "Emotional and Spiritual Care," which is the approach taken at each engagement with persons in inevitable crises, can become nothing more than a simple blessing, either physically or verbally, without a concerted effort to dive into each person's real spiritual needs. The priority of offering a full salvation seems almost too demanding a task in the face of constant distress.

What is the Gospel? As we have seen, doctrine is unquestionably important in evangelism for The Salvation Army. But, to place doctrine as an indication of one's orthodoxy over actually offering Christ

67. Lillian Taiz, *Hallelujah Lads and Lasses: Remaking The Salvation Army in America, 1880–1930* (University of North Carolina Press, 2001), 144, 161, 164, 166.

is anathema to Salvationism. The Gospel must be always incarnated theology, offered salvation, confronting injustice with redemptive love and saving truth. Salvific truth without finding creative means for sharing Christ's reconciling love is, for Salvationists, an impossibility.

At several important junctures of early Salvationist history the picture of a storm with people drowning captivated William Booth's entire agenda. He recounts a "vision" he had once of the culture where the Army had been placed. As with the Church in any time and place, he saw a storm engulfing masses of people. Both personal and institutional forms of sin were the source of the chaos. Offering salvation took many forms: ropes, ladders, plunging in. What shocked Booth was that most who had been saved were unwilling, and thus unresponsive, to those who were yet in distress. They rejected the call of a "Wonderful Being" to dive into the chaos, the "holy strife," to join him in saving others. The Founder of the Army noted that they all worshipped, prayed, fellowshipped, and even asked for the presence of the Rock of Salvation in their midst, but they were unwilling to offer the deliverance they had known. Booth concludes:

> Now then, go to God and tell Him . . . that you are willing to spend the rest of your days struggling in the midst of these perishing multitudes, whatever it may cost you. You must do it. With the light that is now broken in upon your mind and the call that is now sounding in your ears, and the beckoning hands that are now before your eyes, you have no alternative. To go down among the perishing crowds is your duty. Your happiness from now on will consist in sharing their misery, your ease in sharing their pain, your crown in helping them to bear their cross, and your heaven in going into the very jaws of hell to rescue them.[68]

68. William Booth, *Visions* (1906). Find it as the last article entitled "Who Cares?" at www.salvationfactory.org/w-p-content/uploads/2015/Who-Cares-pr.pdf (accessed September 9, 2022). The entirety of *Darkest England* bears the imprint of this sense of the drowning masses. Maritime metaphors are found numerous times, for example, "submerged" (31), "social lifeboat institution" (51), "drain the whole bog" (81, 94), a literal "Salvation Ship" (160–63).

APPENDIX ONE

Comparison of 25 Methodist Articles of Religion with the 11 Salvationist Doctrines[69]

25 ARTICLES OF RELIGION	DOCTRINES OF THE SALVATION ARMY
	1. The Inspiration of Scripture
	2. The One True God
1. Faith in the Holy Trinity	3. The Co-equal Trinity
2. The Word, or Son of God, Who Was Made Very Man	4. The Person of Jesus Christ
3. The Resurrection of Christ	
4. The Holy Ghost	
5. The Sufficiency of the Holy Scriptures for Salvation	
6. The Old Testament	
7. Original or Birth Sin	5. Creation in the Image of God/Fall
8. Free Will	6. Atonement
9. Justification	7. Regeneration
10. Good Works	8. Justification
11. Works of Supererogation	
12. Sin After Justification	9. Continued Obedient Faith
13. The Church	
14. Purgatory	
15. Speaking in a Tongue the People Understand	
16. Sacraments	
17. Baptism	
18. The Lord's Supper	
19. Both Kinds	
20. The One Oblation of Christ, Finished upon the Cross	
21. Marriage of Ministers	

69. The eventual distillation of the Methodist Articles of Religion from the Thirty-Nine Anglican Articles, which shows a strong *via media* approach given its strong dependence upon the Augsburg Confession and Latin theologians for a variety of reasons. Of the Thirty-Nine Articles 3, 8, 13, 15, 17, 18, 20, 21, 23, 24, 29, 33, 35, 39 were removed. See the discussion of the reasons for the removals in Oden, *Doctrinal Standards*, 104–6.

25 ARTICLES OF RELIGION	DOCTRINES OF THE SALVATION ARMY
22. Rites and Ceremonies of Churches	
23. Rulers of the United States of America	
24. Christian Men's Goods	
25. Christian Man's Oath	10. Entire Sanctification
	11. Eschatology[70]

APPENDIX TWO

A General Comparison of Orders of Salvation

Wesleyan	Reformed	Lutheran	Catholic
Prevenient Grace	Common Grace		Prevenient Grace
	Electing Grace	Baptismal Regen.	Baptismal Regen.
	Predestination		
	Mystical Union		Sufficient Grace
	Regeneration		
	Faith		
	Calling	Calling	
	Illumination		Illumination
Convicting Grace	Conversion		
Repentance	Repentance	Repentance	Repentance
Faith			Cooperating Grace
Saving Grace			Regeneration
			Preparation
	a. Justification	*Faith*	
	b. Adoption	Justification	
Initial Sanct.	Sanctification	Sanctification	Infused Grace
	Daily Conversion		Sacramental Grace
Assurance	Repentance	Repentance	Justification
Growth in Grace	Repentance	Repentance	Repentance
	Perseverance		Merit
Evangelical Repentance			
Entire Sanctification			
Assurance of Sanctification			
Growth in Grace			
	Perseverance		Penance
Glorification	Glorification	Glorification	Glorification

70. *The Salvation Army Handbook of Doctrine* (Salvation Books, 2010), xv–xvi. Note also a chapter given to ecclesiology and sacramentalism: *Handbook of Doctrine*, 247–75. Green asserts that Benjamin Field's *The Student Handbook of Christian Theology* (1868) was the immediate source of Booth's initial doctrinal statement. Roger J. Green, *War on Two Fronts: William Booth's Theology of Redemption* (Crest Books, 2017), 34–35.

APPENDIX THREE
The Doctrines of The Salvation Army

We believe that the Scriptures of the Old and New Testaments were given by inspiration of God, and that they only constitute the Divine rule of Christian faith and practice.

We believe that there is only one God, who is infinitely perfect, the Creator, Preserver, and Governor of all things, and who is the only proper object of religious worship.

We believe that there are three persons in the Godhead—the Father, the Son and the Holy Ghost, undivided in essence and co-equal in power and glory.

We believe that in the person of Jesus Christ the Divine and human natures are united, so that He is truly and properly God and truly and properly man.

We believe that our first parents were created in a state of innocency, but by their disobedience they lost their purity and happiness, and that in consequence of their fall all men have become sinners, totally depraved, and as such are justly exposed to the wrath of God.

We believe that the Lord Jesus Christ has by His suffering and death made an atonement for the whole world so that whosoever will may be saved.

We believe that repentance towards God, faith in our Lord Jesus Christ, and regeneration by the Holy Spirit, are necessary to salvation.

We believe that we are justified by grace through faith in our Lord Jesus Christ and that he that believeth hath the witness in himself.

We believe that continuance in a state of salvation depends upon continued obedient faith in Christ.

We believe that it is the privilege of all believers to be wholly sanctified, and that their whole spirit and soul and body may be preserved blameless unto the coming of our Lord Jesus Christ.

We believe in the immortality of the soul; in the resurrection of the body; in the general judgment at the end of the world; in the eternal happiness of the righteous; and in the endless punishment of the wicked.

1.3 Mission and Evangelization in the Catholic Church Today

Daniel A. Keating

The pilgrim Church is missionary by her very nature. (*Ad gentes*, §2)[1]

Introduction

THE AIM OF THIS PAPER is to track the main lines of the Catholic Church's approach to mission and evangelization in the twentieth century and up to today.[2] Mission of course has existed from the very beginning of the Church and the call to spread the Gospel is found in every age, but a *theology* of mission—a sustained theological reflection on mission—is of relatively late vintage.[3] For tracing a theology of mission and evangelization, developments in the twentieth century leading up to and including the Second Vatican

1. Second Vatican Council, *Ad gentes* (December 7, 1965), 459–51 in *The Sixteen Documents of Vatican II* (Daughters of St. Paul, n. d.).

2. A focus on the contemporary period means that I will not be able to give attention to the history of mission through the centuries and to the theological resources from past times that provide the foundation for a theology of mission today. For a brief overview of mission and evangelization in the Catholic Church previous to the last century, see my summary in "Mission and Evangelization," 329–45 in *The Oxford Handbook on Catholic Theology*, ed. Lewis Ayres and Medi Ann Volpe (Oxford University Press, 2019), at 330–31.

3. Scholars of the history of mission typically date the beginning of "missiology" (sustained historical and theological reflection on mission) in the Protestant world to Gustav Warneck (1834–1910), and in the Catholic world to Josef Schmidlin (1876–1944).

Council, along with the crises and challenges following the Council, are paramount. Mission in the Catholic Church at the beginning of the twenty-first century is understood and practiced differently than mission was at the beginning of the twentieth century. Important continuities exist but there have been significant developments. My hope is to trace some of these developments and offer a summary of the main elements of a Catholic understanding of mission and evangelization today.

The Period Leading Up to Vatican II

The papal teaching on mission in the first half of the twentieth century gives us a window onto how mission was then being conceived and carried out, and what issues were emerging. In the nineteenth century, following a long period of missionary stagnation, the Catholic Church experienced a season of explosive missionary growth. With the help of strong papal encouragement numerous missionary religious orders of both men and women sprang up, the end result being that "the approximate number of Catholic missionaries worldwide jumped from three hundred in 1800 to seventy-five hundred in 1920."[4] It was to this context that the popes directed their missionary teaching and directives in the first half of the twentieth century.

Three papal letters are especially useful for assessing a Catholic understanding of mission in this period. The first, *Maximum illud* (*MI*) from Benedict XV in 1919, speaks about mission in traditional terms. Mission is understood as being directed to the nations (*ad gentes*) that have never heard the Gospel message, with a strongly expressed sense of obligation to evangelize the unreached peoples and to win souls for Christ (*MI*, §7). The clear assumption is that mission workers will be celibate men and women (*MI*, §12), with the laity supporting mission work through prayer, financial contribution, and fostering vocations for mission (*MI*, §§31–34). The central pastoral aim of the letter, however, is a keen concern for training local people in mission areas so

4. Stephen B. Bevans and Roger P. Schroeder, *Constants in Context: A Theology of Mission for Today* (Orbis Books, 2004), 226.

that the local church can carry on without foreign missionaries (*MI*, §§15–19).

In *Rerum Ecclesiae* (1926), Pius XI follows Benedict XV's approach closely, with one development worthy of note. Pius emphasizes the value of charitable works accompanying mission, and encourages missionaries to attend specially to the poor who are often the most ready to receive the Gospel. This is not yet the focus on solidarity with the poor or a "preferential option for the poor" that will emerge after the Second Vatican Council, but a door is opened in this direction.

With Pius XII's encyclical letter *Evangelii praecones* (*EP*)[5] in 1951, new concerns and orientations begin to appear. He confirms the traditional view of mission as consisting of the proclamation of the Gospel and the establishment of the Church (*EP*, §22), but hints at a wider concept of mission that includes promoting culture, peace, and justice among nations (*EP*, §23). Works of charity, Pius says, are essential but not sufficient, "for in the first place there must be justice which should prevail and be put into practice" (*EP*, §51). Strikingly, he opens up a new role for the laity in mission, not just indirectly through prayer and financial support but as active workers in the mission field (*EP*, §37). Finally, Pius XII directly addresses the issue of inculturation, that is, the need to respect and make use of what is "naturally good, just or beautiful" in a native culture (*EP*, §56). The promotion of justice, the direct involvement of the laity, and the need for inculturation—all these will receive significant development at the Second Vatican Council.

The Second Vatican Council

Background. The Second Vatican Council's Decree on the Mission Activity of the Church (*Ad gentes*), promulgated in 1965, was arguably the most developed presentation of a theology of mission and evangelization ever offered by the Church's magisterium. Alongside *Ad gentes* were other important statements touching directly on mission found in the Decree on the Laity, *Apostolicam actuositatem* (*AA*), and in the

5. Quotations from Pius XII, *Evangelii praecones* (June 2, 1951) (Paulist Press, 1951).

Pastoral Constitution on the Church in the Modern World, *Gaudium et spes* (*GS*). The forwarding of mission, however, was not really a central concern at the Council, and so this teaching on mission was left largely in the shadows and remained undeveloped for some years following the Council. Still, the principles laid down in *Ad gentes* (*AG*) have proved immensely important for the subsequent development of a theology of mission and so demand our close attention.

Trinitarian Foundation for Mission. The opening sentence of chapter one is perhaps the most important single statement in the document: "The pilgrim Church is missionary by her very nature, since it is from the mission of the Son and the mission of the Holy Spirit that she draws her origin, in accordance with the decree of God the Father" (*AG*, §2). By situating a theology of mission in the missions of the Son and Spirit, the Council decisively locates mission in the very nature of the triune God and the work of the triune God in the world. Mission, then, is to be conceived not primarily as a practical matter and not only as a response of obedience to Christ's command, but as part of the Church's very nature and as an expression of the full unfolding of God's own action in the world. Previous to the Council, "the theological basis for the Church's missionary activity was, as a rule, the *missionary mandate* of the risen Lord."[6] Now the Council draws attention to the truth that mission is to be understood as having both its origin and final goal in the triune God.[7]

The implications of the trinitarian origination of mission and evangelization are profound. The triune God is recognized as the primary agent of mission; the Church participates in and serves the mission of the Son and the Spirit for the salvation and sanctification of the created order. Without minimizing human action in any respect, *Ad gentes* positions the Father, Son, and Spirit at the center of mission and calls the Church to reconsider mission from the perspective of

6. Adam Wolanin, "Trinitarian Foundation of Mission," 47–64 in *Following Christ in Mission: A Foundational Course in Missiology*, ed. Sebastian Karotemprel (Daughters of St. Paul, 1996), 49.

7. It is important to recognize that this theology of mission grounded in the triune God and in the missions of the Son and the Spirit in the world is already implicitly found, for example, in the theology of Thomas Aquinas.

the entire narrative of salvation grounded in the Bible. Conversely, a trinitarian theology of mission requires the Church to reconsider all of Christian life from the perspective of mission. If the Church is missionary "by her very nature" then all aspects of Christian life—theology, pastoral practice, the sacraments, priestly ministry, the lay vocation—need to be understood as having a missionary dimension.

Broader Definition of Mission. In *Ad gentes* we also begin to see a broader, more comprehensive understanding of mission emerge. "The mission of the Church" is that activity which makes the Church "fully present" to all peoples and which leads them on a "firm and free road to full participation in the mystery of Christ" (*AG*, §5). This broader notion of mission entails the witness of a genuine Christian life (*AG*, §11), and includes striving for dignity, peace, and justice in temporal affairs and the works of charity (*AG*, §12). Nonetheless, the Council underlines that proclamation of the Gospel and entrance into the Church through baptism are the "chief means" by which mission is advanced (*AG*, §6), and that direct proclamation can never be forfeited:

> It is not enough that the Christian people be present and be organized in a given nation, nor is it enough to carry out an apostolate by way of example. They are organized for this purpose, they are present for this, to announce Christ to their non-Christian fellow-citizens by word and example, and to aid them toward the full reception of Christ. (*AG*, §15)

One signpost of this broader concept of mission is the appearance of a new term. Alongside the more traditional terms, "mission" and "apostolate," "evangelization" makes an entrance at Vatican II and becomes increasingly the preferred term for describing the missionary activity of the Church.[8] Though Catholics only began to use this term just previous to the Council, it has now become the standard term in Catholic parlance.[9]

8. Appearing only once in pre-Vatican II mission encyclicals (*Evangelii praecones*, §19), the term "evangelization" is found nineteen times in *Ad gentes* and will become even more common in the missionary writings of Paul VI, John Paul II, and Francis.

9. Ironically, the term "evangelization" was first used in Evangelical Protestant circles in the late nineteenth century.

Mission and Salvation. The Council also had to wrestle with an apparent incompatibility: how can we reconcile the acknowledgment that salvation is in principle open to all people, even those who have never heard and responded to the Gospel—which the Council plainly acknowledged[10]—with the ongoing requirement to announce the good news? If someone can potentially be saved apart from an explicit response of faith to the Gospel message, is mission traditionally conceived now passé? *Ad gentes* firmly answers this question by upholding the necessity of mission and the reception of people into the Church:

> Therefore though God in ways known to himself can lead those inculpably ignorant of the gospel to find that faith without which it is impossible to please him (Heb. 11:6), yet a necessity lies upon the Church (1 Cor. 9:16), and at the same time a sacred duty, to preach the gospel. And hence missionary activity today as always retains its power and necessity. (*AG*, §7)

In the postconciliar period this issue will be revisited, and the argument within the Catholic Church *against* the need for mission as traditionally conceived will intensify.

Inculturation. Two further elements in a theology of mission at the Council are worthy of note. The first is an expression of what the Church had traditionally said about the intersection of the Gospel and human culture. The preaching of the Gospel and the practices of the Church do not negate elements present in various human cultures, but they purify them and raise them up, holding on to what is good. "And so, whatever good is found to be sown in the hearts and minds of men, or in the rites and cultures peculiar to various peoples, not only is not lost, but is healed, uplifted, and perfected for the glory of God" (*AG*, §9). In other words, human culture apart from Christ is not barren of his presence, but already possesses "seeds" that can be cultivated as the Gospel brings what is latent to full fruition (*AG*, §22). This perspective, found in the early Fathers of the Church (e.g., Justin Martyr), receives a new emphasis here.

10. See e.g. *Lumen gentium*, §16; *Ad gentes*, §7.

The Role of the Laity. Vatican II also explicitly opened wide the doors to the activity of the laity in many spheres, including that of mission and evangelization. The Council offered a theology of the laity that grounds their activity in the threefold office of priest, prophet, and king: "But the laity likewise share in the priestly, prophetic, and royal office of Christ and therefore have their own share in the mission of the whole people of God in the Church and in the world" (*AA*, §2).[11] Specifically, the missionary role of the laity is directed to the "evangelization and sanctification" of all people and to "the penetrating and perfecting of the temporal order through the spirit of the gospel" (*AA*, §2). By placing the renewal of the temporal order within the sphere of mission, the Council not only broadened the scope of the Church's missionary activity but commissioned the laity to be active in this sphere and opened the way for what will later be called the New Evangelization.

In summary, the Second Vatican Council put the missionary activity of the Church at the center of things, even if it did not pursue the advancement of mission as a central focus. By asserting that the "pilgrim Church is missionary by her very nature" and that missionary activity is "the greatest and holiest task of the Church" (*AG*, §2, §29), and by offering a greatly expanded theology of mission and a broadened understanding of the scope of mission, the Council would seem to have prepared the way for a new season of missionary flourishing. It is more than a little ironic that in the years immediately following the Council the vision for mission was blurred and the impulse for mission blunted.

The Postconciliar Period: Challenge and Response

Among many factors that contributed to the "missionary crisis"[12] following Vatican II, three primary causes may be identified. The first was a call for liberation from unjust social structures as the new locus for the

11. Quotations from *Apostolicam actuositatem*, 333–72 in *The Sixteen Documents of Vatican II* (Daughters of St. Paul, n. d.).

12. Bevans and Schroeder, *Constants in Context*, 251.

Church's mission, especially in Latin America. The second was a new theology of religions that raised serious doubts about the legitimacy of mission. And the third was a postcolonial critique that called into question, and often rejected, the content and methods of the Church's traditional approach to mission in developing countries.[13] It was in the crucible of these challenges that the Church's theology of mission and evangelization was tested, purified, and refined in the postconciliar period. Here I will examine the first two of these challenges.

Theologies of Liberation. The conviction that missionary activity should include working for justice and human development is already present in Pius XII's missionary encyclical *Evangelii praecones* (1951), and received much greater emphasis at Vatican II (*AG*, §11–12). But it was during the gathering of the Latin American bishops in 1968 at Medellín that the topic of liberation became front and center, catalyzing a profusion of writing on the subject of liberation in the 1970s from a distinctively Latin American perspective. The watershed work was written by Gustavo Gutiérrez (*A Theology of Liberation*, 1971), but a wide array of theologians attempted to express a theology of liberation that entailed a new way of conceiving the mission of the Church in the world.[14]

To summarize the main tenets of these theologies of liberation is notoriously difficult, not least because they differ from one another in notable ways. They propose to begin from the existential situation of the poor and oppressed and to interpret the Gospel in terms of the experience of the poor and their liberation from unjust structures and institutions. Narratives from the Old Testament, especially the deliverance of Israel from slavery in Egypt, provide the primary paradigms for liberation from contemporary forms of oppression. Sin is viewed not merely or even primarily in terms of individual moral action, but in terms of social structures of oppression.[15] Many liberation theolo-

13. For this threefold cause for the missionary crisis, see Karl Müller, "Missiology: An Introduction," 25–45 in *Following Christ in Mission*, at 30–31.

14. Among other prominent authors who helped shape liberation theology are Leonardo Boff, Juan Luis Segundo, Jon Sobrino, and José Miguez Bonino.

15. Rebecca S. Chopp, "Latin American Liberation Theology," 409–25 in *The Modern Theologians*, ed. David F. Ford, 2nd ed. (Blackwell, 1997).

gians make explicit use of both Marxist social analysis and philosophy of history, seeking to apply them in ways they believe serve the cause of the Gospel among the poor.

The topic of liberation theology was prominent during the third Synod of Bishops (1974) that took up "Evangelization in the Modern World" as its topic. This in turn led to the promulgation of Paul VI's apostolic exhortation *Evangelii nuntiandi* (*EN*) in 1975.[16] Calling this letter a "meditation on evangelization" (*EN*, §5),[17] he states his goal is to encourage mission "in this time of uncertainty and confusion," in order "to make the Church of the twentieth century ever better fitted for proclaiming the Gospel to the people of the twentieth century" (*EN*, §1, §2). The opening salvo of the letter is a vibrant declaration of the validity of the Church's mission to proclaim the Gospel that sets the stage for all that follows:

> The presentation of the Gospel message is not an optional contribution for the Church. It is the duty incumbent on her by the command of the Lord Jesus, so that people can believe and be saved. This message is indeed necessary. It is unique. It cannot be replaced. It does not permit either indifference, syncretism or accommodation. It is a question of people's salvation. (*EN*, §5)

With respect to the topic of liberation theology, *Evangelii nuntiandi* carefully positions new insights on human liberation within a wider framework that upholds the need for mission, for conversion, and for the role of the Church. And so Pope Paul says that the good news of the Gospel is "liberation from everything that oppresses" the human race, "but which is above all liberation from sin and the Evil One, in the joy of knowing God and being known by him" (*EN*, §9). Notably, Paul broadens the sphere of evangelization to include more than just proclamation and sacramental initiation (*EN*, §17). The Gospel kerygma is a crucial and central aspect of evangelization, but it is only one aspect of the entire evangelizing activity of the Church (*EN*, §22).

16. Quotations from Paul VI, *On Evangelization in the Modern World: Evangelii nuntiandi* (December 8, 1975) (United States Catholic Conference, 1976).

17. The term "evangelization" becomes predominant in this letter, appearing 115 times, while the term "mission" appears just 23 times.

Paul introduces the idea of "evangelizing culture and cultures," while constantly returning to the need for proclaiming the Gospel if human cultures are to be truly evangelized (*EN*, §20). As a summary statement of the full work of evangelization, he writes:

> Evangelization, as we have said, is a complex process made up of varied elements: the renewal of humanity, witness, explicit proclamation, inner adherence, entry into the community, acceptance of signs, apostolic initiative. These elements may appear to be contradictory, indeed mutually exclusive. In fact they are complementary and mutually enriching. Each one must always be seen in relationship with the others. (*EN*, §24)[18]

Paul goes on to address the issue of evangelization and human liberation more concretely. Speaking about the profound links between evangelization and human advancement (*EN*, §29), he rejects at the same time the temptation to reduce the Gospel to a purely temporal project; the Church's contribution to human liberation is gutted if the proclamation of salvation in Christ is neglected. Importantly, Paul asserts that the Church "links human liberation and salvation in Jesus Christ, but she never identifies them" (*EN*, §35), and he firmly rejects the use of violence that some were proposing as a path to liberation (*EN*, §37). In sum, Paul widens a theology of mission and evangelization to include new insights about the Church's mission to the poor, but at the same time he adjusts or rejects certain aspects of liberation theology that were emerging.[19]

18. In his own summary of this complex picture, John Paul II tends to use the term "mission" rather than "evangelization": "Mission is a single but complex reality, and it develops in a variety of ways." *Redemptoris missio* (December 7, 1990) (United States Catholic Conference, 1990), §41.

19. In the 1980s the Congregation for the Doctrine of the Faith (CDF) weighed in on the subject, issuing two important instructions intended to clarify concerns raised about liberation theology: *Instruction on Certain Aspects of the "Theology of Liberation"* (1984) and *Instruction on Christian Freedom and Liberation* (1986). The first instruction offered a sharp critique of certain elements within liberation theology, especially Marxist elements that were deemed inconsistent with a Christian anthropology. The second instruction sought to provide a more positive account of how liberation and evangelization go together.

The fall of the communist governments in Eastern Europe in 1989 and the evident failure of Marxism to transform society dealt a serious blow to the hopes of many that a theology of liberation was the way of the future. But the challenges presented by these theologies of liberation nonetheless provoked the Church to examine the relationship between mission and human liberation and led to a broadened conception of mission.

Theologies of Religion and the Issue of Universalism. An even more severe challenge to mission in the postconciliar period came from various theologies of religion offering a spectrum of positions that called into question the need for, and the validity of, mission.[20] Was the old paradigm of "preaching the Gospel" and "winning souls for Christ" now outdated? If God could bring people to salvation by means that did not include formal entrance into the Church—which Vatican II specifically allowed—then perhaps the mission of the Church was simply to help people of other faiths live their own religious practices well. Was the Church, then, really necessary for salvation, and should the Church any longer seek to make converts from other religions? Was explicit faith in Christ necessary for salvation, or were there alternate paths to salvation, orchestrated by God's Spirit, that existed within the practices of other religions? More radically, is salvation really an issue at all, given the assumption that all (or nearly all but a few of the most hardened) will eventually be saved? A tacit universalism—that all in the end will be saved by the mercy of God—functions more or less openly in these various theologies of religion, and had a profound impact on the views of the laity.[21]

John Paul II composed his encyclical letter *Redemptoris missio* (*RM*) on the twenty-fifth anniversary of *Ad gentes* (December 7, 1990), in

20. For an overview of the various positions taken in contemporary theology of religions, see Gavin D'Costa, *Christianity and World Religions: Disputed Questions in the Theology of Religions* (Wiley-Blackwell, 2009), 3–54.

21. For the theological roots of this culture of universalism and its effects upon the Church, see Ralph Martin, *Will Many Be Saved? What Vatican II Actually Teaches and Its Implications for the New Evangelization* (Eerdmans, 2012), and Michael J. McClymond, *The Devil's Redemption: A New History and Interpretation of Christian Universalism* (Baker, 2020).

large part to answer these questions and doubts about the ongoing need for mission. The stated purpose of the letter is to renew the Church's missionary commitment, with the conviction that "the moment has come to commit all of the Church's energies to a new evangelization and to the mission *ad gentes*" (*RM*, §3).[22] But it is clear from his own summary of the present situation that doubts surrounding mission are uppermost in John Paul's concerns:

> *Is missionary work among non-Christians still relevant?* Has it not been replaced by inter-religious dialogue? Is not human development an adequate goal of the Church's mission? Does not respect for conscience and for freedom exclude all efforts at conversion? Is it not possible to attain salvation in any religion? Why then should there be missionary activity? (*RM*, §4; italics in original)

In a chapter entitled "Jesus Christ, the Only Savior," John Paul offers his principal response. Making ample use of the Scriptures to rehearse the plan of God in Christ, he locates the missionary nature of the Church first in the nature of the trinitarian God, and then in the revelation of the Word made flesh (the Incarnation) (*RM*, §4, §5). He insists that there remains one dispensation of salvation that comes from Christ through the Spirit: "No one, therefore, can enter into communion with God except through Christ, by the working of the Holy Spirit. Christ's one, universal mediation, far from being an obstacle on the journey toward God, is the way established by God himself" (*RM*, §5).

John Paul grants that there is a universal *offer* of salvation, and that "we are obliged to hold that the Holy Spirit offers everyone the possibility of sharing in the Paschal Mystery in a manner known to God" (*RM*, §6), but he maintains that even when we recognize accessibility to salvation apart from formal membership in the Church, "this grace comes from Christ; it is the result of his sacrifice and is communicated by the Holy Spirit" (*RM*, §10). Summing up these truths in tension, he says: "It is necessary to keep these two truths together, namely, the real possibility of salvation in Christ for all mankind and

22. The phrase "new evangelization," which was first used by John Paul II in 1983 ("Address to CELAM"), appears prominently in this letter (16 times).

the necessity of the Church for salvation. Both these truths help us to understand the *one mystery of salvation*, so that we can come to know God's mercy and our own responsibility" (*RM*, §9).

Why mission? asks John Paul. Because true liberation comes from opening ourselves to Christ; because a faith that is alive will make Christ known to others; and because men and women of every age are seeking for new life and "have a right to know the value of this gift" (*RM*, §11). The impetus for mission comes not only from Christ's mandate, but also from the demands of God's life within us.[23]

The Call to Personal Encounter and Missionary Discipleship

Alongside these significant challenges to mission, a fresh appeal to missionary discipleship through personal encounter with Christ appears in the same period, reflected in the primary missionary documents of recent popes. This is one of the more striking and noteworthy developments in a theology of mission over the past generation: the consistent use of the language of personal encounter with Christ and a call to missionary discipleship. We find this first in Pope Paul VI (*EN*, §12): "And among all these signs there is the one to which he attaches great importance: the humble and the poor are evangelized, become his disciples and gather together 'in His name' in the great community of those who believe in Him."

But it is with John Paul II that the language of discipleship becomes front and center. According to George Weigel, "For John Paul II, everything began with discipleship. He was, first and foremost, a Christian disciple whose life had been transformed by his own friendship with the Lord. Everything else—his priestly vocation, his work as a bishop

23. In the years following *Redemptoris missio*, many of the questions concerning the validity of mission continued to be raised, prompting a more sharply stated declaration from the CDF in 2000, *Dominus Iesus* (Libreria Editrice Vaticana, 2000), which concludes with a vigorous call to renew the Church's mission: "Thus, the certainty of the universal salvific will of God does not diminish, but rather increases the duty and urgency of the proclamation of salvation and of conversion to the Lord Jesus Christ" (§22). The CDF followed this in 2007 with a "Doctrinal Note on Some Aspects of Evangelization" in order to further clarify the right and duty to proclaim the Gospel to everyone.

and as pope, his intellectual life, his impact on the world and the Church—flowed from that."[24] In his first encyclical (*RM*, §46), John Paul makes reference to an "ontological community of disciples," and in succeeding writings points to the personal encounter with Christ that gives rise to a life of discipleship: "Every disciple is personally called by name; no disciple can withhold making a response" (*Christifideles laici*, §33); "Conversion means accepting, by a personal decision, the saving sovereignty of Christ and becoming his disciple" (*RM*, §46). In *Veritatis splendor* (*VS*), John Paul describes at greater length what it means to be a disciple:

> This is not a matter only of disposing oneself to hear a teaching and obediently accepting a commandment. More radically, it involves holding fast to the very person of Jesus, partaking of his life and his destiny, sharing in his free and loving obedience to the will of the Father. By responding in faith and following the one who is Incarnate Wisdom, the disciple of Jesus truly becomes a disciple of God. (*VS*, §19)[25]

For his part, Pope Benedict XVI frequently employs the language of personal encounter and links this with the life of the disciple: "Ever since the start of my ministry as Successor of Peter, I have spoken of the need to rediscover the journey of faith so as to shed ever clearer light on the joy and renewed enthusiasm of the encounter with Christ."[26] He links this encounter closely with the call to discipleship and mission: "This is why the Church is missionary by her very nature. We cannot keep to ourselves the words of eternal life given to us in our encounter with Jesus Christ: they are meant for everyone, for every man and woman."[27]

24. George Weigel, "For John Paul II, Everything Began with Discipleship," Interview with *Catholic Herald* (November 27, 2017), at https://catholicherald.co.uk/commentandblogs/2017/11/27/george-weigel-for-john-paul-ii-everything-began-with-discipleship/.

25. John Paul II, *Veritatis splendor* (August 6, 1993) (United States Conference of Catholic Bishops, 1993), §19.

26. Benedict XVI, *Porta fidei* (October 11, 2011), in *Origins* 41, no. 21 (October 27, 2011): 325–32, at §2.

27. Benedict XVI, *Verbum Domini* (September 30, 2010) (United States Conference of Catholic Bishops, 2010), §91.

Following actively in the wake of his predecessors, Pope Francis adopted the language of personal encounter and missionary discipleship to describe the Church on mission in the modern world. In his apostolic exhortation *Evangelii gaudium* (*EG*),[28] Francis consciously echoes the language of Pope Benedict to make his own appeal for the Church as a community of missionary disciples: "The Church which 'goes forth' is a community of missionary disciples who take the first step, who are involved and supportive, who bear fruit and rejoice" (*EG*, §24). For Francis, a missionary is always a disciple who lives constantly in the presence of Jesus himself:

> A true missionary, who never ceases to be a disciple, knows that Jesus walks with him, speaks to him, breathes with him, works with him. He senses Jesus alive with him in the midst of the missionary enterprise. Unless we see him present at the heart of our missionary commitment, our enthusiasm soon wanes and we are no longer sure of what it is that we are handing on; we lack vigor and passion. (*EG*, §266)

This focus on missionary discipleship received significant emphasis in the American Catholic Church through a 2017 conference, attended by three thousand people and more than two hundred Catholic bishops, specifically aimed at unpacking Francis's teaching in *Evangelii gaudium*.[29]

In my view, this emphasis on encounter, conversion, discipleship, and mission provides one important way that the Catholic Church has marked out in order to pursue the universal call to holiness called for by the Second Vatican Council. "*The universal call to holiness* is closely linked to the *universal call to mission*. Every member of the faithful is called to holiness and to mission.... The Church's missionary spirituality is a journey toward holiness" (John Paul II, *RM*, §90). It also provides interesting and important points of contact with Evangelical Protestants concerning the central characteristics of mission and evangelization today.

28. Quotations from Pope Francis, *The Joy of the Gospel: Evangelii gaudium* (November 24, 2013) (United States Conference of Catholic Bishops, 2013).

29. "The Convocation of Catholic Leaders: The Joy of the Gospel," Orlando, FL (July 1–4, 2017).

Characteristics of Catholic Mission and Evangelization Today

Thus far I have sought to trace the lines of a Catholic theology of mission and evangelization so that developments that have come through challenge and crisis may be seen in historical context. But it is also useful to consider the main characteristics of a Catholic theology of mission in a more analytic fashion, noting continuities with the past as well as developments. Toward this end, I offer ten characteristics (others could certainly be added) that mark a Catholic theology of mission and evangelization today.

1. *The Essential Content and Universal Scope of Mission Remain Unchanged.* Perhaps the central continuity with a traditional understanding of mission is the conviction that the core message of the Gospel remains unchanged. Vatican II acknowledged that circumstances and methods vary greatly, but that the mission of the Gospel is "one and the same everywhere and in every condition" and the essential nature of mission does not change (*AG*, §6). In the same way, the universal destination of mission, that is, the conviction that mission must continue to all peoples that have not heard the Gospel (mission *ad gentes*), has not abated, but rather been re-proposed with renewed vigor. Here we see a profound continuity with the traditional missionary teaching of the Church.

2. *Doctrines of the Trinity and the Incarnation: The Narrative of Salvation.* A theology of mission rooted in the triune God and the missions of the Son and the Spirit receives special emphasis during and after the Second Vatican Council. Communicating this trinitarian theology of mission from within the entire narrative of Scripture to those engaged in missionary and evangelistic work remains an important task within the Catholic Church.

3. *The Holy Spirit as the Principal Agent in Mission.* A signal truth underlined in Catholic teaching since the Council is the explicit recognition of the Holy Spirit as "the principal agent of evangelization" (*EN*, §75). In a sense there is no new content here—this has always been true—but there is a new awareness of the sovereign action of the Spirit and the need to follow this lead in the entire work of mission.

"We Christians are called to an apostolic courage based upon trust in the Spirit. *He is the principal agent of mission!*" (*RM*, §31).[30]

4. Broadening the Scope of Mission. The Church's understanding of mission has significantly broadened since Vatican II. Though the terms are used variously (e.g., mission, evangelization, evangelizing mission, proclamation; see the appendix), there are two primary senses of "evangelization" or "mission." The narrower sense is the preaching of the Gospel and establishment of the local church in a given area, including catechesis and sacramental initiation. At the core of this is the act of proclamation. The broader sense encompasses the total mission of the Church and includes the full application of the social teaching of the Church and a concern for human development in the world.[31] Joining these together, a full understanding of mission would include: (1) the witness of Christian living so that people can see a way of life in action; (2) the proclamation of the Gospel, the kerygma, and the signs of the kingdom; (3) catechesis and sacramental initiation for full membership in the Church; (4) charitable action that reveals the love of God to people; (5) the application of the social teaching of the Church to promote the common good, to care for the poor, and to contribute to human development, peace, and justice—in short, to evangelize the wider culture.[32]

30. For the role of the Holy Spirit in mission, see Samuel Jacobs, "How Must Catholics Evangelize? Evangelization and the Power of the Holy Spirit," 38–48 in Ralph Martin and Peter Williamson, eds., *John Paul II and the New Evangelization: How You Can Bring the Good News to Others* (Servant, 2006); for the impact of the Charismatic Renewal in contemporary evangelization, see Peter Hocken, "Ecumenical Issues in Evangelization," 276–87 in *John Paul II and the New Evangelization*, at 277–78.

31. For the two senses of mission, see Pontifical Council for Interreligious Dialogue, *Dialogue and Proclamation* (May 19, 1991), in Pontifical Council for Interreligious Dialogue, *Interreligious Dialogue: Official Teaching of the Catholic Church (1963–2005)* (Pauline Books & Media, 2006), §8; see also Avery Dulles, "Vatican II and Evangelization," 1–12 in *The New Evangelization: Overcoming the Obstacles*, ed. Stephen Boguslawski and Ralph Martin (Paulist, 2008), 1–3.

32. Francis George, "Evangelizing Our Culture," 43–58 in *The New Evangelization*, at 44, writes: "Culture is the object of our evangelization and not just the sea in which we swim. To form gospel-shaped people, the Church must work to create gospel-friendly cultures." The language of "evangelizing culture" does not appear in Vatican II's *Ad gentes*, but appears in Paul VI, *Evangelii nuntiandi*, §20.

5. *Proclamation as the Core of Mission.* Even as the definition of mission and evangelization has broadened, a Catholic theology of mission places firm emphasis on proclamation as the core of evangelization. The full evangelization of culture "will not take place if the Gospel is not proclaimed" (*EN*, §20). "Proclamation is the permanent priority of mission . . . . In the complex reality of mission, initial proclamation has a central and irreplaceable role" (*RM*, §44). "Proclamation is the foundation, center, and summit of evangelization" (*Dialogue and Proclamation*, §10).[33]

6. *A Recognition of the Need for Missionary Disciples.* Presupposed by this emphasis on proclamation is that the one proclaiming has had a personal encounter with Christ through the Spirit. The Church has recognized with greater clarity the need for missionaries themselves to encounter God personally, in order to be able to proclaim the Gospel to others persuasively and effectively. Personal conversion is the prerequisite for proclamation, and the task of mission in the Church today is understood to occur within the context of a community of missionary disciples.

7. *The Laity in Mission.* Recapturing a role for the laity (a role that was more prevalent in the early Church), Vatican II underlined that mission and evangelization—both at home and abroad—must involve the full and direct role of the laity. "No longer reserved to clerics and religious with a special missionary vocation, evangelization is now seen as the responsibility of the whole church."[34] The calling of the laity into the task of evangelization, thereby increasing their responsibility for owning and propagating the faith, is one of the most important new developments in the past century. "The mission *ad gentes* is incumbent upon the entire People of God. Whereas

33. Pope Francis also devotes attention to the priority of proclamation: "This first proclamation is called 'first' not because it exists at the beginning and can then be forgotten or replaced by other more important things. It is first in a qualitative sense because it is the *principal* proclamation, the one which we must hear again and again in different ways, the one which we must announce one way or another throughout the process of catechesis, at every level and moment" (*Evangelii gaudium*, §164).

34. Avery Dulles, "John Paul II and the New Evangelization: What Does it Mean?," 25–39 in *John Paul II and the New Evangelization*, at 6.

the foundation of a new church requires the Eucharist and hence the priestly ministry, missionary activity, which is carried out in a wide variety of ways, is the task of all the Christian faithful" (*RM*, §71).

8. The Poor and Human Development. Charitable work and concern for the poor has always marked the mission of the Church. What is *new* in the Catholic Church's present approach to mission is a special emphasis on the poor and a commitment to work for justice and human dignity within the structures of human society. While "it is not the Church's mission to work directly on the economic, technical or political levels, or to contribute materially to development" (*RM*, §58), the Church does have a direct mission to promote human dignity and justice through her social teaching and through the direct involvement of the laity in the temporal order.

9. Inculturation. Adaptation to the needs of particular cultures, likewise, has always been the missionary principle of the Church, however successful from age to age, and the Church can point to magnificent examples of cultural accommodation in her history. The recently coined term "inculturation" captures both the impact of the Gospel on a given culture and the impact of that culture on how the local church takes shape. There is a two-way street here. Though there is no essential change in the Gospel itself, through successful inculturation of the Gospel there is a mutual impact on the culture as a whole and on the local church as it grows to maturity within that culture.[35]

10. Mission and Ecumenism. A final characteristic of mission and evangelization is the new ecumenical climate within which mission occurs at the start of the twenty-first century. The Catholic Church was cautiously slow to engage the ecumenical movement in the

35. Arji A. Roest Crollius, "Inculturation," 149–63 in *Following Christ in Mission: A Foundational Course in Missiology*, ed. Sebastian Karotemprel (Pauline Books & Media, 1996), at 53, offers a useful working definition of inculturation: "Inculturation is the integration of the Christian experience of a local Church into the culture of its people, in such a way that this experience not only expresses itself in elements of this culture, but also becomes a force that animates, orients and renews this culture, creating a new unity and communion, not only within the culture in question but also as an enrichment of the Church universal."

twentieth century, but has now taken up a vigorous role in cooperation with other Christians at many levels, including common mission. "We can already give a greater common witness to Christ before the world in the very work of evangelization. Christ's command urges us to do this; the duty of preaching and of giving witness to the Gospel requires this" (Paul VI, *EN*, §77). Though significant differences remain that place limits on doing common mission together, many areas of fruitful mission are now in place.[36] Notably, a full Catholic *theology* of mission must now take account of the goal of full Christian unity as part of the missionary aim. This concluding quote from Pope John Paul II on the link between unity and common mission provides an excellent bridge to a discussion between Evangelicals and Catholics on mission and evangelization today: "The fact that the Good News of reconciliation is preached by Christians who are divided among themselves weakens their witness. It is thus urgent to work for the unity of Christians, so that missionary activity can be more effective" (*RM*, §50).

APPENDIX

Frequency of Key Terms in Select Missionary Documents

	EN	*RM*	*EG*	*Dial/Proclam*
"Mission"	23	152	134	43
"Evangelization"	115	57	115	21
"New Evangelization"	none	16	11	none
"Evangelizing Mission"	1	1	1	21

36. For ways that Catholics are encouraged to join in common mission with other Christians, see the Pontifical Council for Promoting Christian Unity, *Directory for the Application of Principles and Norms on Ecumenism*, (1993), p. 50.

1.4 The Role of Doctrine in Evangelization

Christian D. Washburn

IN THE CATHOLIC CHURCH TODAY, there is a hesitancy to speak of doctrine within the context of evangelization. In the index of the Pontifical Council for the Promotion of the New Evangelization's *Compendium on the New Evangelization*, a collection of magisterial texts from 1939–2012 with over 1,100 pages, the entry on doctrine contains only two references, both of which refer to the same page. Contrast this with other entries in the index. There are more entries on culture (43), Oceania (16), America (11), migrants (6), and relativism (4).[1] This near-allergic reaction to speaking about Catholic doctrine is also found in more popular works on evangelization. In Sherry Weddell's *Forming Intentional Disciples*, for example, the few references are always negative in nature. Weddell approvingly quotes Fr. Raniero Cantalamessa, OFM Cap., the papal preacher: "The immense wealth of doctrine and institutions can become a handicap if we are trying to present all of that to a person who has lost all contact with the Church and no longer knows who Jesus is."[2] Again: "Transmitting the faith is an organic, whole-person, whole-life concept that goes far

1. Pontifical Council for the Promotion of the New Evangelization, *Compendium on the New Evangelization: Texts of the Pontifical and Conciliar Magisterium, 1939–2012* (United States Conference of Catholic Bishops, 2015), (doctrine) 1073, (culture) §§1071–1072, (Oceania) §§1100–1101, (America) §1054, (migrants) §1097, (relativism) §§1108–1109.

2. Sherry A. Weddell, *Forming Intentional Disciples: The Path to Knowing and Following Jesus* (Our Sunday Visitor Publishing Division, 2012), 168.

beyond instruction in facts or doctrines."[3] Weddell states, "Intellectual assent to the doctrines of the Catholic faith alone, without charity and good works, is what the Church calls *fides informis*; it is a 'dead' faith that does not save (Jas 2:18–26)."[4] None of these statements are false, but they envision doctrine as a handicap, as something to move beyond, and finally as a sign of a dead faith—hardly a positive account of the importance of doctrine in evangelization!

It is true that evangelizing is not just teaching doctrine but also proclaiming "Jesus Christ by one's words and actions, that is, to make oneself an instrument of his presence and action in the world."[5] Minimizing the importance of doctrine in evangelization, however, is seriously misguided. The sheer amount of time that the magisterium of the Church has spent simply on defining articles of faith should demonstrate this. Twenty-one ecumenical councils as well as at least 1,500 diocesan, national, and provincial synods have met to discuss and to define articles of faith.[6] Some of these councils spent years working carefully on these definitions. In many cases, these councils directly tied the faithful's salvation to adherence to its defined doctrines. The Council of Trent, for example, tied the faithful's justification—and therefore one's salvation—to adherence to its doctrine on justification:

> No one can be justified unless he faithfully and firmly accepts (*fideliter firmiterque receperit*) the Catholic doctrine of justification, to which

3. Weddell, *Forming Intentional Disciples*, 52.
4. Weddell, *Forming Intentional Disciples*, 108.
5. CDF, *Doctrinal Note on Some Aspects of Evangelization* (Paulist Press, 2012), §2.
6. On the number of ecumenical councils, see Christian D. Washburn, "Conciliar Infallibility and Error in the Thomistic Ecclesiology of St. Robert Bellarmine, S.J.," *The Journal of Early Modern Christianity* 8 (2021): 251–73. Nelson H. Minnich, "What Is an Ecumenical Council? The Sixteenth-Century Teachings of the Theologian Roberto Bellarmino and the Canonist Domenico Giacobazzi," 1–21 in Nelson H. Minnich, *The Decrees of the Fifth Lateran Council (1512–17): Their Legitimacy, Origins, Contents and Implementation* (Routledge, Taylor & Francis Group, 2016). Vittorio Peri, "Il numero dei concili ecumenici," *Aevum* 37 (1963): 430–501. Mario Fois, "I concilii del secolo XV," 162–214 in *Problemi di storia della Chiesa: Il medioevo dei secoli XII–XV*, Cultura e storia 16 (Vita e Pensiero, 1976), 165. Remigius Bäumer, "Die Zahl der allgemeinen Konzilien in der Sicht von Theologen des 15. und 16. Jahrhunderts," *Annuarium Historiae Conciliorum* 1 (1969): 288–313.

> the holy council has decided to add the following canons, so that all may know, not only what they should hold and follow, but also what they should shun and avoid.[7]

Moreover, for centuries catechism class and the catechism were called "Christian Doctrine." This was not just true for Catholic children but also in the evangelization of the New World.[8] Two of the most popular catechisms were written by Saint Robert Bellarmine, entitled *A Short Christian Doctrine* and *A More Copious Explanation of Christian Doctrine*.[9] It is estimated that these two catechisms went through between 350 and 500 editions[10] and were translated into at least sixty languages, including Chinese, Congolese, Coptic, Ethiopian, Hebrew, Hindustani, and Peruvian.[11] In 1598, Pope Clement VIII wrote of Bellarmine's catechism:

> I exhort in the Lord the Venerable Patriarchs, Archbishops, Bishops, and their beloved sons Vicars, Abbots, and all parish priests existing everywhere, and others to whom it concerns, that in so far as they are able, they adopt and see that others adopt this book and use it in the teaching of Christian doctrine in their respective churches, dioceses, and parishes.[12]

7. Council of Trent, Session 6, *Decree on Justification* (January 13, 1547), ed. Peter Hünermann, Helmut Hoping, Robert L. Fastiggi, Anne Englund Nash, and Heinrich Denzinger, *Compendium of Creeds, Definitions, and Declarations on Matters of Faith and Morals* 43rd edition (Ignatius Press, 2012), 1550, cf. 1650, 1700, 1770 (hereafter DH).

8. Robert Ricard, *The Spiritual Conquest of Mexico: An Essay on the Apostolate and the Evangelizing Methods of the Mendicant Orders in New Spain, 1523–1572* (University of California Press, 1982), 96–108.

9. Robert Bellarmine, *Dottrina Christiana Breve Composta Per Ordine Di Papa Clemente VIII* (Appresso Luigi Zannetti, 1598). Robert Bellarmine, *Dichiaratione Piu Copiosa della Dottrina Christiana* (Appresso Luigi Zannetti, 1598).

10. (350) Sacra Rituum Congregatio, *Urbis et Orbis Concessionis Tituli Doctoris et extensionis ejusdem tituli ad universam ecclesiam nec non officii et missae sub ritu dupl. de comm. doctorum pontificum in honorem S. Roberti S. R. E. Card. Bellarmino e Societate Jesu* (Sacra Rituum Congregatione, 1931), 143. (500) Pietro Braido, *Lineamenti di Storia della Catechesi e dei Catechismi: Dal "Tempo delle Riforme" all'età Degli Imperialismi (1450–1870)* (Elle di Ci., 1991), 83.

11. James Brodrick, *The Life and Work of Blessed Robert Francis Cardinal Bellarmine, S.J.: 1542–1621*, 2 vols. (Burns, Oates and Washbourne, Ltd., 1928), 1:396.

12. Clement VIII, *Pastoralis Romani Pontificis*, in *Bullarium Societatis Iesu* (Ex Typographia a SS. Conceptione, 1892), 1:129.

In 1633, Pope Urban VIII recommended the same catechisms' use in the East Indies.[13] In 1742, Pope Benedict XIV recommended Bellarmine's catechism to be used in every diocese of the world.[14] So, Christian doctrine was the foundation of the Church's efforts to evangelize.

Correct doctrine is associated with almost every aspect of living a Christian life and therefore has a type of governing centrality in evangelizing. This paper will argue that doctrine has a more important role in evangelization than is currently recognized. To this end, this paper will examine what doctrine is. It will then examine how doctrine frames evangelization with respect to its end and its means. It will then examine doctrine's role in perfecting the intellect, which unites the believer to God. Finally, the paper will explain its important role in attaining and living the life of holiness that is expected of those who are evangelized.

What Is Doctrine?

Doctrine is any truth pertaining to faith and morals taught by the Church as necessary for acceptance by the faithful.[15] The phrase "faith and morals" (*fides et mores*) has a long history.[16] The term "faith" here refers to those doctrines that are of a speculative nature, such as the Trinity or the Real Presence of Christ in the Eucharist. In

13. Urban VIII, *Ex debito* (February 18, 1633), in *Collectanea S. Congregationis De Propaganda Fide: Seu Decreta, Instructiones, Rescripta Pro Apostolicis Missionibus* (Ex Typographia Polyglotta, 1907), 1:18n72.

14. Benedict XIV, *Etsi minime*, in *Opera Omnia* (In Typographia Aldina, 1845), 15:140.

15. John Hardon, SJ, *Modern Catholic Dictionary* (Eternal Life, Inc., 2000), 168.

16. Piet Fransen, "A Short History of the Meaning of the Formula 'Fides et mores,'" 287–318 in *Hermeneutics of Councils and Other Studies*, ed. H. E. Mertens and F. de Graeve (Leuven University Press, 1985). David Stagaman, "Piet Fransen's Research on *Fides et Mores*," *Theological Studies* 64 (2003): 69–77. Maurice Bevenot, "Faith and Morals in Vatican I and in the Council of Trent," *Heythrop Journal* 3 (1962): 15–30. John Mahoney, *The Making of Moral Theology* (Clarendon, 1987), 116–74. Johann Beumer, "Res fidei et morum: Die Entwicklung eines theologischen Begriffes in den Dekretem der drei letzten Okumenischen Konzilien," *Annuarium Historiae Conciliorum* 2 (1979): 112–34. Teodoro López Rodriguez, "'Fides et mores' en Trento," *Scripta Theologica* 5 (1973): 175–221. Marcelino Zalba, SJ, "'Omnis et salutaris veritas et morum disciplina': Sentido de la expresión 'mores' en el Concilio de Trento," *Gregorianum* 54 (1973): 679–715.

contemporary usage the term "morals" refers to those teachings which concern the goodness or badness of human acts, such as the immorality of contraception or abortion.

Doctrines have various levels of authority. The *Professio fidei* (1989) and the CDF's instruction *Donum veritatis* (1990) together indicate four levels of magisterial teaching, each with a corresponding degree of required assent. The first level of magisterial teaching consists of definitive declarations of revealed truth. This level has various other names in Catholic theology, such as the primary object of infallibility, dogma, and articles of faith. These teachings, contained within the two sources of revelation—namely, Scripture and Apostolic Tradition—have been formally revealed by God and proposed definitively as such by the Church to the faithful, who have the obligation of believing them.[17] These truths require the assent of supernatural faith which can only be bestowed by God himself. The second degree is definitive declarations of nonrevealed truth, sometimes also known as the secondary object of infallibility. These doctrines are held to be infallible but not revealed. This extends "to those matters without which that deposit cannot be rightly preserved and expounded."[18] These secondary objects require the faithful to firmly accept and hold them. The third degree of magisterial teaching is nondefinitive obligatory teachings. One must assent to these doctrines with an act of religious submission (*obsequium*) of intellect and will. The fourth degree of magisterial teaching concerns prudential judgments, which are applications of Christian doctrine or admonitions for a particular time and place.[19] This paper is primarily concerned with the first level of doctrine, i.e., articles of faith.

It must be noted that the first two levels of doctrine are considered "irreformable." The term "irreformable" means simply that the doctrine cannot be transformed or metamorphosed into a new doctrine with some other meaning. The First Vatican Council was clear that

17. Pietro Parente, Antonio Piolanti, and Salvatore Garofalo, *Dictionary of Dogmatic Theology*, trans. Emannual Doronzo (Bruce, 1951), 81.

18. CDF, *Mysterium ecclesiae* (June 24, 1973), §3 (DH 4536).

19. CDF, *Donum veritatis*, §24.

> the doctrine of faith which God revealed has not been handed down as a philosophic invention to the human mind to be perfected but has been entrusted as a divine deposit to the Spouse of Christ, to be faithfully guarded and infallibly interpreted. Hence, also, that understanding of its sacred dogmas must be perpetually retained, which Holy Mother Church has once declared; and there must never be recession from that meaning under the specious name of a deeper understanding.[20]

Since irreformability is confined to the doctrine's meaning and not the terms in which it is presented, it does not exclude reformulation in new terms.[21] The council then quoted Saint Vincent of Lerins, who maintained that doctrine must remain "with the same sense and the same understanding,"[22] even when there is doctrinal or linguistic development.

Teachings that are irreformable will always be true and binding on all the faithful including the magisterium itself. The binding character of level one and level two teachings extends even to popes and councils, whether local or ecumenical. So, there are limits to a pope's or a council's authority. Every pope is bound to and cannot teach contrary to the content of revelation as found in Sacred Scripture and Apostolic Tradition, and to the infallible decrees of previous councils and popes. Popes are not like the Oracle of Delphi or the president of the Mormon church, who can issue new revelation or invalidate either natural or supernatural revelation. On this point, the First Vatican Council was clear that "the Holy Spirit was not promised to the successors of Peter that they might disclose a new doctrine by His revelation."[23]

20. First Vatican Council, *Dei Filius* (April 24, 1870) (DH 3020). See also Canon 3: "If anyone says that, as science progresses, at times a sense is to be given to dogmas proposed by the Church different from the one that the Church has understood and understands, let him be anathema." First Vatican Council, *Dei Filius* (DH 3043).

21. One must distinguish between "the substance of the ancient doctrine of the deposit of faith . . . and the way in which it is presented." John XXIII, Opening Speech to the Vatican II Council (*Gaudet mater ecclesia*), AAS (1962): 791; trans. *The Documents of Vatican II*, ed. Walter M. Abbott (America Press, 1966), 715.

22. First Vatican Council, *Dei Filius* (DH 3020).

23. First Vatican Council, *Dei Filius* (DH 3070).

The aforementioned four levels of magisterial teaching, which reflect the degree of certitude that the Church has about a particular authoritative teaching, should not be confused with the "hierarchy of Catholic doctrine."[24] This hierarchy of doctrine "is a principle of organic structure" recognizing that the different doctrinal truths are "organized" around a center.[25] For Catholics the mystery of the Trinity "is the central mystery of Christian faith and life" and "is therefore the source of all the other mysteries of faith, the light that enlightens them. It is the most fundamental and essential teaching in the 'hierarchy of the truths of faith.'"[26] The second central mystery are those doctrines which concern Christ the incarnate Word, who was born of the Virgin Mary, and who suffered, died, and rose for our salvation. The mystery of the Holy Spirit, who is present in the Church, sanctifying it and guiding it until the glorious coming of Christ, our Savior and Judge, is also part of the third central mystery. The fourth central mystery concerns Christ's Mystical Body, the Church.[27]

Doctrine Determines Who Should Be Evangelized

The Sacred Scriptures repeatedly testify to the universality of the mission of the Church. Christ our Lord testifies that "all nations" need to be evangelized: "Go therefore and teach all nations, baptizing them in the name of the Father, and of the Son, and of the Holy Spirit, teaching them to observe all that I have commanded you. And behold, I am with you always, until the end of the world" (Matt 28:18–20; cf. Luke 24:46–48; John 17:18, 20, 21; Acts 1:8).[28] Our Lord reaffirms in the Gos-

24. "In comparandis doctrinis meminerint existere ordinem seu 'hierarchiam' veritatum doctrinae catholicae, cum diversus sit earum nexus cum fundamento fidei christianae." Second Vatican Council, *Unitatis redintegratio* (November 21, 1964), in *Acta Apostolicae Sedis* 62 (1965): 90–112, at §11. See also *Catechism of the Catholic Church*, 2nd ed. rev. in accordance with the official Latin text promulgated by Pope John Paul II (Libreria Editrice Vaticana, 2000), §90; and CDF, *Mysterium ecclesiae*, §4.

25. Joseph Ratzinger and Christoph Schönborn, *Introduction to the Catechism of the Catholic Church* (Ignatius Press, 1994), 42.

26. *Catechism of the Catholic Church*, §234.

27. Sacred Congregation for the Clergy, *General Catechetical Directory* (United States Catholic Conference, 1997), §43.

28. All scriptural references in the text are to the *ESV Study Bible* (Crossway, 2008).

pel of Mark that the good news is to be proclaimed to "every creature" (Mark 16:15). The Church has accepted and followed this commission. The Second Vatican Council teaches that

> the Catholic Church strives constantly and with due effect to bring all humanity and all its possessions back to its source in Christ, with Him as its head and united in His Spirit.[29]

It is particularly striking that the council envisions not only all humanity, but also its possessions, returning to Christ.

Some contemporary Catholic and non-Catholic theologians argue that it is unnecessary and unacceptable to evangelize certain groups of humans. Pluralist theologians, for example, argue that the various religions are equally legitimate ways of attaining salvation, so evangelization is, in the end, unnecessary.[30] Other theologians argue that Jews should not be evangelized as this is a form of supersessionism which is inherently antisemitic.[31] Rabbi Abraham Joshua Heschel, an observer at the Second Vatican Council, said that he would rather go to Auschwitz than convert to Catholicism, because for Heschel conversion meant the destruction of the Jewish people.[32]

The magisterium has repeatedly condemned indifferentism, i.e., the belief that all religions have the same positive value.[33] It is not the case that the Jewish people are a special exception to the universal need for Christ. Although the Jewish people were God's chosen people according to the doctrine of the Church,[34] both Sacred Scripture

29. Second Vatican Council, *Lumen gentium* (November 21, 1964), §13 (DH 4133).

30. Terrence Merrigan, "Religious Pluralism and *Dominus Iesus*," *Sacred Heart University Review* 20 (2000): 63–78.

31. Steven Paas, "The Bible and Israel," 12–39 in *Israelism and the Place of Christ: Christocentric Interpretation of Biblical Prophecy*, ed. Steven Paas (LIT, 2018), 28.

32. Doris Donnelly, "Lovingly Observant: An Interview with Susannah Heschel," *America* (June 18, 2007), at http://americamagazine.org/issue/618/article/lovingly-observant. Ruth Langer, "A Jewish Response to Gavin D'Costa, *Vatican II: Catholic Doctrines on Jews and Muslims*," *Louvain Studies* 40, no. 3 (2017): 273–85. Joshua Furnal, "Abraham Joshua Heschel and *Nostra Aetate*: Shaping the Catholic Reconsideration of Judaism During Vatican II," *Religions (Basel, Switzerland)* 7 (2016): 1–12, at 12.

33. Pius IX, *Syllabus of Errors* (December 8, 1864) (DH 2915–2918).

34. Second Vatican Council, *Lumen gentium*, §9 (DH 4122).

and the magisterium teach that the Jewish law has no power to free anyone from original sin. Saint Paul teaches that "For by works of the law no human being will be justified in His sight, since through the law comes knowledge of sin" (Rom 3:20). The Council of Trent follows Scripture's teaching that "even the Jews by means of the letter of the law of Moses were unable to liberate themselves and to rise from that state."[35] Moreover, the sacraments of the Old Law, like circumcision and the Passover meal, no longer have any positive value because Christ instituted the Church and the seven sacraments. The Council of Florence denounced "all who after that time observe circumcision, the sabbath, and other legal prescriptions as strangers to the faith of Christ and unable to share in eternal salvation."[36] Clearly, then, Catholic doctrine teaches that those not in the Church need to be evangelized.

Doctrine Teaches Why Everyone Needs to Be Evangelized

The teaching of Sacred Scripture, Tradition, and the magisterium is that the condition of man is such that he comes into the world unable to help himself. The Council of Trent solemnly teaches that those in the state of original sin are "enemies of God."[37] It also defines just exactly how we are enemies:

> It is necessary that each one admits and confesses that all men, having lost innocence through the sin of Adam (cf. Rom 5:12; 1 Cor 15:22), "became unclean" (Is 64:6) and, according to the apostle, were "children of wrath" (Eph 2:3), as the council taught in its decree on original sin. So completely were they the slaves of sin (cf. Rom 6:20) and under the power of the devil and of death that not only the Gentiles by means of the power of nature [can. 1] but even the Jews by means of the letter of the law of Moses were unable to liberate themselves

35. Council of Trent, *Decree on Justification* (DH 1521, 1551).

36. "Therefore, she denounces all who after that time observe circumcision, the sabbath, and other legal prescriptions as strangers to the faith of Christ and unable to share in eternal salvation, unless they recoil at some time from these errors." Council of Florence, *Decree for the Jacobites* (February 4, 1442) (DH 1348).

37. Council of Trent, *Decree on Justification* (DH 1528).

> and to rise from that state, even though their free will, weakened and distorted as it was, was in no way extinct.[38]

These truths are frankly biblical and part of God's revealed Word. This also explains, for example, why in baptism we perform exorcisms on babies and adults alike. Those in the state of original sin are, as the council teaches, "under the power of the devil." Moreover, one should note that according to the council there is nothing one can do to "liberate" oneself from this state. It does not matter how good one tries to be in the state of original sin. The only way out of this state is by Christ bestowing his justifying grace either through sacramental baptism or by baptism of desire.[39] Finally, Trent says that "no one can be justified unless he faithfully and firmly accepts" these teachings about man's condition.[40]

In addition to being "under the power of the devil," those in the state of original sin are also "under the power of death" according to the council. By death the council does not mean biological death but principally eternal death. The point is that if one dies in the state of original sin, then one descends immediately to the hell of the damned. Trent here is simply reaffirming what was taught infallibly by other ecumenical councils. The Council of Florence (1439) taught:

> As for the souls of those who die in actual mortal sin or *with original sin only* [emphasis mine], they go down immediately to hell, to be punished, however, with different punishments.[41]

The Second Council of Lyon (1274) solemnly taught the same.[42] According to three ecumenical councils, one does not have to commit a single mortal sin in order to go to hell. It is sufficient to die in the state of original sin.[43]

38. Council of Trent, *Decree on Justification* (DH 1521).

39. Council of Trent, *Decree on Justification* (DH 1524). One should of course add baptism of blood.

40. Council of Trent, *Decree on Justification* (DH 1550).

41. Council of Florence, *Laetentur caeli* (July 6, 1439) (DH 1306).

42. Council of Lyon II, Session 4 (July 6, 1274) (DH 858).

43. Christian D. Washburn, "*Ex inimico amicus*: Catholic Teaching on Initial Justification," in *Justified in Jesus Christ: Catholics and Evangelicals in Dialogue*, ed. Steven Hoskins and David Fleischacker (University of Mary Press, 2017), 5–36.

All of mankind is in this dire condition, and there is nothing in man's nature that can liberate him from this captivity. Original sin cannot "be taken away by the powers of human nature."[44] The Second Vatican Council counsels:

> Often men, deceived by the Evil One, have become vain in their reasonings and have exchanged the truth of God for a lie, serving the creature rather than the Creator [cf. Rom 1:21, 25]. Or some there are who, living and dying in this world without God, are exposed to final despair. Wherefore, to promote the glory of God and procure the salvation of all of these, and mindful of the command of the Lord, "Preach the gospel to every creature" [Mark 16:16], the Church fosters the missions with care and attention.[45]

Man's salvation is one of the two primary ends of evangelization. Out of charity, then, we are called to evangelize all people to help them reach their end.

Evangelization and Proclamation

In evangelization, Catholic doctrine provides the central content of proclaiming the saving truth to the world. Faith comes by hearing, so one of the main ways that individuals are evangelized is through the proclamation of the Gospel. Ratzinger notes that the modern preacher is tempted to leave out entirely dogma and doctrinal formulas from his preaching, choosing instead to focus on those issues that are modern. Ratzinger warns, however, that the result of this is a form of preaching that becomes utterly subjective. Authentic preaching, therefore, "depends on the objective arch spanning and upheld by the pillars: Scripture-Dogma-Church-Today; not one of them can be taken away without the whole thing eventually collapsing."[46]

44. Council of Trent, Session 5, *Decree on Original Sin* (June 17, 1546) (DH 1513). Council of Trent, *Decree on Justification* (DH 1521, 1551).

45. Second Vatican Council, *Lumen gentium*, §16 (DH 4140).

46. Joseph Ratzinger, *Dogma and Preaching: Applying Christian Doctrine to Daily Life*, unabridged, trans. Michael J. Miller and Matthew J. O'Connell, ed. Michael J. Miller (Ignatius Press, 2011), 7.

There are three basic norms for governing the content of preaching. The first is the two sources of divine revelation—namely, Scripture and Apostolic Tradition. This norm has propositional content; Scripture is after all contained in a book. Some argue that at the Second Vatican Council the Church moved away from a propositional understanding of revelation to a relational understanding.[47] Even if this were true one is still left with many propositions that need to be conveyed.

The second norm is the living magisterium of the Church. The magisterium sometimes solemnly defines, for example, the meaning of Sacred Scripture. The Church can authoritatively interpret the word of God in two distinct ways that are important for preaching. First, the magisterium can offer at least one authentic meaning of a particular text of Scripture. Second, the magisterium can prohibit an erroneous interpretation, i.e., it can teach what a particular biblical text does not mean.[48] The Council of Trent did this for the following verses: Romans 5:12, John 3:5, Luke 22:19, 1 Corinthians 11:24, John 20:22–23, and James 5:14.[49] It infallibly determined, for example, that the words "This is my Body" are to be understood properly and not merely figuratively.[50] One can immediately see the consequence of such a magisterial decision, i.e., that Christ is truly present body, blood, soul, and divinity in the Eucharist. The council also taught that the water mentioned in John 3:5 is water in the proper sense of the term. First, this definition impacts the content of preaching when

47. Anthony Towey, "*Dei Verbum*: Fit for Purpose?," *New Blackfriars* 90 (2009): 206–18.

48. Examples of this type of intervention can be found in: DH 443, 1922, 1950, 1975, 1976, 3447.

49. The Council of Trent taught on the meaning of the following passages: (Rom 5:12) DH 1514, (John 3:5) DH 1615, (Luke 22:19) DH 1752, (1 Cor 11:24) DH 1752, (John 20:22–23) DH 1703, (Jas 5:14) DH 1716.

50. Council of Trent, Session 13, *Decree on the Sacrament of the Eucharist* (October 11, 1551) (DH 1637). Christoph Rasperger wrote a book on two hundred different interpretations given to the words "This is my body" by Protestants. Christoph Rasperger, *Ducentae paucorum istorum et quidem clarissimorum Christi verborum: Hoc est Corpus meum; interpretationes quibus continentur vocum novitates, deprevationes, errores, haereses, contra dictiones . . . theologorum . . . ex propriis . . . scriptis fideliter collectae* (Ingolstadt: Excudebat A. Weissenhorn cum cohaeredibus suis, 1577).

evangelizing, i.e., one must preach, for example, a water baptism. Second, this determines the sacramental culmination of this evangelization, in this case a water baptism.

Evangelization, the Act and Virtue of Faith, and Friendship with God

The proximate end of evangelization is that the unevangelized starts to believe in God and accepts Christ's teaching, thereby becoming justified and a friend of God. Doctrine plays an important role in this process. Both the Council of Trent and the First Vatican Council are clear that this faith which justifies is a dogmatic faith. The Council of Trent speaks of justifying faith: "Adults are disposed for that justice when, awakened and assisted by divine grace, they conceive faith from hearing and are freely led to God, believing to be true what has been divinely revealed and promised."[51] Later in the nineteenth century, the First Vatican Council taught that this justifying faith is a dogmatic faith when it affirmed:

> This faith, which is the beginning of human salvation, the Catholic Church professes to be a supernatural virtue, by means of which, with the grace of God inspiring and assisting us, we believe to be true what He has revealed, not because we perceive its intrinsic truth by the natural light of reason, but because of the authority of God Himself, who makes the revelation and can neither deceive nor be deceived.[52]

This dogmatic faith is a justifying faith since it is accompanied by the virtue of love.

This dogmatic faith is perfecting, even of the unjustified. Catholic doctrine teaches that one can have the supernatural virtue of faith or make a supernatural act of faith without the supernatural virtue of love. In Catholic theology this is called unformed faith (*fides informis*). Some magisterial reformers entirely rejected the notion of an unformed faith. Luther called the distinction between formed and unformed "blasphemous and satanic," and Calvin, "childish babble."[53]

51. Council of Trent, *Decree on Justification* (DH 1526).

52. First Vatican Council, *Dei Filius* (DH 3008, 3032).

53. Martin Luther, *Lectures on Galatians*, in *Luther's Works* (Concordia, 1965), 26:270. Calvin, *Institutes of the Christian Religion*, 3.2.8.

For Catholics this unformed faith is perfecting of the human person when a person who is not justified assents to the articles of faith, and the supernatural virtue of faith elevates man, even if he has not yet achieved justification.

While Trent is clear that "nothing that precedes justification, neither faith nor works, merits the grace of justification,"[54] theologians generally hold that faith justifies "*per modum dispositionis*."[55] Prior to one's justification this dogmatic faith is dispositive to initial justification, although it does not efficiently justify the sinner. Again, this unformed faith is a supernatural gift bestowed only by God. So, it is by means of this dispositive dogmatic faith that one comes to be justified in baptism. The council describes this initial justification:

> This disposition or preparation is followed by justification itself, which is not only the remission of sins but the sanctification and renewal of the interior man through the voluntary reception of grace and of the gifts, whereby from unjust man becomes just, and from enemy a friend, that he may be "an heir in hope of eternal life" (Tit 3:7).[56]

It is in the moment of one's justification that one is transformed from an enemy into a friend of God. This is what God desires for all of humanity.

When discussing the role of faith in the life of the new believer, one may hear a common objection to the importance of the articles of faith, which is taken from Saint Thomas Aquinas: "The act of the believer does not terminate in a proposition, but in a thing," namely God.[57] The point of citing this clause is that ultimately propositional claims or articles of faith are to be surpassed so that the Christian

54. Council of Trent, *Decree on Justification* (DH 1532).

55. Robert Bellarmine, *Disputationes Roberti Bellarmini Politiani Societatis Jesu, de controversiis Christianae fidei, adversus hujus temporis haereticos*, 4 vols. (Paris: Triadelphorum, 1613), 15.1.4, vol. 4, col. 731.

56. Council of Trent, *Decree on Justification* (DH 1528).

57. "Actus autem credentis non terminatur ad enuntiabile sed ad rem." Saint Thomas Aquinas, *Summa Theologiae* II-II, q. 1, a. 2, ad 2. All translations of Aquinas, unless otherwise noted, are from *Summa Theologiae*, ed. John Mortensen and Enrique Alarcón, trans. Laurence Shapcote, OP, Latin/English Edition of the Works of St. Thomas Aquinas 13–20 (The Aquinas Institute for the Study of Sacred Doctrine, 2012).

resides in the thing itself. Propositional claims have no importance in themselves other than as signs signifying invisible realities.

To isolate this clause from its broader theological context, however, is to be unfaithful to the thought of Saint Thomas. In discussing the purpose of propositional doctrines as part of the object of faith, Saint Thomas answers the question of "Whether the object of faith is something complex, by way of a proposition?" To this question, Aquinas responds:

> Accordingly, the object of faith may be considered in two ways. First, as regards the thing itself which is believed, and thus the object of faith is something simple, namely the thing itself about which we have faith. Secondly, on the part of the believer, and in this respect the object of faith is something complex by way of a proposition.[58]

Thomas's point is that God, the First Truth, is absolutely simple; but due to limitations of the human intellect the object of faith is cognizable only through a multiplicity of concepts. This is reflected in the use of propositions about God that are not simple but complex. Here I am not going to explain Thomas's theory of cognition, but instead I will explain the important consequences of his theory for evangelization. For Saint Thomas, propositions about the faith are indeed truth-bearing propositions. Assenting to these articles of faith allows one not just to grasp the particular content of these propositions but to attain the very object of those propositions. In other words, when one believes what God has revealed, one also attains God himself. Second, even assenting to articles of faith that do not concern God directly (for example, concerning the Blessed Virgin Mary), one still attains God himself in assenting to these. Why? For Aquinas the formal object of the act of faith is always God himself, so one assents to these articles on account of the God who is Truth.[59] This act of faith, whereby God himself is attained, can only be given by God himself graciously uniting himself to us. Where does this leave us with propositional doctrines? As Romanus Cessario states, "The mediation of

58. Aquinas, *Summa Theologiae* II-II, q. 1, a. 2.
59. Aquinas, *Summa Theologiae* II-II, q. 1, a. 1; q. 1, a. 3.

propositions, however, does not impede but achieves the attainment of real truth."[60] For they are a means of attaining God.

Conversely, correct doctrine protects the evangelized from the harm that is done to their souls by incorrect doctrine. The denial of level one doctrines, i.e., dogmas, is called heresy, which is a sin that fundamentally harms man. Toward the end of *Ineffabilis Deus* defining the Immaculate Conception, Pius IX warns that

> Therefore, if any people (which God forbid!) will presume in their hearts to think otherwise than what has been defined by Us, let them henceforth know and understand that they are condemned by their own judgment, and they have made shipwreck of their faith and defected from the unity of the Church.[61]

Anyone who denies the Immaculate Conception, then, has made a shipwreck of his faith. This passage must, of course, be understood with the necessary caveats, such as one must *knowingly* and *willingly* deny the doctrine of the Immaculate Conception after it has been *sufficiently proposed* to him. Nevertheless, Pius IX's language is remarkable and echoes Saint Paul in 1 Timothy 1:19. For Catholic theology and doctrine, formal heresy makes "a shipwreck of one's faith." Another way to think about this is while intellectual assent to an article of faith ennobles man by bringing him to a closer union to God, the sinful denial of an article of faith is harmful to man by making him an enemy of God. If, as said earlier, one recalls that in Catholic theology, faith in God unites one to God himself, then heresy severs one from God. To summarize, the point of a propositional doctrine is that it, in part, brings the one evangelized into contact with the First Truth.

Not only does formal heresy disunite one from God, it also does so in a radical way. Catholic theology teaches that the denial even of a single article of faith means that the believer has no faith at all. Pope Francis explains:

> Since faith is one, it must be professed in all its purity and integrity. Precisely because all the articles of faith are interconnected, to deny

60. Romanus Cessario, *Christian Faith and the Theological Life* (Catholic University of America Press, 1996), 72.

61. Pius IX, *Ineffabilis Deus* (December 8, 1854) (DH 2804).

> one of them, even of those that seem least important, is tantamount to distorting the whole.[62]

This is not only because of the interconnectedness of the articles but also on account of the motive of faith. We base our belief in the articles of faith on the authority of God alone, the authority who can neither deceive nor be deceived.[63] Now to reject even one article of faith is to reject in principle God's authority, since the foundation of every article is that same authority. Aquinas explains it this way: "Though he intends to assent to Christ, yet he fails in his choice of those things wherein he assents to Christ, because he chooses not what Christ really *taught*, but the suggestions of his own mind."[64]

Doctrine, Holiness, and Evangelization

In evangelizing all nations, the Catholic Church does not just want to bring everyone to a knowledge of Christ and to be interiorly renewed; she also wants all men to live lives of virtue. Some Catholics think of holiness primarily in terms of whether one is in the state of sanctifying grace. For the Catholic, sanctifying grace is the *sine qua non* of being in friendship with God. Sanctifying grace, however, is an entitative habit, not an operative habit ordered to action. The Council of Trent teaches that the three theological virtues of faith, hope, and charity are infused with sanctifying grace at baptism[65] so that a Christian can actively live a life of virtue.

62. Francis, *Lumen fidei* (June 29, 2013) (Ignatius Press, 2013), §48. "To reject any article of the faith is to reject the faith itself. This is like pulling one stone out of an arch; it is like putting one hole in the hull of a ship. The whole arch tumbles down; the whole ship sinks. A man who has the faith, accepts God's word. Now, God's word has set up the Church as man's infallible teacher and guide. If a man, therefore, rejects one article of the faith, and says that he believes all the other articles, he believes these by his own choice and opinion, not by faith. Rejecting one article of the faith, he rejects the whole authority of the Church, and he rejects the authority of God which has set up and authorized the Church to teach truth. Hence, it is entirely incorrect to say that a man may have lifeless or formless faith in some articles of the Creed while he rejects others; such a man has not the faith at all, living or lifeless." Paul J. Glenn, *A Tour of the Summa* (Herder, 1960), 191.

63. First Vatican Council, *Dei Filius* (DH 3008).

64. Aquinas, *Summa Theologiae* II-II, q. 11, a. 1.

65. Council of Trent, *Decree on Justification* (DH 1530).

Faith allows us to think with the mind of Christ, which Sacred Scripture instructs us to do. To think like Christ is to become more like Christ. Saint Paul writes, "We destroy arguments, and every lofty opinion raised against the knowledge of God and take every thought captive to obey Christ" (2 Cor 10:5). Again, Paul writes, "Have this mind among yourselves, which is yours in Christ Jesus" (Phil 2:5). Another way to put this is that having our minds filled with the data of sacred doctrine is itself perfecting of the intellect. Bellarmine, explaining Acts 15:8–9, states:

> Faith is said to purify hearts, since it frees man from the filth of errors and false opinions about God and divine things. Faith, not so much efficiently as formally, is like a penetrating light driving out the darkness, because light and darkness cannot remain together. What then is purity of heart unless it is justice, whether its beginning or its end?[66]

There is a second moral aspect of supernatural faith which, according to Saint Thomas, "inclines man to believe, by giving him a certain affection for the good, even when that faith is lifeless."[67]

For the newly evangelized, the act of faith is intimately connected to living the Christian life. The virtue of faith is "the foundation and root of all justification."[68] For example, the Council of Trent explains the manner whereby an adult sinner moves from faith to hope and then to love of God:

> Adults are disposed for that justice when, awakened and assisted by divine grace, they conceive faith from hearing and are led to God, believing to be true what He has divinely revealed and promised, especially that the sinner is justified by God's grace "through the redemption which is in Christ Jesus" (Rom 3:24); when, understanding that they are sinners and turning from the fear of divine justice, which

66. "Idem probat illud Apostoli Petri Actorum 15 Fides purificans corda eorum. Ubi fides dicitur corda purificare, quoniam liberat hominem a sordibus errorum & falsarum opinionum de Deo, rebusque divinis. Quod quidem facit fides non tam efficienter, quam formaliter, quomodo lux intrans pellit tenebras, cum simul morari non possint lux & Tenebrae. Porro puritas cordis quid est nisi iustitia, vel inchoata, vel perfecta?" Bellarmine, *De controversiis*, 15.1.17, vol. 4, col. 775.

67. Aquinas, *Summa Theologiae* II-II, q. 5, a. 2, ad 2.

68. Council of Trent, *Decree on Justification* (DH 1532).

> gives them a salutary shock to the consideration of God's mercy, they are raised up in hope, confident that God will be merciful to them because of Christ; and they begin to love God as the source of all justice and are thereby moved by a certain hatred and detestation for sin, that is, by that repentance.[69]

One can extend Trent's analysis. The articles of faith tell us much more than just that God is merciful to the sinner; they also tell us that suffering has meaning, that eternal life is possible, as well as the nature of eternal life and the beatific vision. So, we come to hope that we will have a share in these realities. The theological virtues of hope and charity are dependent on the virtue of faith because doctrine determines both what we hope for and what love is, as well as whom and how we should love.

It is equally true that the articles of faith specify and inform us about the nature of the virtue of love. At the beginning of the *Summa Theologiae*, Saint Thomas asks the question whether anything other than philosophy is required to know truth. Of course, he says yes, sacred doctrine is also required. Thomas's answer is affirmative, not only because we could not, on our own, know supernatural truths, but also because in our present condition we do not even know what we ought with respect to natural knowledge. In our present condition, we simply do not know how to love one another, and doctrine teaches us what acts are loving acts.[70]

Catholic doctrine specifies what the Christian life filled with virtue will be like. It teaches us positively that in the Christian life of virtue, the gifts of the Holy Spirit and the beatitudes are like ladders to help us climb to perfection.[71]

Sacred doctrine also teaches what love is not. From divine revelation, the extraordinary magisterium, and/or the ordinary universal

69. Council of Trent, *Decree on Justification* (DH 1526).

70. Aquinas, *Summa Theologiae* I, q. 1, a. 1.

71. Christian D. Washburn, "Fruitful Married Love: The Catholic Church's Teaching on Marriage, Abortion, and Contraception," in *Walking with Jesus Christ: Catholic and Evangelical Visions of the Moral Life*, ed. Steven Hoskins and Christian D. Washburn (Saint Paul Seminary Press, 2024), 129–54.

magisterium, we know that the following acts are not loving acts, although the world, without doctrine, often thinks that they are. These include contraceptive acts,[72] simultaneous polygamy,[73] prostitution,[74] fornication,[75] homosexual acts,[76] the direct and voluntary killing of an innocent life,[77] abortion,[78] and euthanasia.[79]

72. Pontifical Council for the Family, "*Vade mecum* for Confessors Concerning Some Aspects of the Morality of Conjugal Life," *Origins* 26 (March 13, 1997): 617–25. John C. Ford and Germain Grisez, "Contraception and the Infallibility of the Ordinary Magisterium," *Theological Studies* 39 (1978): 258–312.

73. Trent: "If anyone says that Christians are permitted to have several wives simultaneously, and that such a practice is not forbidden by any divine law (Matt 19:4–9): let him be anathema." DH 1802.

74. CDF, *Doctrinal Commentary on the Concluding Formula of the Professio Fidei* (June 29, 1998), §11.

75. CDF, *Doctrinal Commentary on the Concluding Formula of the Professio Fidei*, §11.

76. CDF, "Notification Regarding Sister Jeannine Gramick, SSND, and Father Robert Nugent, SDS," 488–91 in *Documenta inde a Concilio Vaticano Secundo expleto edita (1966–2005)* (Libreria Editrice Vaticana, 2006), 491.

77. John Paul II, "Therefore, by the authority which Christ conferred upon Peter and his Successors, and in communion with the Bishops of the Catholic Church, I confirm that the direct and voluntary killing of an innocent human being is always gravely immoral. This doctrine, based upon that unwritten law which man, in the light of reason, finds in his own heart (cf. Rom. 2:14–15), is reaffirmed by Sacred Scripture, transmitted by the Tradition of the Church, and taught by the ordinary and universal Magisterium." *Evangelium vitae* (March 25, 1995) (United States Catholic Conference, 1995), §57.

78. John Paul II, "Therefore, by the authority which Christ conferred upon Peter and his Successors, in communion with the Bishops—who on various occasions have condemned abortion and who in the aforementioned consultation, albeit dispersed throughout the world, have shown unanimous agreement concerning this doctrine—I declare that direct abortion, that is, abortion willed as an end or as a means, always constitutes a grave moral disorder, since it is the deliberate killing of an innocent human being. This doctrine is based upon the natural law and upon the written Word of God, is transmitted by the Church's Tradition and is taught by the ordinary and universal Magisterium." *Evangelium vitae*, §62.

79. John Paul II, "Taking into account these distinctions, in harmony with the Magisterium of my Predecessors and in communion with the Bishops of the Catholic Church, I confirm that euthanasia is a grave violation of the law of God, since it is the deliberate and morally unacceptable killing of a human person. This doctrine is based upon the natural law and upon the written word of God, is transmitted by the Church's Tradition and taught by the ordinary and universal Magisterium." *Evangelium vitae*, §65.

Conclusion

While doctrine is not the most important thing in proclaiming the Gospel, it plays a foundational role in the project of evangelizing the whole world. Doctrine tells us who needs to be evangelized, and indeed we learn that there are no exceptions to Christ's Great Commission. Doctrine also teaches us about why every man needs to be evangelized, because they are born in the state of sin and there is no other answer to man's fundamental condition than Jesus Christ. Doctrine provides the content of the proclaimed word. It also provides the content of what is received in faith. This faith in what God has revealed disposes us to receive the grace of justification, without which we cannot be saved. Doctrine also teaches the evangelized what they are to hope for and how they are to love. Moreover, doctrine purifies the intellect, uniting the believer to God. Doctrine and especially dogma, the teaching of God himself, plays a central role in the entire process of evangelizing the world.

SECTION 2.
Fall 2023

November 2023
Convergence/Agreement Statement

Topic: Evangelization and Salvation

TOPICS UNDER CONSIDERATION

1. Urgency for doing evangelism
2. What is and is not "on the books" regarding evangelization?
3. Contextualization
4. Role of kerygma
5. Role of the Spirit
6. Explicit and implicit faith/knowledge of the Gospel (cognitive content and profession of faith)
7. Fate of the unevangelized/universalism (hell is real; punishment is eternal; affects content and motive of evangelism)
8. Definition of evangelism/content of the message/the agents, the motive, the manner, and the goal of evangelization
9. Points of divergence: the range of and idea of what is acceptable in evangelism

PREAMBLE

Catholics and Evangelicals agree that evangelization is a participation in the missions of the Son and Spirit by which God is reconciling the world to himself. We seek Christian unity because our lack of a unified witness is a scandal to the world and a hindrance to evangelization. Jesus prayed on the night before he died that they may be one (John 17).

CONTENT OF THE MESSAGE

Evangelicals and Catholics agree that the content of the Gospel kerygma can be summed up as the Lord Jesus Christ, who was crucified for our sins and is now risen from the dead as Lord of all, who pours out his Holy Spirit and gives eternal life to all who repent and believe.

THE AGENTS

The Holy Spirit is the primary agent of evangelization. Jesus entrusted the Church's mission in a particular way to the apostles, but the work of evangelization is also incumbent upon all members of the Church in every age.

For Catholics, the bishops, as successors of the apostles, have a guiding role in the work of evangelization, even as the initiative in evangelistic efforts often arises from the laity.

For some Evangelicals, pastors and ecclesiastical leaders have a guiding role in the work of evangelization. For other Evangelicals, para-church and lay-led movements often guide the work of evangelism.

Motivations

Evangelicals and Catholics agree that we evangelize in obedience to Christ's command, out of love for the lost and for the sake of their salvation, all to the glory of God.

We agree that everyone in a state of sin is liable to eternal condemnation and is captive of Satan. Hell and its punishments are eternal. Because of this, urgency is among the great motives to evangelize the lost.

Catholics understand the state of sin that deserves eternal condemnation to be either the state of original sin or actual mortal sin.

Evangelicals understand that all sins, whether original or actual, deserve eternal condemnation.

The Manner

Catholics and Evangelicals agree that evangelization is carried out through the verbal proclamation of the kerygma, accompanied by the witness of the fruit of the Spirit in the life of the Church. Catholics and some Evangelicals also hold that signs and wonders have an important role to play in evangelization.

Catholics and Evangelicals stand united against universalism, pluralism, syncretism, indifferentism, and latitudinarianism.

We agree that that the unevangelized need the grace of Jesus Christ. We also agree that for the unevangelized, the gift of faith is a grace and that an indispensable component of faith is cognitive assent to revealed truth(s).

Catholics say that faith is primarily an assent of the intellect to revealed truth. Some Evangelicals say that faith is primarily trust in Christ's atoning work. Other Evangelicals say that faith is both intellectual assent to revealed truth(s) and fiduciary (heartfelt) trust in Christ.

We agree that everyone in a state of original sin is worthy of eternal condemnation/death and is captive of Satan. Hell and its punishments are eternal. Because of this, urgency is among the great motives to evangelize them/the lost.

We agree that universal salvation of all souls or what is known as universalism is contrary to this truth of the Gospel and that it weakens the motive for evangelization.

We affirm the reality of hell and that the punishments of hell are real.

2.1 Pentecostals on Justification and Evangelization: Historical and Contemporary Perspectives

Alex Mayfield

Soul winning is the one big business of the Church upon earth.[1]

Introduction

THE GOAL OF THIS PAPER is to explore the relationship between evangelization and justification within the Pentecostal tradition. While both theological topics could—and have—filled volumes of Pentecostal treatises, this paper will focus on the theological interaction of these two conceptual areas throughout Pentecostal history and up to today. To better frame this discussion, the paper will be organized around two broad questions that bring this relationship into focus: (1) must the justified evangelize? and (2) must one be evangelized to be justified? On one level, it is quite impossible to separate these two questions. The concept of justification is integral to any theology or practice of evangelization, and likewise, a basic concept of evangelization is the natural outgrowth of a fully developed theology of justification. The reception of the Gospel and the communication of the Gospel are part of a wholly united and divinely orchestrated speech act. All the same, I believe this split can help identify

1. Aimee Semple McPherson, *Declaration of Faith* (Foursquare Missions Press, 2005), 29. This is a reprint of the original, which was published in 1923.

and explore some of the distinctive Pentecostal approaches to these subjects. In each section, I will explore the question chronologically, moving from historical church statements and publications to later developments, mostly among Pentecostal theologians. Each section will end with a brief analysis.

Finally, a few caveats are in order. In this paper, I am restraining myself to perspectives from what is sometimes called the "Classical Pentecostal" tradition.[2] Today, the Pentecostal/Charismatic Movement is a phenomenon that cuts across national and theological boundaries and constitutes a sizeable portion of the global Christian population.[3] In contrast, the Classical Pentecostal tradition commonly refers to denominational movements that trace their origins to the early Pentecostal revivals of the twentieth century. Coming largely from Wesleyan Holiness groups, these Pentecostals typically have strong and specific theologies of sanctification, baptism in the Spirit, and tongues-speech.[4] As experientially oriented, these historical communities have also tended to embed theology in sources other than theological treatises and position papers.[5] Thus, while I will pull from official ecclesial documents, I will also rely on analysis of more popular forms of publication to fill in the gaps, so to speak. Likewise, I will track theological developments through the work of

2. This a common—if not contested—categorization used within Pentecostal scholarship that refers to the "first wave" of Pentecostals who left, or were kicked out of, their denominations and forced to form new ones. See Vinson Synan, "Preface," in *A Century of the Holy Spirit: 100 Years of Pentecostal and Charismatic Renewal*, ed. Vinson Synan (Thomas Nelson, Inc., 2001), digital edition.

3. The Center for the Study of Global Christianity estimated that there were about 644,260,000 Pentecostal/Charismatics in 2020. By their estimate, that means roughly one in four Christians is Pentecostal/Charismatic. See Gina A. Zurlo, Todd M. Johnson, and Peter F. Crossing, "World Christianity and Mission 2020: Ongoing Shift to the Global South," *International Bulletin of Mission Research* 44, no. 1 (2020): 8–19.

4. For more on this Wesleyan connection, see Donald W. Dayton, *Theological Roots of Pentecostalism* (Francis Asbury Press, 1987).

5. For example, Mark Cartledge argues that testimony is "central to the ordinary expression of [Pentecostal] faith," being a means both of conveying theology and creating Pentecostal communities. These testimonies were often published and republished in periodicals. Mark J. Cartledge, *Testimony in the Spirit: Rescripting Ordinary Pentecostal Theology* (Ashgate Publishing, 2010), 16–18.

academic Pentecostal theologians. While these are important figures in the movement, there can be a disconnect between these types of sources and the life of most Pentecostal communities. Theological developments are not evenly distributed, and older historical viewpoints coexist beside newer approaches. With these caveats laid down, I'll proceed.

Must the Justified Evangelize?

HISTORICAL VIEWPOINTS

Like many evangelical revivals of the late nineteenth century and early twentieth century, early Pentecostal revivals had a firm focus on the priority of world evangelization. The 1906 revival at the Azusa Street Mission, for example, commissioned and sent multiple parties of missionaries and evangelists around the world. Operating on faith principles, these Pentecostals often went to far-flung places with little to no economic support, believing simply that God had called them. Within the first five months of the revival, thirty-eight missionaries were commissioned and sent; within the first two years, the Pentecostal message had reached over fifty nations.[6] Just one example of these was Alfred Garr. Originally commissioned to India, Alfred Garr believed that God had miraculously given him the ability to speak a dialect of India. Fully convinced, he and his family set sail in 1906.[7] Garr also provides a particularly Pentecostal wax on the priority of evangelization. During this earliest period, the phenomenon of tongues-speech was commonly understood as a xenoglossic phenomenon. Many Pentecostals believed that the experience of tongues was the gift of an unknown language. Thus, the miraculous gift of a foreign language was a divine solution to the hurdles of world

6. These are the counts provided by Mookgo Solomon Kgatla, "The Influence of Azusa Street Revival in the Early Developments of the Apostolic Faith Mission of South Africa," *Missionalia* 44, no. 3 (2016): 321–35, at 324.

7. Allan Anderson, "The Missionary Spirit: Alfred and Lillian Garr and the Hong Kong Pentecostal Mission" (lecture, Princeton Theological Seminary, Princeton, NJ, December 1–2, 2008), https://www.academia.edu/11607929/The_Missionary_Spirit_Alfred_and_Lillian_Garr_ and_the_Hong_Kong_Pentecostal_Mission.

evangelization. Many would-be missionaries, Garr among them, boarded boats fully expecting that they would be able to preach in a foreign language as the Spirit led.[8] These individuals quickly realized that such was not the case (at least in general), and the xenoglossic understanding largely faded in the movement. That said, the foundational belief that Spirit baptism was an empowerment for mission did not go away, and the Pentecostal belief in divine healing would become instrumental in many contexts as a tool for evangelization.

As the heady days of revival died down and denominational bodies took shape in the 1910s and 1920s, the prioritization did not fade. When the Assemblies of God formed in 1914 in Hot Springs, Arkansas, they listed five reasons for their formation, two of which focused on ensuring a more effective evangelical witness.[9] Christ's Great Commission (Matt 28:19–20) commanded that believers should ensure that the Gospel was "taught, preached, and published in all the world."[10] Two years later, when the Assemblies adopted their "Fundamental Truths," their ecclesiological and ministerial identity was firmly established in an evangelistic mode. Article 8 defines the Church as a "living organism . . . with divine appointments for the fulfillment of her great commission."[11] Article 9 defines ministry completely in terms of evangelization, stating, "A divinely called and Scripturally ordained ministry for the evangelization of the world, is the command of the Lord, and the chief concern of the Church. Mk. 16:15–20; Eph. 4:11–13." While the "Fundamental Truths" have been modified over the years, this evangelistic impulse remains an essential aspect of ecclesiology and ministry in the Assemblies of God's doctrinal statements.[12]

8. For more on this, see Gary B. McGee, "Shortcut to Language Preparation? Radical Evangelicals, Missions, and the Gift of Tongues," *International Bulletin of Missionary Research* 25, no. 3 (July 2001): 118–22.

9. *Minutes of the General Council of the Assemblies of God in the United States of America, Canada, and Foreign Lands* (1914), 4.

10. *Minutes of the General Council of the Assemblies of God* (1914), 4.

11. *Minutes of the General Council of the Assemblies of God in the United States of America, Canada, and Foreign Lands* (1916), 11.

12. The current articles on the Church and the Ministry both list evangelization as the first priority. See *Constitution and Bylaws of the General Council of the Assemblies of God* (2021), 11–16.

Other Classical Pentecostal denominations had a similarly strong emphasis on evangelization during their founding periods. When the first General Assembly of the Church of God (Cleveland) met in 1906, the minutes reported that "strong men wept" in their anxiety to proclaim the Gospel, and the assembly felt that all should do their best to "work with greater zeal and energy for the spread of the glorious gospel of the Son of God than ever before."[13] In 1923, Aimee Semple McPherson penned her "Declaration of Faith," which would go on to become a foundational document for the International Church of the Foursquare Gospel. In it, Semple McPherson emphatically declares that

> soul winning is the one big business of the Church upon earth; and that therefore every weight and hindrance which would tend to quench the flame or hamper the efficiency of world-wide evangelism should be cut off and cast away as unworthy of the Church.[14]

In the same year, Semple McPherson founded the Echo Park Evangelistic and Missionary Training Institute. It was intended for those who "really intend to become Evangelists and feel the burning all of God for service at home or abroad."[15] Besides her own church, the school for evangelization was the first institution built by the denomination.

Finally, while the founding documents of the Pentecostal Holiness Church did not include an explicit statement on evangelism, the impulse was expressed elsewhere. For example, the baptismal formula listed in the church's first by-laws begins with a wax on the Great Commission and admonishes the witnessing congregation that "it is our bounden duty as professors of His grace to conform to this great commission."[16] Similarly, the same by-laws included a specific section mandating missionary societies in each local church. The Pentecostal Holiness Advocate, the official publication of the church,

13. *Minutes of the Annual Assembly of the Churches of East Tennessee, North Georgia, and Western North Carolina* (1906), 4.

14. Semple McPherson, *Declaration of Faith*, 29.

15. "Angelus Evangelistic Training School," *Bridal Call* (July–August 1922): 35. Today the school has grown into Life Pacific University, an accredited four-year institution.

16. *Constitution and General Rules of the Pentecostal Holiness Church* (1911), 21.

was likewise awash with passionate calls for evangelization of the world, and special issues were dedicated to various mission fields.[17] Eventually, the church added Article 14 to its "Articles of Faith" in 1977, which affirms that "it is the responsibility of every believer to dedicate his life to carrying out the work of the Great Commission (Matthew 28:18–20; Mark 16:15–20; Acts 1:8)."

CONTEMPORARY DEVELOPMENTS

Looking back, we can see that the earliest period of the Pentecostal movement placed a high priority on evangelism, so much so that some groups could be said to have subsumed their ecclesiology into a theology of evangelism. In subsequent decades, pastors, evangelists, and theologians would build on this tradition by supplying more robust theological frameworks for the theology and practice of evangelism. I will draw attention to just two approaches that relate to the above, larger question: (1) evangelism as participation in the divine life and (2) holistic proclamation.

EVANGELISM AND DIVINE LIFE

Through their reliance on Matthew 28:19–20 as an anchoring text, many early Pentecostal doctrinal statements and professions discussed evangelism through a language of commandment, duty, or obligation. The justified "must" evangelize because it is an imperative given by Christ. More recent theological reflection, however, has moved toward a more integrated approach that synergistically weds the evangelistic imperative with the dynamics of justification and sanctification. Looking back to a previous round of this dialogue, the contribution by Jackie and Cheryl Johns sets the stage well: "Justification is the inauguration and continuation by grace of a right relation with God. . . . Sanctification, on the other hand, while inextricably tied to justification, is for Wesleyan-Pentecostals the process of sharing Divine life."[18]

17. For example, an entire issue in 1923 was dedicated to evangelistic work in China. See *The Pentecostal Holiness Advocate*, June 7, 1923.

18. Jackie David Johns and Cheryl Bridges Johns, "Life in the New Creation: Justification and Sanctification Revisited," 173–82 in *Justified in Jesus Christ: Evangelicals and*

In this framework, justification and sanctification describe a trajectory for the believer's life. Through Christ and in the indwelling of the Spirit, we are bound up and brought into the divine life as active participants who are being conformed to the likeness of Christ. Steven Studebaker describes this as a "redemptive soteriology" in which "God's act of justifying the believer recreates in the believer the redemptive work of Christ."[19]

Building on a similar trajectory, Assemblies of God theologian Frank Macchia argues that the indwelling Spirit creates a new reality in which *finitum capax infiniti*, the humblest of finite human actions, can now bear the weight of the divine.[20] We are turned into temples of God, and this has specific consequences for our relationship with others. As Macchia explains:

> To lay claim to the privilege of being the one who is taken by the Spirit into the divine life involves taking in the other as well. Jesus opened his blessing to Israel only on the condition that the Pharisees receive it at the banquet table with the outcasts (Luke 15). And the blessing of Abraham is to occur only when the Jews bless the nations and are blessed with their fellowship in return.[21]

To say it another way, if we are taken into the *vita Dei*, then we are also taken into the *missio Dei*. To share in the life of God also means we share in God's mission. Justification, then, necessarily implies evangelization.

Just as justification-sanctification is not the transference of a moral category or enactment of a divine legal fiction, the sharing of the divine mission is not the sharing of a mere duty or obligation. Rather, the Spirit enables our finite evangelical witness to bear the weight of the divine by providing both the opportunity and means through which the good news can be effectively proclaimed. Both

Catholics in Dialogue, ed. Steve Hoskins and David Fleischacker (University of Mary Press, 2017), 180.

19. Steven M. Studebaker, "Pentecostal Soteriology and Pneumatology," *Journal of Pentecostal Theology* 11, no. 2 (2003): 248–70, at 269.

20. Frank D. Macchia, *Justified in the Spirit: Creation, Redemption, and the Triune God* (Eerdmans, 2010), 80–88 [digital edition].

21. Macchia, *Justified in the Spirit*, 259 [digital edition].

provisions deserve attention. Amos Yong, the prominent Assemblies of God missiologist, describes how the Spirit enables effective proclamation in a pluralistic world of different languages and cultures:

> Among the many miracles of Pentecost, the most important for our purposes is that it made possible the encounter of human beings with each other that, left to themselves, would not have entered into relationship. Whether such was a miracle of speech or of hearing is not of concern here. The crucial issue is that understanding occurred across linguistic lines: "in our own languages we hear them speaking about God's deeds of power."[22]

For Yong, Acts 2 documents not just a linguistic miracle but a communicative one. When we are taken up in the divine life, the Spirit goes before us into the world and establishes the very ground on which we can communicate with the other. Human proclamation is necessarily bound up in cultural-linguistic frameworks, which make the act of translation and effective communication nigh impossible. However, the Spirit enables a dialogical approach to proclamation that infuses the finite with the infinite and enables the effective proclamation of the Gospel. All mission is pneumatologically infused mission.[23]

Likewise, the Spirit can also provide the means for effective proclamation through supernatural manifestations. Early Pentecostals expected miraculous xenoglossy to enable world evangelization. Perhaps the disappointment explains why the linking of miraculous phenomena with evangelization is missing from most early doctrinal statements. That is not the case with more recent doctrinal and theological works. The current edition of the Assemblies of God's "Fundamental Truths" states that believers should pursue Spirit baptism because it explicitly "enables them to evangelize in the power of the Spirit with accompanying supernatural signs (Mark 16:15–20; Acts 4:29–31; Hebrews 2:3, 4)."[24] Of these signs, healing has come to be one of the most prominent forms of Spirit-enabled witness to

22. Amos Yong, *The Missiological Spirit: Christian Mission Theology in the Third Millennium Global Context* (James Clarke, 2015), 40–41.

23. Yong, *The Missiological Spirit*, 51–52.

24. *Constitution and Bylaws of the General Council of the Assemblies of God* (2021), 15.

the power of God. Healing crusades and evangelists are normative within Pentecostal and Charismatic traditions.[25] Practical evangelistic reflection on this form of evangelism has sometimes been dubbed "power encounter" or "encounter evangelism."[26] This evangelistic model depends on the effective demonstration of the supernatural power of God within a public setting. Depending on the context, these demonstrations of power are openly contrasted with the relative weakness of supernatural beings in traditional religions.[27] In this mode, evangelism describes the supernatural encounter between the power of the Holy Spirit and the various spirits, powers, and principalities of this world.

HOLISTIC PROCLAMATION

Pentecostal evangelistic supernaturalism does not necessarily have to be defined by miraculous speech acts and power encounters. Through an engagement with their own Wesleyan heritage and the broader Evangelical world, many modern Pentecostal theologians have begun fleshing out a pneumatologically informed approach to holistic mission.[28] In his discussion of justification-sanctification, Macchia observes that entrance into the divine life begins a process whereby the believer is put right. This rightwising of the self, however, is not just an individualistic process. As Macchia asks, "How can we be rightwised with God 'by faith' or in conformity by the Spirit to the faithfulness of Christ in isolation from others?"[29] If justifica-

25. Veli-Matti Kärkkäinen, *Spirit and Salvation* (Eerdmans, 2016), esp. ch. 10.

26. One of the most influential books espousing this approach is John Wimber's *Power Evangelism* (Harper & Row, 1986). Upon reading medieval accounts of missionary bishops and monks, such as Boniface, it is apparent that Pentecostals were not the first to endorse this sort of confrontational approach.

27. Such accounts are legion in early Pentecostal missionary literature, especially in relation to the practice of divine healing and idol removal. For a detailed look at this dynamic, see my own work, Alex Mayfield, "The Heathen City," 141–84 in *The Kaleidoscopic City* (Baylor University Press, 2023).

28. For just a few more examples, Brian Woolnough and Wonsuk Ma, eds., *Holistic Mission: God's Plan for God's People* (Wipf & Stock, 2011); Miguel Alvarez, *Integral Mission: A Paradigm for Latin American Pentecostals* (Wipf & Stock, 2017).

29. Macchia, *Justified in the Spirit*, 255 [digital edition].

tion-sanctification entails a person being caught up into the divine life, then it also entails that their social relationships and the social systems that they are part of are, in some way, also caught up with them in the process of rightwising. The interconnected nature of human existence implies that justification, and thus evangelism, have an unavoidable social component.

This social component is often expressed in two ways. The first takes a more sectarian approach, much along the lines of Stanley Hauerwas.[30] The Church, as the community of the rightwised, is meant to be a representation of God's Kingdom in miniature. The Church witnesses to the Gospel through the proclamation of the Word, but it also witnesses and proclaims the Gospel through its specific way of life. As Yong puts it, Spirit-empowered mission extends "to the work of the church as a social body in an imperial world."[31] The life of the community is itself a form of evangelistic proclamation meant to woo and win the lost. Yong goes on to stress that this sort of Spirit-empowered witness "involves all-of-life discipleship, with concomitant holiness of behavior and practice that reaches beyond one's community."[32] To make an evangelistic play on Hauerwas's more famous maxim: The Church does not have an evangelistic strategy; it is an evangelistic strategy.

The second way that Pentecostals express their concerns for the social component of evangelism is via forms of charity and development work. While various forms of these works have been part of the Pentecostal tradition from its inception, recent decades have seen a downtick in giving toward purely evangelistic causes and a larger uptick in giving toward the development and charitable arms of Pentecostal denominations.[33] Likewise, many prominent Pente-

30. Stanley Hauerwas and William H. Willimon, *Resident Aliens: Life in the Christian Colony* [Expanded Twenty-Fifth Anniversary Edition] (Abingdon Press, 2014), esp. 39–40.

31. Amos Yong, *Mission After Pentecost: The Witness of the Spirit from Genesis to Revelation* (Baker Academic, 2019), 189.

32. Yong, *Mission After Pentecost*, 217.

33. As described in more detail in Jerry Ireland, *The Missionary Spirit: Evangelism and Social Action in Pentecostal Missiology* (Orbis, 2021), ch. 4 [digital edition].

costal missiologists have drawn attention to how participation in the *missio Dei* entails participating in acts of justice, addressing human suffering, and serving the community.[34] In these developments, Pentecostals have largely followed the general trend of global Evangelicalism's embrace of more holistic forms of proclamation. With that said, this move has not been without controversy among Pentecostals—as with Evangelicals writ large. Missiologist Jerry Ireland has argued that these approaches have undercut a traditional focus on bringing the Gospel to places where Christ is not known.[35] Responding to similar concerns, the Assemblies of God issued a position paper in 2015 that addressed the growth of ministries of compassion, social transformation, and peacemaking. While it endorsed all of these as expressions of the Gospel, it stressed that the "Assemblies of God's main focus of ministry has been, and continues to be, worldwide evangelism and discipleship."[36] Similarly, in 2010, the Church of God passed a resolution in which the denomination reaffirmed its "total, unreserved commitment to understanding the scope of the Great Commission and the essential structure necessary for superior evangelism performance."[37] While holistic proclamation is good, most Classical Pentecostals see themselves as being in the "soul-winning" business.

ANALYSIS

In reviewing the above, it seems clear that when asked, "Must the justified evangelize?" the Pentecostal tradition, from its beginning to today, responds with a resounding, "Yes!" Pentecostals believe that evangelization, be it in the form of verbal or holistic proclamation, is

34. For examples, see Wonsuk Ma and Julie Ma, *Mission in the Spirit: Towards a Pentecostal/Charismatic Missiology* (Regnum, 2010); Murray W. Dempster, "Pentecostal Social Concern and the Biblical Mandate of Social Justice," *Pneuma: The Journal of the Society for Pentecostal Studies* 9 (1987): 129–53.

35. For a summary brief of these critiques, see Ireland, *The Missionary Spirit*, esp. ch. 1.

36. General Presbytery of the Assemblies of God, "Church Mission and Peacemaking," August 1–3, 2015, https://ag.org/Beliefs/Position-Papers/Church-Mission-and-Peacemaking.

37. *Minutes 2010—Church of God Book of Discipline, Church Order, and Governance* (2010), 12.

at the core of the Church's identity. Rather than being a moral duty or obligation, evangelization is the natural outgrowth of the process of justification-sanctification. We are brought, through Christ and in the power of the Spirit, into the *vita Dei*, and thus, we are also brought into the *missio Dei*. As such, the Spirit empowers the Church for a faithful, supernatural witness to the Gospel and goes before us to establish the ground on which communication to the fallen world is even possible. While there are some disagreements about the prioritization of forms of public proclamation, Pentecostals remain committed to preaching Christ where he is not yet known and truly becoming an apostolic community that is propelled forward by the Spirit to seek and save the lost.

Must One Be Evangelized to Be Justified?

Unlike the first question, the second involves heading into the murky waters known as theologies of religions. I would like to make two more caveats before I dive in. First, traditional Evangelical approaches to this area have often utilized a tripartite formula of exclusivism, inclusivism, and pluralism to demarcate positions on the soteriological value of other religions.[38] More recent work in the past decades, however, has brought these terms under increased scrutiny, and attempts to offer qualifications and more complex categorical frameworks have not really offered any clarity. In short, these terms oversimplify a topic that is necessarily complex, and as Yong has observed, one can hold classical exclusivist, inclusivist, or pluralist positions at the same time.[39] For my part, I will try to avoid these terms or at least use them sparingly. The second caveat is a simple one drawn from Christian

38. Defining these terms is problematic for reasons to be discussed. Peter Kreeft offers a simplified overview: "Exclusivists say that the religions of the world contradict each other. . . . Inclusivism says that deep down, perhaps at some 'mystical' level, religions do not contradict each other. . . . Pluralism says we cannot know which it is." In terms of soteriology, this usually is translated in relation to the exclusivity of Christ's salvific work. Peter Kreeft, *Between One Faith and Another: Engaging Conversations on the World's Great Religions* (IVP Books, 2017), 1–2.

39. Amos Yong, *Beyond the Impasse: Toward a Pneumatological Theology of Religions* (Wipf & Stock, 2014), 28.

and Missionary Alliance theologian Gordon T. Smith: "The Bible is not explicit on what happens to one who has never heard or had the opportunity to hear specifically of Jesus."[40] At times, Pentecostals will go beyond Scripture to fill in this gap, so to speak. However, within their doctrinal statements and positions, most groups have tended to mirror the ambiguity within the biblical witness. Thus, the answer to this second question can never be quite as resounding as the answer to the first.

HISTORICAL VIEWPOINTS

None of the founding documents of classical Pentecostal denominations included any statements about the eternal fate of those who have not heard the Gospel (i.e., the unevangelized). However, doctrinal statements about salvation and the eternal rewards do offer some insights.

SALVATION

Regarding salvation, all early Pentecostal denominations take a classical Protestant approach. The Pentecostal Holiness Church's 1911 by-laws state that "We believe, teach, and firmly maintain the Scriptural doctrine of justification by faith alone."[41] The Assemblies of God's 1916 "Fundamental Truths" describes that the believer is saved "by the washing of regeneration and renewing of the Holy Ghost" and that this is possible because the believer has been "justified by grace through faith."[42] The 1915 *Doctrines and Disciplines* of the Apostolic Faith Mission at Azusa Street states that the process of repentance includes godly sorrow for sin, the confession of sin, and "restitution and faith in Jesus Christ." Likewise, the Foursquare Church's 1923 Declaration of Faith goes on to say that "upon sincere repentance, godly sorrow for sin, and a whole-hearted acceptance of the Lord

40. Gordon T. Smith, "Religions and the Bible: An Agenda for Evangelicals," 9–29 in *Christianity and the Religions: A Biblical Theology of World Religions*, ed. Edward Rommen and Harold Netland (William Carey, 1995), 25.

41. *Constitution and General Rules of the Pentecostal Holiness Church* (1911), 3.

42. *Minutes of the General Council of the Assemblies of God* (1916), 10.

Jesus Christ, they who call upon Him may be justified by faith."[43] Here, we see a theology of conversion that generally relies upon classical Evangelical theologies of justification by faith in Christ. While some doctrinal statements do not explicitly include the "in Christ," this omission was not likely strategic, as subsequent decades of clarification showed. When the Church of God finally adopted a doctrinal Declaration of Faith in 1948, it stated that "justification, regeneration, and the new birth are wrought by faith in the blood of Jesus Christ."[44] Similarly, the Pentecostal Holiness Church included an official doctrinal exegesis in its by-laws in 1945. Written by then Overseer J. H. King, it stated that "faith is the result of divine persuasion effected by the promises of God" and that this faith "includes confidence and trust" in Christ.[45] In conclusion, Classical Pentecostals have always stressed that repentance unto salvation is only possible when a person has explicit knowledge of the good news of Jesus Christ.

ETERNAL REWARDS

Pentecostal doctrinal statements on eternal rewards also take a similar path toward increased clarity. In the Article on "The Lake of Fire," in the Assemblies of God's 1916 "Fundamental Truths," hell awaits anyone "not found written in the Book of Life, the fearful and unbelieving, and abominable, and murderers and whoremongers, and sorcerers, and idolaters and all liars."[46] The 1923 Foursquare Declaration of Faith describes hell as reserved for those "who have rejected the mercy, love and tenderness of the crucified Savior, . . . in spite of every entreaty and warning of the Holy Spirit."[47] The Pentecostal Holiness Church's parallel article states that "everlasting banishment from the presence of the Lord, and unending torture in hell, [are] the wages of the persistently wicked." When the Church of God embraced an official doctrinal statement in 1948, they adopted a sparse statement

43. Semple McPherson, *Declaration of Faith*, 10.
44. *Minutes of the 4th Assembly of the Church of God* (1948), 31.
45. *Discipline of the Pentecostal Holiness Church* (1945), 15.
46. *Minutes of the General Council of the Assemblies of God* (1916), 13.
47. Semple McPherson, *Declaration of Faith*, 28.

that they believed in the "eternal punishment for the wicked."[48] These approaches tend to cleave closely to biblical language, especially from Revelation 19–20. Because of this, they inherit the general ambiguity regarding the fate of the unevangelized. These early statements could be read broadly to imply that damnation is only possible through outright rejection of God or the egregious violation of the moral law as provided by natural revelation. In at least some cases, this intentional ambiguity might be purposeful. Sometimes called an inclusivist, J. H. King saw other religions as demonically inspired but tended to be hopeful about the fate of the unreached.[49] Likewise, early Pentecostal leader Charles Fox Parham's theology could be described as having a very high Christology that still held out hope for those who had not heard the Gospel.[50] For the most part, however, the Pentecostals' priority on evangelization led them to reject anything that might undercut the evangelistic impulse, like the idea that the unreached might be saved through some sort of post-mortem experience or through their own works.[51]

To that end, by 1973, the Assemblies of God's Article on the "Lake of Fire" was renamed to "The Final Judgment," and it makes it clear that "the wicked dead will be raised and judged according to their works," and that it is these who are not written in the Book of Life

48. *Minutes of the 4th Assembly of the Church of God* (1948), 31.

49. Tony G. Moon, "J. H. King and a Pentecostal Theology of Religions and Interreligious Ecumenism: Lessons Learned and Suggestions for Future Research," *Journal of Pentecostal Theology* 22 (2013): 312. From 2007 to 2010, Tony G. Moon and Tony Richie held heated debates in the *Journal of Pentecostal Theology* about the exact nature of King's inclusivist position. Their final responses provide helpful summaries of their ultimate positions. See Tony Richie, "Getting Back to the Heart of the Matter: The Way Forward and a Final Response to Tony Moon," *Journal of Pentecostal Theology* 18 (2009): 141–49; Tony G. Moon, "J. H. King and a Pentecostal Theology of Religions and Interreligious Ecumenism: Lessons Learned and Suggestions for Future Research," *Journal of Pentecostal Theology* 22 (2013): 301–17.

50. For more, see Tony Richie, "Eschatological Inclusivism: Exploring Early Pentecostal Theology of Religions in Charles Fox Parham," *Journal of the European Pentecostal Theological Association* 27, no. 2 (2007): 138–52.

51. Amos Yong and Tony Richie, "Missiology and the Interreligious Encounter," 96–119 in *The Missiological Spirit*, 105–6.

and are destined for the lake of fire.[52] Three years later, the Assemblies put forth a position paper that stated, "All who do not know God with a personal knowledge of salvation plus all who do not keep on obeying the gospel" are destined for eternal punishment.[53] Moreover, they emphatically stated that "there will be no second chance" for salvation following death.[54] To my knowledge, no other Classical Pentecostal denominations have taken the step of issuing an official position on this subject, but similar perspectives continue to be common in the pulpit and the pews.

CONTEMPORARY DEVELOPMENTS

On both a popular and academic level, more recent decades have also seen movements toward approaches that attempt to be less pessimistic about the fate of the unevangelized while also not de-emphasizing the importance of evangelization. On a more popular level, this was most radically demonstrated by the Church of God in Christ minister Carlton Pearson. As a rising star in the Pentecostal world, Pearson began teaching a variant of universal reconciliation that he called the "Gospel of Inclusion" around 2001. He argued that people, whether in this life or the next, will be punished for their sins, but that hell is not an eternal reality and that all people will ultimately be reunited with God. Nevertheless, people should push their own and others' reconciliation with God to avoid needless suffering. Pearson was declared a heretic by his denomination and was quickly shunned by the Pentecostal and Charismatic community.

Theologians have been a bit more careful than Pearson in their exploration of the fate of the unevangelized. The most provocative foray into the arena was that of Clark Pinnock. While a Baptist, Pinnock borrowed heavily from the Pentecostal tradition, and his work continues to be engaged with by Pentecostal theologians. Veli-Matti Kärkkäinen summarizes the crux of Pinnock's argument in his 1992 book, *A Wideness in God's Mercy*:

52. *Minutes of the 35th Council of the Assemblies of God* (1973), 122.

53. General Presbytery of the Assemblies of God, "Eternal Punishment," August 17, 1976, https://ag.org/Beliefs/ Position-Papers/End-Times-Eternal-Punishment.

54. General Presbytery of the Assemblies of God, "Eternal Punishment."

> The key to hope for the unevangelized lies in Pinnock's idea of the faith principle: according to the Bible, people are saved by faith, not by the content of their theology. Since God has not left anyone without witness, people are judged on the basis of the light they have received and how they have responded to that light. Obviously, people cannot be held responsible for not responding to a revelation they never received.[55]

Protecting his Evangelical bona fides, Pinnock goes on to argue that the drive for evangelism is not to urge others "to turn to Jesus because God hates them and delights in sending them to hell. . . . No, our mission is to the announce the wonderful news . . . of God reconciling the world to himself in Jesus Christ and the beginning of the age of salvation."[56] Pinnock's insistence on the faith principle aligns well with the more vaguely worded doctrinal statements of some Pentecostal groups. However, it is a broadening that also seems to go against the wider trajectory of Classical Pentecostalism in the twentieth and twenty-first centuries.

This does not mean Pentecostals are completely pessimistic about the fate of the unevangelized. Church of God theologian Tony Richie continues to argue for an optimistic Pentecostal engagement with other faiths and hopes for the creation of a Pentecostal theology of religions that is "neither naïve nor narrow," that "neither compromises nor confines either Christ or God's grace, or the Holy Spirit's presence and power."[57] Perhaps meeting the call, the work of Amos Yong continues to push forward in this area. Among other observations, Yong has highlighted the way typical Evangelical exclusivist approaches lead to a de facto position of *extra ecclesiam nulla salus*, in which salvation is ecclesiologically mediated via proclamation and

55. Veli-Matti Kärkkäinen, *An Introduction to the Theology of Religions: Biblical, Historical, & Contemporary Perspectives* (IVP Academic, 2003).

56. Clark H. Pinnock, *A Wideness in God's Mercy: The Finality of Jesus Christ in a World of Religions* (Zondervan Academic, 1992), 177–78.

57. Tony Richie, "Neither Naïve Nor Narrow: A Balanced Pentecostal Approach to Christian Theology of Religions," *Cyberjournal for Pentecostal-Charismatic Research* 15 (2006), http://www.pctii.org/cyberj/cyberj15/richie.html.

not Christian initiation.[58] This approach introduces a whole host of questions about the level of comprehension required to be saved. Are children able to understand enough to be saved? At what age? Can those with cognitive difficulties be saved? What happens if someone rejects Christ based on a faulty understanding of the Gospel? Is a misguided understanding of the Gospel damnable? If so, which of us in this dialogue—holy as we try to be—is going to hell for our misinterpretation of Scripture?[59] If *extra ecclesiam nulla salus* is mediated through proclamation and not Christian initiation, it does seem as if God's grace can be severely limited by a single human's capacity. Simply put, most Pentecostals—and I would venture to guess most Evangelical groups—do not have a high enough ecclesiology to support the position Yong is critiquing.

While this critique is a good one, it does not answer the main question of this section or define the Church's relationship to an unbelieving—and at times nonreceptive—world. Here again, Macchia can be helpful by redefining the Church in relation to the kingdom of God. While he defends the doctrine of election, he insists that this cannot be interpreted as an "unqualified identification between the church and Christ, the Spirit, or the kingdom of God." Rather, "only *Christ's* witness is identical without qualification with the kingdom of God."[60] In such a scenario, the Spirit-empowered community of the Church must assume a humbler and more dialogical position in relation to the world and God's kingdom. While much more can be said about the Church, we are no less than a "loving fellow traveler with the world's religions" who confidently points others to the superiority of Christ.[61] Macchia's approach does not necessarily resolve the question of the salvation of unevangelized people, and it may introduce more ecclesiological questions.

58. Yong, *Beyond the Impasse*, 26.

59. Amos Yong, "The Christian Spirit, Practices, and the Religions: Theology of Religions in Pentecostal and Pneumatological Perspective," *The Asbury Journal* 62, no. 2 (2007): 5–31, at 15–16.

60. Frank D. Macchia, *Baptized in the Spirit: A Global Pentecostal Theology* (Zondervan, 2009), 190.

61. Macchia, *Baptized in the Spirit*, 188.

However, his argument, along with those of Richie and Yong, at least illustrates that Pentecostals are attempting to break through the impasse to find an approach that synthesizes the particularity of Christian witness, the evangelistic impulse, and confidence in the gratuitousness of God's grace.

ANALYSIS

How, then, could one characterize the response of Classical Pentecostals when asked, "Must one be evangelized to be justified?" It would likely sound like a confident "Yes" accompanied by a much quieter "Probably." Historically, Pentecostals have clung to narrow definitions of justification that have placed the emphasis on an individual's faith in the atoning work of Christ. Salvation, then, does necessitate some sort of cognitive assent to specific dogmas. To my knowledge, no Classical Pentecostal group has tried to define the doctrinal threshold by which someone might be saved. In fact, almost all would likely be adamantly against such an attempt due to the way it patently restricts God's grace. At the same time, Pentecostals have tended to avoid adopting full-throated inclusivist positions because, on one level or another, these stances are perceived as threatening the exclusivity of Christ's atoning work or undermining the mandate of the Great Commission and the apostolic witness of the Church. In short, Pentecostals, like many in the Evangelical camp, are attempting to sail between two unacceptable positions. Venture too far to one side, and we are grabbed by the Scylla of restricting God's grace via human limitation; venture too far to the other, and we are pulled down by Charybdis and lose the prioritization of evangelism. If we have sailed close to one side, it is Scylla's, but only just.

Conclusions

For the sake of the dialogue, I would like to end this paper by summarizing a few of the key points above in as concise a manner as possible. Surveying the above, several conclusions are apparent regarding the Classical Pentecostal tradition.

Classical Pentecostals have always and continue to believe that:

Evangelization of the lost is one of the chief purposes of the Church;

The desire for and participation in the evangelization of the lost is a fundamental outcome of the justified-sanctified life;

While not required, miraculous phenomena, such as divine healing or other supernatural manifestations of power, should be expected to accompany evangelistic efforts;

The evangelistic witness of the Church should be accompanied by a correspondingly winsome social ethic;

The Church's social ethic is not the same as nor does it stand in place of the active evangelization of the lost;

The scriptural witness suggests—and certainly does not preclude—eternal separation from God as the fate of the unevangelized, yet their eternal fate is ultimately up to God.

2.2 The Destiny of the Unevangelized: A Reformed Perspective

Dennis W. Jowers

Introduction

THE CONFESSIONAL DOCUMENTS of the Reformed churches deny that any mentally competent adult can attain salvation without believing the Gospel of Jesus Christ. The answer to question 60 of the Westminster Larger Catechism, "Can they who have never heard of the gospel, and so know not Jesus Christ, nor believe in him, be saved by their living according to the light of nature?" for example, reads as follows: "They who, having never heard the gospel, know not Jesus Christ, and believe not in him, cannot be saved, be they never so diligent to frame their lives according to the light of nature, or the laws of that religion which they profess; neither is there salvation in any other, but in Christ alone, who is the Saviour only of his body the Church."[1] Likewise, the framers of the Westminster standards declare in chapter 10, section 4 of the Westminster Confession of Faith:

> Others, not elected, although they may be called by the ministry of the Word, and may have some common operations of the Spirit, yet they never truly come unto Christ, and therefore cannot be saved: much less can men, not professing the Christian religion, be saved in any other way whatsoever, be they never so diligent to frame their lives according to the light of nature, and the laws of that religion

1. *The Confession of Faith; the Larger and Shorter Catechisms, with the Scripture Proofs at Large: Together with the Sum of Saving Knowledge* (Johnstone, Hunter, & Co., 1894), 125.

> they do profess. And, to assert and maintain that they may, is very pernicious, and to be detested.[2]

The framers of the Canons of Dordt, likewise, condemn those who assert that pagans may, by the right use of means at their disposal, attain the benefits that those who believe in Christ attain through explicit faith in him. The fifth error they reject under the Third and Fourth Heads of Doctrine, specifically, is that of persons "who teach that corrupt and natural man can so well use common grace, by which they mean the light of nature, or the gifts left after the Fall, that he can gradually obtain by this good use a greater grace: viz., the evangelical or salutary grace, and salvation itself."[3]

The belief of the Reformed churches, then, is plain: no mentally competent adult shall ever attain salvation without first believing the Gospel of Christ. In the following, we intend, first, to refute the arguments most commonly employed to prove that mentally competent adults may attain salvation without professing the Christian faith; and, second, to state the reasons that constrain the Reformed churches to reject that claim.

Arguments Against the Reformed Position

Scripture, many Christians assert, implicitly teaches that some mentally competent adults who never profess faith in Christ before death may be saved nonetheless. This opinion's proponents, customarily referred to as inclusivists, advance four principal arguments in its defense.

1. Faith in God without explicitly Christian faith. First, they assert, God justifies human beings on the basis of faith in the sense of at least implicit trust in God rather than faith in the sense of assent to a specific set of claims. "For grace," writes J. N. D. Anderson, "it is not so much knowledge as a right attitude that matters."[4]

2. *The Confession of Faith*, 46.

3. *Bekenntnisschriften der reformierten Kirche*, ed. E. F. Karl Müller (A. Deichert, 1903), 855.

4. J. N. D. Anderson, *Christianity and Comparative Religion* (Tyndale Press, 1970), 99.

a. The saints of Israel. In order to supply biblical warrant for their contention, such persons typically adduce the saints of Israel who lived and died before Christ's Incarnation. Clark Pinnock, for example, asserts:

> [One] class of people saved without professing Christ were the Jews who lived before Jesus was born. Forefather Abraham was saved by faith, as is clear in Genesis. "Abraham believed the Lord, and he credited it to him as righteousness" (Ge 15:6). All who have faith are sons of Abraham and are blessed with him (Gal 3:7). The Old Testament describes a large number of believing Israelites who trusted in God, though the Messiah had not yet come to them. Yet they exercised saving faith, as did Abraham, and experienced forgiveness, as did David. Their theological knowledge was deficient, measured by New Testament standards, and their understanding of God was limited because they had not encountered Jesus, in whom alone one sees the Father. Nonetheless, they knew God and belonged to the great cloud of witnesses who encourage us (Heb 12:1). Without actually confessing Jesus Christ, they were saved by his work of redemption.[5]

It is incontestable that Abraham, Isaac, and Jacob did not explicitly confess that Jesus of Nazareth is Lord as Christians do today. It is just as incontestable, however, that God proclaimed the Gospel to Abraham and that Abraham believed it. For, as Paul writes in Galatians 3:8, "Scripture, foreseeing that God would justify the Gentiles by faith, proclaimed the gospel beforehand [προευηγγελίσατο] to Abraham that 'in you all the nations will be blessed' [Gen 12:3]."[6] The context of Paul's remarks renders it unlikely in the extreme that Paul would employ the term προευηγγελίσατο here to refer to anything other than the proclamation of "the gospel of Christ" (τὸ εὐαγγέλιον τοῦ Χριστοῦ) to which he refers in Galatians 1:7. For Paul writes in Galatians 1:8–9:

> If we or an angel from heaven proclaim a gospel [εὐαγγελίζεται] to you other than the gospel which we proclaimed [εὐαγγελισάμεθα] to you,

5. Clark H. Pinnock, *A Wideness in God's Mercy: The Finality of Jesus Christ in a World of Religions* (Zondervan Academic, 1992), 163.

6. All translations of Scripture are my own.

> let him be anathema. As we said before and now I say again, if anyone proclaims a gospel [εὐαγγελίζεται] to you other than that which you received, let him be anathema.

One who anathematizes those who preach gospels other than the one, true Gospel in one breath is unlikely to designate as "the Gospel" some message other than the one, true Gospel in the next. According to Paul, therefore, Abraham believed the Gospel of Christ, which Paul identifies elsewhere as "the power of God unto salvation for everyone who believes" (Rom 1:16).

Unless one wishes to assert that one can believe "the Gospel of Christ" without believing in Christ himself, therefore, one cannot, without contradicting Scripture, deny that Abraham believed in the Savior in whom Christians of Paul's time believed: the same Savior in whom Christians believe today. That later Old Testament saints such as Moses, Gideon, David, and Hezekiah likewise believed in the Messiah who was yet to come seems evident from (a) their familiarity with the ancient lore of Israel about Abraham and God's covenant with him; (b) the trust in Yahweh they exhibited in their exploits recorded in Scripture; and (c) New Testament authors' explicit identification of these persons as bona fide saints. The last consideration proves, in the main at least, that these figures' exploits are the fruit of saving faith in Christ.

It is true, admittedly, that Abraham's physical descendants sometimes forgot important truths about Yahweh. Abraham and God's covenant with him and his seed, nevertheless, must have loomed large in the people's collective memory. For God instructed Moses to introduce himself to Israel's elders with the words, "Yahweh, the God of your fathers, appeared to me, the God of Abraham, Isaac, and Jacob" (Exod 3:16). Near the end of Israel's captivity in Egypt, where the children of Israel worshipped other gods (Josh 24:14), therefore, the memory of Abraham must have remained fresh; and how could it have remained fresh without vivid recollection of God's promises to Abraham, which primarily account for his significance to later generations? It seems, then, that the average Israelite knew of Abraham and of God's promises to him. If, in Abraham's case, the right kind of belief of those promises constituted saving faith in Christ, the same kind of belief on others' part would presumably have constituted saving faith in Christ in their case as well. The saints of Israel who lived and died before Christ's advent, therefore, are not counterexamples to the principle that all mentally competent adults can attain salvation only through faith in Jesus. As Jerome rightly observes:

> The saints who were of old, moreover, were justified by faith in Christ. Abraham, indeed, saw the day of Christ and was gladdened [John 8:56]. And Moses judged the reproach of Christ greater riches than the treasure of Egypt, for he looked to the reward [Heb 11:26]. And Isaiah saw the glory of Christ, as John the Evangelist mentions [John 12:41]. And Jude writes generally about all: "I want to remind you," he says, "although you once knew all these things, that although Jesus delivered the people from the land of Egypt, he afterwards destroyed those who did not believe" [Jude 5].[7]

For to them as well as to us, Jerome might have added, the Gospel was preached. "We have been evangelized [ἐσμεν εὐαγγελισμένοι]," writes the author of Hebrews, "just as they were" (Heb 4:2). Nevertheless, inclusivists contend, Scripture depicts certain figures as saints, who did not share even the faith of Abraham. Such figures fall into three classes: first, those who lived before God promised Abraham a seed in whom all nations would be blessed (Gen 15:6); second, those who lived before Christ's advent as strangers to the congregation of Israel; and, third, those who, although alive after Christ's advent, possessed no knowledge or only scant knowledge of Jesus himself.

b. Pre-Abrahamic saints. The first class includes such notables as Adam, Eve, Abel, Enoch, and Noah. To Adam and Eve, God addressed the *protevangelium*, i.e., Scripture's initial statement of the Gospel, in Genesis 3:15. In this passage, speaking ostensibly to the serpent, but manifestly for Adam and Eve's benefit, God says: "Enmity will I put between you and the woman and between your seed [זַרְעֲךָ] and her seed [זַרְעָהּ]; he [הוּא] will bruise your head, and you will bruise his heel." Since Eden presumably contained no poisonous snakes, and concern

7. Jerome, *Commentarii in epistulam Pauli apostoli ad Galatas* at Gal 2:16a (CCSL 77A:60).

for her safety did not deter Eve from engaging in a tête-à-tête with the serpent in Genesis 3:1–5, it seems unlikely in the extreme that Adam and Eve would have construed God's words in Genesis 3:15 as a promise of humanity's collective triumph over snakes.

They are likely, instead, to have regarded God's promise as a pledge that one of their seed would defeat the fiend who had beguiled them and thereby introduced death and misery into the world. That the pronoun הוּא (=he), whose antecedent is זַרְעָהּ, i.e., her seed, is masculine and singular certainly gives the impression that the promised seed who is to bruise the serpent's head will be an individual man rather than an agglomeration of human beings. This impression strengthens when one realizes that throughout the Hebrew Bible, whenever an author employs זֶרַע (=seed) in an unmistakably collective sense and refers to the זֶרַע in question with a pronoun, the pronoun is invariably plural.[8] Eve's response to the birth of her son Seth, moreover, suggests that she understood the seed promised in Genesis 3:15 to be an individual man: "Then Adam knew his wife again, and she bore a son and called his name Seth. 'For God has appointed for me another seed [זֶרַע] instead of Abel because Cain slew him'" (Gen 4:25).

Adam and Eve, therefore, probably regarded the promised seed in Genesis 3:15 as an individual man who would ultimately triumph over their primordial adversary: i.e., "the great dragon, the ancient serpent, who is called the devil and Satan" (Rev 12:9). That pre-Abrahamic figures such as Adam, Eve, Abel, Seth, Enoch, and Noah believed that Eve's seed would purchase the salvation of God's people through vicarious suffering appears overwhelmingly likely, moreover, from the divine institution of sanguinary, anticipatorily piacular sacrifice. That God instituted sanguinary sacrifice appears from the favor he showed to Abel and his offering. For the author of Hebrews observes that it was by faith that Abel offered God a greater sacrifice than Cain's (Heb 11:4), and "faith comes from hearing and hearing from the word of Christ" (Rom 10:17). As the fathers of the

8. We owe this insight to Jack Collins, "A Syntactical Note (Gen 3:15): Is the Woman's Seed Singular or Plural?," *Tyndale Bulletin* 48 (1997): 139–48, at 142–45.

First Vatican Council rightly observe in the third chapter of the dogmatic constitution, *Dei Filius*:

> That faith, which is the beginning of human salvation, the Catholic Church professes to be a supernatural virtue, whereby, God's grace inspiring and assisting us, we believe the things revealed by him to be true, not on account of the intrinsic truth of the things perceived by the light of natural reason, but on account of the authority of God himself revealing [*propter auctoritatem ipsius Dei revelantis*], who can neither be deceived nor deceive. [DH 3008]

Of saving faith, the framers of the Westminster Confession of Faith likewise assert, "By this faith, a Christian believeth to be true whatsoever is revealed in the Word, for the authority of God himself speaking therein."[9] Those who yield such faith to God obey his command to believe what he asserts simply because he asserts it: a command implicit, for example, in 1 John 5:10: "He who believes not God has made him a liar." To exhibit a praiseworthy, divine faith such as Abel exhibited, then, is to comply with a divine command.

To worship God as one lists without the warrant of God's command, by contrast, is ἐθελοθρησκία (Col 2:23), will-worship: the sin of Nadab and Abihu, whom God consumed with fire from heaven because they burned incense to him without his authorization (Lev 10:1–4). "Every word that I command you, you shall take care to do it; you shall not add to it or diminish from it" (MT Deut 13:1; ET Deut 12:32). For Abel to have devised and enacted a novel mode of worshipping God would have been not a praiseworthy exhibition of his faith, but a presumptuous indulgence of his fancy. One might argue, admittedly, that in worshipping God by sacrificing livestock to him, Abel may have simply followed the dictates of the natural law.[10] If, however, Abel had deduced from naturally known premises alone that he should offer sacrifice, the sacrifice he offered on that basis would not have manifested divine faith: i.e., belief of some proposition, "not on account of the intrinsic truth of things perceived by the

9. Westminster Confession of Faith 14.2 (*The Confession of Faith*, 52).

10. Cf. Thomas Aquinas, *Summa Theologiae* II-II, q. 85, a. 1, corp. (https://www.corpusthomisticum.org/sth3082.html).

light of natural reason, but on account of the authority of God himself revealing." Inasmuch as "by faith Abel offered to God a greater sacrifice than Cain's" (Heb 11:4), then, he must have offered sacrifice in response to a divine command.

It is one thing, an objector might protest, however, to demonstrate that God commanded Abel to slay animals in sacrifice to him. It is something else entirely to prove that God intended for Abel's sacrifice to be anticipatorily piacular: i.e., an expression of trust in the efficacy of a genuinely expiatory sacrifice to be offered in time to come. Nevertheless, the faith that Abel exhibited in sacrificing the firstlings of his flock must have consisted in a belief in some mystery that God revealed to him. Faith is, after all, "the certainty of what is hoped for, the conviction of matters unseen" (Heb 11:1): i.e., the belief of things one must accept on the basis of God's testimony because they are not evident to our natural reason. In what, one might ask, did the faith whereby Abel offered a greater sacrifice than Cain consist? Scripture supplies the beginnings of an answer to this question in Hebrews 11:13, where the author of Hebrews asserts of Abel, Enoch, Noah, Abraham, Sarah, Isaac, and Jacob: "In faith died all these, not having received the promises [τὰς ἐπαγγελίας], but beheld and hailed them from afar." All seven saints beheld and hailed from afar a set of promises, then, by which the author evidently means promised benefits. Since Abraham unquestionably beheld and hailed from afar the salvation of his spiritual children through the promised seed, it stands to reason that the rest of the "all these" of Hebrews 11:13, including Abel, Enoch, and Noah, also foresaw by faith the eventual deliverance of God's people by that seed. The faith which Abel praiseworthily expressed through his sacrifice, therefore, consisted at least partially in the belief that Abraham's seed would redeem sinful human beings. It seems difficult to fathom, however, how one could express that faith by slaughtering animals in sacrifice to God unless the sacrifice were anticipatorily piacular: i.e., intended to foreshadow and express reliance upon a future, greater sacrifice that would accomplish what the sacrifice of beasts merely prefigured. Whether or not Abel prophesied verbally that Eve's promised seed would die for the sins of God's people, then, his sacrifices implicitly expressed his faith that God would sacrifice the seed of Eve and thereby atone for his people's iniquities.

Nevertheless, one might observe, even if the Old Testament saints had believed that an individual seed of Eve would die for the sins of God's people and thereby propitiate God's wrath against them, trusting that seed for their salvation would have amounted to crass idolatry if they had conceived of that seed as a mere man. "Cursed be the man who trusts in man," thunders Yahweh through the prophet Jeremiah (Jer 17:5). "I, I am Yahweh," speaks the same God through Isaiah, "and besides me there is no savior" (Isa 43:11). If the saints of the Old Testament believed in Christ unto salvation, therefore, they must have believed in him as God incarnate: the Lord of glory, whom the rulers of this world crucified (1 Cor 2:8). Scripture, admittedly, does not expressly state that the antediluvian saints expected their redeemer to be God in human flesh.

It seems unreasonable, however, to deem the first believers in God's Messiah so naïve as to expect a mere man's death to satisfy God's wrath against humankind's first sin and the countless sins that followed in its train. Adam and Eve were no simpletons, for God would hardly have appointed a pair of buffoons to be his vicegerents over the Earth (MT Ps 8:5–9; ET Ps 8:4–8). The image of God, in which he created Adam, moreover, included knowledge of the sort that God imparts to the saints through Scripture. Hence Paul urges the Christians of Colossae to "put on the new man, who is being renewed unto knowledge in accordance with the image of him who created him" (Col 3:10). From the severity of their punishment and their indebtedness to God for everything good they could possibly have or be, then, it seems that Adam and Eve could and would have inferred that they had committed no trifling offense. That the gravity of an offense increases in direct proportion to the dignity of the party offended, furthermore, appears self-evident. Patricide and matricide, for example, are manifestly graver crimes than fratricide, and fratricide is just as manifestly a graver crime than the destruction of subhuman property. That God is of infinite dignity, moreover, can hardly have escaped the attention of the earliest human beings.

That the slightest sin against a being of infinite dignity merits a correspondingly infinite punishment, therefore, is bound to have occurred to persons who reflected in a penitent frame of mind on such matters even in those early days. For the antediluvian saints knew that their lives would extend beyond the grave. According to the author of Hebrews:

> In faith died all these [i.e., Abel, Enoch, Noah, Abraham, Sarah, Isaac, and Jacob], not having received the promises, but beheld and hailed them from afar and confessed that they were strangers and sojourners upon the earth. For those who say such things show that they seek a homeland. And if they had remembered that from which they departed, they had opportunity to return. But now they seek a better homeland, i.e., a heavenly one. (Heb 11:13–16a)

If the earliest saints knew that an eternal, glorious inheritance awaited them if they believed God's promise of redemption through a male descendant of Eve (Gen 3:15), they cannot have been unaware that those who withheld such belief would suffer at least eternal deprivation of this inheritance. Indeed, without gravely impugning God's justice and honesty, one cannot deny that even before the Fall Adam and Eve knew what consequences would ensue upon their transgression of God's command to forgo the tree of the knowledge of good and evil's fruit. God is not a thimblerigger, who promised one penalty and then inflicted on Adam and Eve another that exceeded what he originally threatened so radically as to beggar comprehension. Adam and Eve's awareness of their punishment's indescribable severity, of its limitless duration, and of the unfailing justice of the God who imposed it must surely have borne in upon them that no mere man or angel's death could suffice to pay the debt of punishment they had incurred.

Neither they, nor Abel, nor Enoch, nor Noah, however, despaired of regaining God's favor. "In faith," writes the author of Hebrews, "all these died, not having received the promises, but beheld and hailed them from afar" (Heb 11:13). Inasmuch as Eve, Abel, Enoch, and Noah attained heavenly glory, their faith cannot have rested on a foolhardy presumption that God would show them mercy in the absence of a sacrifice on their behalf that satisfied the demands of divine justice.

These saints cannot, therefore, have expected redemption through the suffering of a merely human seed. “Cursed be the man who trusts in man” (Jer 17:5), avers the God who is the same yesterday, today, and forever (Heb 13:8). Inasmuch as an offense’s gravity increases in direct proportion with the dignity of the party offended, the suffering of finitely valuable creatures can never compensate for the slightest offense against a being of infinite dignity.

The infinite duration of unredeemed humanity’s punishment and the justice of the God who inflicts it manifestly imply that only an infinitely valuable sacrifice could propitiate God’s wrath against human sins. As we have already observed, the antediluvian saints were not grievously uninformed dolts. The failure of these saints to despair of their salvation, then, demonstrates either (a) that they inferred that God would unite his nature to that of the seed descended from Eve in such a way as to render that seed’s human suffering infinitely valuable; or (b) more likely, that God stated in words that the promised seed of Eve would be God incarnate. One need merely recall that Abraham inferred from God’s promises that the Almighty would raise Isaac from the dead if necessary to fulfill his covenant engagements (Gen 22:5; Heb 11:19) to realize that Old Testament saints were capable of inferring from God’s promises highly counterintuitive, theologically insightful conclusions. It seems more plausible, however, to suppose that God verbally promised the first saints that he would make the promised seed adequate to his task: a task that only one who was both divine and human could achieve.

c. Holy pagans? Nevertheless, argue those who deny faith in Christ’s indispensability to the salvation of mentally competent adults, the Old Testament depicts certain persons who died after Abraham, but before our Savior’s advent, as righteous although they appear not to have reposed their hope for salvation in a coming Messiah’s redeeming work. Such persons commonly adduce Job, Jethro, Rahab, the queen of Sheba who came to Solomon, the widow of Zarephath, the Shunammite woman, Naaman, the mariners who cast Jonah overboard, and the Ninevites who repented at Jonah’s preaching as examples of holy persons who likely knew nothing of God’s promise of redemption by a Messiah.

Job, however, must surely have known of God's promise of redemption through the suffering of God incarnate. For he offered sacrifices for his children, which he evidently intended to be at least anticipatorily piacular; "He offered burnt offerings according to their numbers for all of them, for he said, 'Perhaps my sons have transgressed or cursed God in their hearts'" (Job 1:5). The praise that God heaps on Job suggests that Job offered these sacrifices not out of superstition, but in response to a divine command. Responding to Bildad's criticisms, moreover, Job says: "I know that my redeemer lives and at the last will stand on the earth. And after they tear off this, my skin, in my flesh I will see God, whom I will see for myself, and my eyes will behold and not another" (Job 19:25–27). Job seems, then, to have believed: (a) that his own and his children's sins, if forgiven, would be forgiven on account of a redeemer's suffering, which his burnt offerings typified; (b) that his redeemer would be God; (c) that his redeemer would stand on the earth and be as visible to the naked eye as any human being might be; and (d) that he, Job, would be resurrected in his body and see his incarnate Redeemer with his physical eyes.

Job, moreover, plainly enjoyed partial access to Scripture, for he states in Job 23:12b, "More than my portion I have treasured the words of his mouth [מֵחֻקִּי צָפַנְתִּי אִמְרֵי פִיו]." Job, then, cherished the words of Yahweh, presumably conveyed to him in Scripture, trusted Yahweh to save him through a future expiatory sacrifice of God incarnate, and expected to see after his death and resurrection God incarnate standing on the earth. The beliefs Job enunciates are precisely what one would expect of someone who believed God's promise of a divine-human redeemer descended from Eve. His example, therefore, does not falsify the principle that mentally capable adults can achieve salvation only through faith in Christ.

Rahab, admittedly, constitutes a difficult case. The author of Hebrews testifies that "by faith Rahab the harlot did not perish together with the disobedient because she received the spies in peace" (Heb 11:31), and James poses in James 2:25 the rhetorical question: "Was Rahab also not justified by works when she received the messengers and sent them out another way?" God justifies the saints by works when he, through their works, manifests to the world that he has sanctified them in what Reformed theologians often term demonstrative justification. God sanctifies, however, only those whom he justifies by faith alone in what is termed constitutive justification.[11] One cannot reasonably deny, therefore, that Rahab possessed justifying faith.

Yet Scripture never explicitly asserts that Rahab believed in God incarnate or that she expected to rise bodily from the dead and behold God incarnate standing on the earth. The closest thing to an account of Rahab's faith that Scripture supplies appears in Joshua 2:9–11:

> I know that Yahweh has given to you the land and that dread of you has fallen on us and that all who dwell in the land despair before you. For we have heard that Yahweh dried the waters of the Red Sea before you when you came forth out of Egypt and what you did to the two kings of the Amorites beyond the Jordan, Sihon and Og, whom you destroyed. We heard, and our hearts melted, and the spirit of man will no longer stand before you, for Yahweh, your God, he is God in the heavens above and in the earth beneath.

Especially noteworthy among Rahab's remarks are her statements: (a) "I know that Yahweh has given to you the land"; and (b) "Yahweh, your God, he is God in the heavens above and in the earth beneath." By these words, Rahab shows that she considers Israel's God the only true God and believes God has given Canaan into the Israelites' hands. That Rahab regarded Yahweh, to whom she refers by the tetragrammaton, as the only true God suffices to block inferences from her salvation to the possibility of salvation through faith in God as he is known from natural revelation alone. Rahab's God was the God of Abraham, Isaac, and Jacob; she was no mere theist. Rahab, admittedly, may have inferred that God had given her land to the Israelites from Israel's victories over Heshbon and Bashan and/or reports of the Israelite ambassadors' announcement to Sihon that God had granted Israel the land across the Jordan (Deut 2:29).

Rahab's belief that God had granted Israel the Amorites' land, however, may also have derived from prior knowledge of God's promises

11. Cf., e.g., Mark W. Karlberg, *Covenant Theology in Reformed Perspective* (Wipf & Stock, 2000), 170–173.

to Abraham: promises that included God's declaration that in Abraham's seed all nations would be blessed (Gen 12:3; 22:18). If Abraham's belief of that declaration constituted belief of the Gospel on his part (Gal 3:8), it seems that such belief could have constituted belief of the Gospel on Rahab's part as well. Johannes Braun speculates that the spies shared with Rahab God's promises that Abraham's descendants would inherit Canaan and that the Messiah would be born there.[12] One need merely consider how unlikely it was that any Canaanite in Rahab's circumstances would not only confess that Yahweh was the one true God, who had given Canaan into Israel's hand, but also hazard her life to facilitate Yahweh's victory over her people, to see that Braun's hypothesis is not farfetched. Rahab's example, then, scarcely falsifies the principle that mentally capable adults can achieve salvation only through faith in Christ.

As for the Old Testament's other putatively holy pagans, suffice it to say that if the principle just mentioned is correct, either they were not holy, or they were not pagans. Of none of these figures does Scripture assert definitively that he or she attained eternal salvation. Of those whom one might plausibly deem saints, moreover, viz. Jethro, the queen of Sheba, the widow of Zarephath, the Shunammite woman, and Naaman, each enjoyed the opportunity to consult someone capable of teaching the rudiments of the Gospel for several hours at least.

d. Holy pagans after Christ's advent? Little time need be expended on the last category of purportedly holy pagans: those who knew little or nothing of Jesus after his advent. Scripture supplies scant basis for assessing what the magi or the Syro-Phoenician woman knew about Jesus and says nothing about their eternal destiny. The only non-Jewish New Testament figure with a serious claim to have been regenerate before he knew of Jesus is Cornelius, whom Scripture characterizes as "pious and God-fearing with all his house, performing many charitable deeds for the people [i.e., the Jews] and praying to God constantly" (Acts 10:2) even before he heard the Gospel from

12. Johannes Braun, *Commentarius in epistolam ad Hebraeos* (Amsterdam: Ex officina Henrici & Viduae Theodori Boom, 1705), 797–98.

Peter. While narrating his encounter with Cornelius to Jewish believers in Jesus, however, Peter indicates that Cornelius "proclaimed to us [i.e., to Peter and his companions] how he saw an angel in his house standing and saying, 'Send to Joppa, and summon Simon, who is called Peter, who will speak words to you through which you and all your house will be saved'" (Acts 11:13–14). The angel's words presuppose that Cornelius was unregenerate when Peter first preached to him. Scripture, then, supplies no evident instances of mentally capable adults who experienced salvation before they consciously believed in the redeemer promised in Genesis 3:15.

2. Hebrews 11:6. Nevertheless, argue those who affirm the salvability of mentally capable adults who die without attaining saving faith in Jesus, Scripture explicitly states only two credenda that one must believe in order to please God: viz., that God exists and that he rewards those who earnestly seek him. "Without faith, it is impossible to please him," writes the author of Hebrews, "for one who approaches him must believe that he is and that he is a rewarder of those who earnestly seek [ἐκζητοῦσιν] him" (Heb 11:6). Scripture never states, however, that belief in any god a man's imagination may devise, coupled with belief in that god's willingness to reward those who seek him, might suffice for salvation. Scripture teaches, rather, that "those who know not God and obey not the gospel . . . will suffer the penalty of eternal destruction" (1 Thess 5:8–9; cf. also 1 Cor 6:9; Gal 5:19–21; Rev 21:8; 22:15, etc.). Outside of Christ, moreover, even the true God is a terror to human beings: a judge, whose wrath no mere man can placate, from whom everyone outside of Christ should expect eternal torment.[13] The author of Hebrews' words in Hebrews 11:6 cohere with the rest of Scripture, then, only if they teach the necessity of (a) belief in the one true God; and (b) of faith that this God will honor his promise to rescue from eternal damnation those who seek him rightly: i.e., who seek him through the Lord Jesus.

3. Divine impartiality. Those who ascribe salvation to certain mentally capable adults who never believe in Christ before death contend,

13. This is a common theme in Protestant theology. Cf. especially John Colquhoun, *A View of Faith from the Sacred Records* (Thomsons, 1824), 99–100.

nonetheless, that one cannot deny the possibility of such persons' salvation without implicitly charging God with προσωποληψία, respect of persons. Scripture explicitly denies that God displays respect of persons in passages such as Deuteronomy 10:17, 2 Chronicles 19:7, Acts 10:34, Romans 2:11, Galatians 2:6, Ephesians 6:9, Colossians 3:25, and 1 Peter 1:17. The same Scripture, however, implies that one can treat others differently without displaying respect of persons if one deprives no one of his just due. When those who labored for twelve hours murmur against the employer in Jesus' parable of the workers in the vineyard because he pays those who labored one hour as much as he pays them, for example, the employer, who obviously represents God, replies, "Friend, I do you no wrong; did you not agree with me for a denarius? Take what is yours, and go. I want to give to this last as I also give to you. Is it not my right to do as I wish with my own? Or is your eye evil because I am good?" (Matt 20:13–15).[14]

4. **God's putatively universal salvific will.** To establish that mentally capable adults who die without ever coming to explicit faith in Christ may attain salvation, some inclusivists argue finally, one need merely invoke the principle that God sincerely desires every human being's salvation. For if God seriously intends to save every human being, he must supply some opportunity to be reconciled with God to all human beings, even if they never encounter the Gospel before death. This intuition, it seems, underlies the Second Vatican Council's declaration in *Gaudium et spes*, §22: "Since Christ died for all men, and since the ultimate vocation of man is in fact one, and divine, we ought to believe that the Holy Spirit in a manner known only to God offers to every man the possibility of being associated with this paschal mystery" (DH 4322).

Scripture, nevertheless, teaches unmistakably that God achieves whatever he desires. "My counsel shall stand, and I will do all my pleasure," declares Yahweh in Isaiah 46:10. "What his soul desires," says Job, "that he does" (Job 23:13). "Our God is in the heavens," writes the anonymous psalmist; "he does all his pleasure" (Ps 115:3). Jehoshaphat,

14. Cf. Augustine's remarks to this effect in his *Contra duas epistolas Pelagianorm*, 2.13 (CSEL 60:473–74).

likewise, prays to the Almighty, "In your hand are power and might, and there is no one who can withstand you" (2 Chron 20:6). Indeed, writes the apostle Paul, "All things are from him and through him and to him" (Rom 11:36). The Almighty, writes the same apostle, "effects all things [τὰ πάντα ἐνεργοῦντος] in accordance with the counsel of his will" (Eph 1:11). In a universe in which there is only one uncaused cause, matters could not be otherwise. Hence, Aquinas rightly observes:

> It is necessary that the will of God always be fulfilled . . . . Something may lie outside the order of some particular active cause, but nothing lies outside the order of the universal cause under which all particular causes are comprehended. For if any particular cause fails to achieve its effect, this is on account of some other particular cause, which impedes it and is contained under the order of the universal cause. In no way, therefore, can an effect lie outside the order of the universal cause . . . . Since, then, the will of God is the universal cause of all things, it is impossible for the divine will not to achieve its effect.[15]

Passages such as 1 Timothy 2:4, according to which God "wills that all men be saved and come to the knowledge of the truth," pose no difficulty for this doctrine because they refer not to God's decretive will, i.e., in Thomistic and Salesian terminology his *voluntas beneplaciti*, but to his preceptive will, his *voluntas signi*.[16] In other words, God imposes on all a duty to believe the Gospel. Therefore, Christians should pray that all may believe just as they pray that God's will, i.e., his preceptive will, may be done by all in the Lord's Prayer. Nor need passages such as John 3:16, "For God so loved the world that he gave his only-begotten Son that everyone who believes in him might not perish, but have everlasting life," belie the interpretation we have offered for 1 Timothy 2:4 and kindred passages. For one might conceive of the salvation of the world as the outcome of a long process

15. Aquinas, *Summa Theologiae* I, q. 19, a. 6 corp. (https://www.corpusthomisticum.org/sth1015.html; translations my own).

16. Cf. Aquinas, *Summa Theologiae* I, q. 19, a. 11 corp. (https://www.corpusthomisticum.org/sth1015.html), and the fifteenth of the *Entretiens spirituels* of Francis de Sales (*Œuvres complètes* [Berche et Tralin, 1898], 5:214–23).

near the end of which, even before Christ's second advent, the vast majority of human beings then alive will be saved (Matt 11:29). Passages of Scripture that arguably anticipate such an outcome include Psalm 22:28 (MT; v. 27 ET): "All the ends of the earth will remember and turn to Yahweh; all families of the nations will bow down before you." Of Yahweh, writes the author of Psalm 66, "All the earth will bow down to you. They will sing praise to you. They will sing praise to your name." One reads, likewise, in Psalm 86:9: "All nations whom you have made will come and bow down before you, my Lord, and they will glorify your name." One could easily multiply such passages, which appear to point to a mass conversion of the human race to Christianity in the future.

As the salvation of each human being is a process, explains B. B. Warfield, so is the salvation of the world:

> What is chiefly of importance for us to bear in mind here, is that God's plan is to save, whether the individual or the world, by process. No doubt the whole salvation of the individual sinner is already accomplished on the cross: but the sinner enters into the full enjoyment of this accomplished salvation only by stages and in the course of time. Redeemed by Christ, regenerated by the Holy Spirit, justified through faith, received into the very household of God as his sons, led by the Spirit into the flowering and fruiting activities of the new life, our salvation is still only in process and not yet complete. We still are the prey of temptation; we still fall into sin; we still suffer sickness, sorrow, death itself. Our redeemed bodies can hope for nothing but to wear out in weakness and to break down in decay in the grave. Our redeemed souls only slowly enter into their heritage. Only when the last trump shall sound and we shall rise from our graves, and perfected souls and incorruptible bodies shall together enter into the glory prepared for God's children, is our salvation complete. The redemption of the world is similarly a process. It, too, has its stages: it, too, advances only gradually to its completion. But it, too, will ultimately be complete; and then we shall see a wholly saved world.[17]

17. B. B. Warfield, *The Plan of Salvation* (Presbyterian Board of Publications, 1915), 129.

Hence Warfield rightly concludes, "There is no antinomy, therefore, in saying that Christ died for his people and that Christ died for the world. His people may be few to-day: the world will be His people to-morrow."[18] Even if one balks at Warfield's optimistic eschatology, it seems, one can reconcile one's knowledge that God's intentions will inevitably be achieved with texts that seem to ascribe to God an intention to save the world by properly understanding the extension of "world." During autumn in any forest one can find vastly more acorns than trees. Although acorns find their proper fulfillment only by growing into full-scale trees, those who planted the forest are untroubled by the undeveloped acorns' fate if the forest is full of tall, majestic trees. Likewise, one can argue that inasmuch as God's people are his treasured possession (Exod 19:5; Deut 7:6; 14:2; Tit 2:14; 1 Pet 2:9), his inheritance (Deut 4:20; 32:9; Ps 28:9; 33:12; Eph 1:18), and the apple of his eye (Deut 32:10; Zech 2:12 [MT; v. 8 ET]), they to him are as trees in the forest of this world. Abraham Kuyper, accordingly, asserts that the world God seeks to save is:

> the general Ego of believing humanity—a limitation in which the additional term "believing" is no contradiction if only it is understood how wrong it is to suppose that the real stem of humanity shall be lost, and that merely an aggregate of elect individuals shall be saved. On the contrary, it should be confessed that in hell there is only an aggregate of lost individuals, who were cut off from the stem of humanity, while humanity as an organic whole is saved, and as such forms "the body of Christ." By "believing humanity," therefore, we understand the human race as an organic whole, so far as it lives, i.e. so far as unbelief has turned again to faith or shall turn.[19]

This conception of the focus of God's saving activity, naturally, should instill in the saints not arrogance, but a mixture of wonder and delight at God's kindness to them combined with shame and confusion at God's decision to save them rather than others who might seem worthier of the honor.

18. Warfield, *The Plan of Salvation*, 133.

19. Abraham Kuyper, *Encyclopedia of Sacred Theology: Its Principles*, trans. J. Hendrik de Vries (Scribner's, 1898), 283–84.

Conclusion: A Summary of the Reasons Why One Should Reject Inclusivism

In sum, one should reject the claim that mentally capable adults who never attain conscious faith in Christ may be saved nonetheless for three principal reasons. First, Scripture characterizes saving faith in Christ as a necessary and sufficient condition of eternal salvation in Romans 10:8–13:

> This is the word of faith, which we preach: that if you confess with your mouth the Lord Jesus and believe in your heart that God raised him from the dead, you will be saved. For with the heart one believes unto righteousness, and with the mouth confession is made unto salvation. For Scripture says, "Everyone who believes in him will not be put to shame." For there is no distinction between Jew and Gentile; the same Lord of all is rich unto all who call upon him. For everyone who calls on the name of the Lord will be saved.

Second, Scripture teaches that all persons whom Jesus has saved know him and that their salvation consists, at least in large part, in the knowledge of God in Christ. "I am the good shepherd," Jesus says, "and I know mine, and they know me just as the Father knows me, and I know the Father" (John 10:14). If "this is eternal life, that they know you, the only true God, and Jesus Christ whom you sent" (John 17:3), how can persons who do not believe in Christ conceivably possess eternal life?

Third, Scripture portrays the difference between the saved and the unsaved as sufficiently stark that one would notice if God delivered one from this present evil age (Gal 1:4) and translated one into the kingdom of the Son of his love (Col 1:13). If everyone in Christ is a new creation (2 Cor 5:17), whom God has called out of darkness into his marvelous light (1 Pet 2:9), in whose heart God has shone with the light of the knowledge of the glory of God in the face of Jesus Christ (2 Cor 4:6), who has been crucified with Christ so that it is now not so much he who lives as Christ who lives in him (Gal 2:20), how can he possibly be unaware that he is a follower of Christ? These three considerations warrant Reformed Christians in denying that mentally capable adults who die before they come to saving faith in Christ will enjoy eternal salvation.

2.3 Evangelization and Universalism

Michael Sirilla

THE SECOND VATICAN COUNCIL affirms that "the pilgrim Church is of its very nature missionary."[1] Postconciliar popes have placed evangelization at the center of our pastoral focus. John Paul II said, "No believer in Christ, no institution of the Church, can avoid this supreme duty: to proclaim Christ to all people."[2] But evangelization, sharing Christ, is frequently hindered by what Ralph Martin identifies as "a lack of conviction that being a Christian is really necessary in order to be saved."[3] The motive for evangelization is the glory of God, the salvation of souls, and the love of Christ and neighbor. The message of evangelization is the good news, namely, that Jesus, the Son of God, died for our sins to save us from eternal damnation and for justification, adoption as a son or daughter of God. This, in turn, enables the believer who dies in Christ's grace to enter the eternal kingdom of God in heaven, enjoying the beatific vision of the triune God for all eternity. This is truly the best conceivable news, because there is no greater good conceivable than eternally participating in the life and the divine nature of the triune God (2 Pet 1:4) who is infinite goodness himself. A critically essential but consistently overlooked part of the Gospel is the doctrine of eternal punishment and separation from

1. Vatican Council II, *Ad gentes* (December 7, 1965), 1011–42 in *Decrees of the Ecumenical Councils*, ed. Norman P. Tanner, trans. Robert Murray (Sheed and Ward, 1990), §2.

2. John Paul II, *Redemptoris missio* (December 7, 1990) (United States Catholic Conference, 1990), §3.

3. Ralph Martin, *Will Many Be Saved? What Vatican II Actually Teaches and Its Implications for the New Evangelization* (Eerdmans, 2012), 5.

God in hell that Jesus Christ taught and that the apostles faithfully handed on in their preaching. In order to understand how great the good news is, to appreciate what it means to need and to have a Savior, it is important to grasp not only what Christ saves us *for* but also what he saves us *from*: everlasting separation from God in hell. Insofar as the opinion of universalism denies the permanence of the punishments of hell, it impedes evangelization by removing a principal motivation for conversion to Christ: a healthy fear of unending punishment and definitive estrangement from God. After all, if everyone will ultimately be saved, why endure the opprobrium heaped upon those who proclaim Christ and his Church as the sole means of salvation? It simply is not worth the suffering.

Universalism in the strong sense holds that every creature punished in hell, every human and every fallen angel, will eventually be delivered from that punishment and enter the eternal kingdom of heaven. Universalism in the weak sense holds that some but not all of the creatures in hell will eventually be saved, whether it be all humans but not demons, or all Christians but no non-Christians. This essay establishes that universalism, in addition to being simply false and contrary to the Gospel, also undermines Christ's mandate to evangelize and make disciples of all nations (Matt 28:18–20). After a brief identification of universalism, its nature, some of its principal proponents, and a few reasons for espousing this position, I will provide a compendium of Scripture passages and authoritative writings of Church Fathers on the eternal duration of the punishments of hell. Following that is a survey of magisterial teachings of the Church on the eternality of hell as a divinely revealed mystery of faith, showing that the eternity of hell is a dogma of divine and Catholic faith (*de fide divina et Catholica*). Finally, I address a few specific theological objections and problems raised by universalists in response to the teaching on hell's eternity—especially as those difficulties relate to proposing the Gospel of Christ through evangelization.

Universalism

In the strong sense, universalism is the opinion that every created rational and intellectual being will be saved, including those who die without faith in God or in Jesus Christ. Origen espoused this position in his work *On First Principles* when speaking of the state of glory of the resurrected body:

> Into this condition [a glorified body], then, we are to suppose that all this bodily substance of ours will be brought, *when all things shall be re-established in a state of unity*, and when God shall be all in all. And this result must be understood as being brought about, not suddenly, but slowly and gradually, seeing that the process of amendment and correction will take place imperceptibly in the individual instances during the lapse of countless and unmeasured ages, some outstripping others, and tending by a swifter course towards perfection, while others again follow close at hand, and some again a long way behind; and thus, through the numerous and uncounted orders of progressive beings who are being reconciled to God from a state of enmity, the last enemy is finally reached, who is called death, so that he also may be destroyed, and no longer be an enemy. When, therefore, *all rational souls shall have been restored to a condition of this kind*, then the nature of this body of ours will undergo a change into the glory of a spiritual body.[4]

Saint Gregory of Nyssa in some places seems to teach that the punishment of hell is eternal[5] and then, in other works, he argues for some form of universal restoration (ἀποκατάστασις).[6] Saint Ambrose of Milan may be a representative of universalism in the weak sense as he seemed to limit eternal punishment only to non-Christians. For him, it appears that all Christian sinners will be liberated from

4. Origen, *De principiis*, 3.6.6 (emphasis mine), in *Ante-Nicene Fathers* [hereafter ANF], ed. Alexander Roberts, James Donaldson, and A. Cleveland Coxe, trans. Frederick Crombie (Hendrickson Publishers, Inc., 1999), 4:346–47.

5. For example, in his homily against those who do not accept criticism, *Adversus eos qui castigationes aegre ferunt*.

6. In *The Great Catechism*, ch. 26.

punishment eventually by God's mercy.[7] The weaker senses of universalism do not significantly obstruct the impetus for evangelization since people who have reached the age of reason, according to these views, would certainly have to convert to Christ in order to be saved. For this reason, they are mentioned in passing, the focus of this essay being on universalism in the strict sense.

A recent, notorious example of universalism in the strongest sense possible is found in David Bentley Hart's book *That All Shall Be Saved: Heaven, Hell, and Universal Salvation* (Yale University Press, 2019). He dismisses those he labels "hopeful universalists" such as Karl Barth, Hans Urs von Balthasar, and others who are more or less open to the possibility of universal salvation. He argues that strict universalism is categorically true and can be known with certitude. It is beyond the scope of this essay carefully to evaluate and reply to his specific arguments for universalism, but it will be shown that his opinions run contrary to the consensus of the Fathers and the magisterial teachings of the Catholic Church who authoritatively interpret Scripture as asserting an eternal punishment in hell. For a thorough understanding of the history of universalism and the history of church teaching against it, see Michael J. McClymond's two-volume exhaustive study, *The Devil's Redemption: A New History and Interpretation of Christian Universalism* (Baker Academic, 2018). In these volumes, McClymond, professor of modern Christianity at St. Louis University, mounts a robust critique of universalism from biblical, philosophical, and theological points of view.

The philosophical concerns forming the basis for universalism commonly arise from the claim that a punishment is just only if it is remedial in the sense that it brings about the reformation of the one being punished. Eternal punishment necessarily implies no reformation, no remediation in this sense and so it cannot be just. Some universalists are also moved by a set of biblical concerns and exegetical questions, such as the proper interpretation of Peter's proclamation

7. See his commentary on Psalm 1 in *Enarrationes in xii Psalmos Davidicos*, 47; and his *Expositio in Psalmum cxviii*, serm. 20.

of the restoration of all things at Christ's second coming, narrated in Acts 3:19–21. These objections and others will be addressed in this essay.

The Eternal Duration of Hell in Scripture, Tradition, and Magisterial Teaching

SCRIPTURE

This section identifies a few seminal passages in both Old and New Testaments that consistently have informed the Church's understanding of the nature of the punishment in hell. These are the kinds of pericopes for which the Church has provided authentic interpretations (directly or indirectly) in the magisterial documents looked at below. In the Old Testament, endless punishment, especially by fire, is connected to the divine judgment of condemnation. In Judith 16:17 (which the Catholic Church holds as canonical), after saving her town and Jerusalem from destruction by the Assyrian general, Judith concludes her song of thanksgiving, singing, "Woe to the nations that rise up against my people! The Lord Almighty will take vengeance on them in the day of judgment; fire and worms he will give to their flesh; they shall weep in pain forever."[8] In Isaiah 33:14, within the prophecies of deliverance from enemies, we read, "The sinners in Zion are afraid; trembling has seized the godless: 'Who among us can dwell with the devouring fire? Who among us can dwell with everlasting burnings?'"[9] And in Isaiah 66:24, speaking of God's judgment and his reign, we hear, "And they shall go forth and look on the dead bodies of the men that have rebelled against me; for their worm shall not die, their fire shall not be quenched, and they shall be an abhorrence to all flesh." These passages may be interpreted as hyperbolic invectives against the enemies of Israel (with the exception, perhaps, of Isaiah

8. All Scripture citations are from the Revised Standard Version, Catholic Edition (Ignatius Press, 1994) unless otherwise noted.

9. See also Isa 33:12 and 14:11, "Your pomp is brought down to Sheol, the sound of your harps; maggots are the bed beneath you, and worms are your covering." The eternal duration of punishments is not mentioned in v. 11; Christ makes reference to worms, for example, in Mark 9:44.

66:24), but Daniel 12:2 directly talks about the general resurrection of the dead and the final judgment: "And many of those who sleep in the dust of the earth shall awake, some to everlasting life, and some to shame and everlasting contempt."

In the New Testament, Jesus warns, "And if your hand or your foot causes you to sin, cut it off and throw it from you; it is better for you to enter life maimed or lame than with two hands or two feet to be thrown into the eternal fire" (Matt 18:8). In describing his second coming and the general judgment, Jesus says, "Then he will say to those at his left hand, 'Depart from me, you cursed, into the eternal fire prepared for the devil and his angels.' . . . And they will go away into eternal punishment, but the righteous into eternal life" (Matt 25:41, 46).

Saint Paul encourages the Thessalonians with these words:

> This is evidence of the righteous judgment of God, that you may be made worthy of the kingdom of God, for which you are suffering—since indeed God deems it just to repay with affliction those who afflict you, and to grant rest with us to you who are afflicted, when the Lord Jesus is revealed from heaven with his mighty angels in flaming fire, inflicting vengeance upon those who do not know God and upon those who do not obey the gospel of our Lord Jesus. They shall suffer the punishment of eternal destruction and exclusion from the presence of the Lord and from the glory of his might. (2 Thess 1:5–9)

And the letter to the Hebrews says that eternal judgment is an *elementary* doctrine: "Therefore let us leave the elementary doctrines of Christ and go on to maturity, not laying again a foundation of repentance from dead works and of faith toward God, with instruction about ablutions, the laying on of hands, the resurrection of the dead, and eternal judgment" (Heb 6:2).

This warning in Jude's epistle would be evacuated of meaning if no human is actually undergoing a punishment of eternal fire:

> Now I desire to remind you, though you were once for all fully informed, that he who saved a people out of the land of Egypt, afterward destroyed those who did not believe. And the angels that did not keep their own position but left their proper dwelling have been

> kept by him in eternal chains in the nether gloom until the judgment of the great day; just as Sodom and Gomor'rah and the surrounding cities, which likewise acted immorally and indulged in unnatural lust, serve as an example by undergoing a punishment of eternal fire. (Jude 5–7)

Here, the eternal punishment of those who are condemned is reaffirmed; but it also says that those who are "undergoing" (ὑπέχουσαι, which is the *present tense*, active, participle of ὑπέχω "to undergo") eternal (αἰωνίου) fire are "set before" (πρόκειται which is third person, plural, present, middle, *indicative*) the readers of this epistle as an example. In other words, the biblical text here asserts that there are some humans actually suffering in hell in the present, and that they serve as a warning against sin.

It is important to note that some universalists like Hart argue that the word αἰώνιος (used in Jude 7 and elsewhere) can be used to signify long-lasting but not without end, even though "eternal" is certainly one of its several meanings. This term is used in the New Testament seventy-one times, and in sixty-four of those instances it refers to God or eternal life. In those instances, according both to universalists and to traditional Christians, it bears the meaning of duration without limit or being outside of time altogether; it is not taken as meaning "for a long time but with an endpoint." It would seem to make better sense, then, to interpret the other instances of αἰώνιος in reference to hell in the same vein unless there appear something—however slight—in the text or context suggesting an end to those punishments. But there are no such indications.

In fact, some New Testament passages explicitly rule out an endpoint. For instance, Christ warns that in hell, "the worm does not die, and the fire is not quenched" (Mark 9:47–49). The undying worm and unquenched fire exclude the termination of the punishment. And in Revelation 14:9–11 we read, "The smoke of their torment goes up for ever and ever; and they have no rest, day or night." Other passages in the New Testament indicate the notion that the punishment of hell is definitive and without limits, for example, the "great chasm" that cannot be crossed in Luke 16:26; the "second death" in Revelation 20:14; the "vessels of wrath made for destruction" in Romans 9:22;

and those who "shall not see life" because they disobey the Son in John 3:36.

There are also passages listing sins that render one unable to enter or inherit the kingdom of heaven. We see these in 1 Corinthians 6:9–10, "Do you not know that the unrighteous will not inherit the kingdom of God?" and Galatians 5:19–21, "Those who do such things [fornication, impurity, etc.] shall not inherit the kingdom of God." See also Revelation 19:2–3, "He has judged the great harlot who corrupted the earth with her fornication, and he has avenged on her the blood of his servants. . . . The smoke from her goes up for ever and ever" and Revelation 20:9b–10, "Fire came down from heaven and consumed them, and the devil who had deceived them was thrown into the lake of fire and sulfur where the beast and the false prophet were, and they will be tormented day and night for ever and ever."[10]

With reference to Peter's sermon in Acts 3, specifically verse 21 where he speaks of the "restoration [ἀποκαταστάσεως] of all things," some universalists argue that this would include the restoration of the damned. But from the larger context of the sermon, backing up to verse 19 we see that this is not an announcement of the cessation of the punishments of hell but of the renewal of the world—the new heavens and new earth—that Christ will bring about at his second coming, as foretold by the prophets:

> Repent therefore, and turn again, that your sins may be blotted out, that times of refreshing may come from the presence of the Lord, and that he may send the Christ appointed for you, Jesus, whom heaven must receive until the time for establishing all that God spoke by the mouth of his holy prophets from of old. (Acts 3:19–21)

One prophetical passage Peter likely had in mind is Isaiah 66:17, "For behold, I create new heavens and a new earth; and the former things shall not be remembered or come into mind." This chapter in Isaiah describes the new Jerusalem, described in virtually the same terms in Revelation 21:1–2, the heavenly Jerusalem. But recall that

10. Contrast these pericopes to Rev 4:9, "The living creatures give glory and honor and thanks to him who is seated on the throne, who lives for ever and ever." On the eternity of God, see, for example, Rev 5:13; 7:12; 10:6; Gal 1:5; and Heb 13:21.

both Isaiah and the author of Revelation speak of the everlasting punishment of the damned.

CHURCH FATHERS AND ECCLESIASTICAL WRITERS

The writings of the early Church Fathers are an indispensable theological source for understanding the revealed mysteries of faith. Learned and holy men, the Fathers were members of the magisterium as bishops and popes in the early Church. They were in a privileged position as men historically proximate to Christ's earthly life and those of the apostles. As such, it is generally recognized by Catholics and Orthodox that God gave them singular graces to understand and establish the orthodox faith as they continued the apostles' mission to institute churches throughout the world. For this reason, the Church teaches that we are not at liberty to interpret Scripture contrary to the unanimous consensus of the early Church Fathers.[11]

The Fathers often repeat the words of Scripture on the eternal punishment of hell. Among the Apostolic Fathers, we have Saint Ignatius of Antioch (d. ca. 108) who warns the Ephesians about false teachers: "Any one who corrupts by wicked doctrine the faith of God, for which Jesus Christ was crucified . . . shall go away into everlasting fire, and so shall every one that hearkens unto him."[12] And in the *Martyrdom of Polycarp* (second century), the temporal nature of the suffering of martyrdom is contrasted with the everlasting duration of the suffering in hell:

> And, looking to the grace of Christ, they [the martyrs] despised all the torments of this world, redeeming themselves from eternal punishment by [the suffering of] a single hour. For this reason, the fire of their savage executioners appeared cool to them. For they kept before their view escape from *that fire which is eternal and never shall be quenched*.[13]

11. Council of Trent, Session 4, "Second Decree: Acceptance of the Latin Vulgate Edition of the Bible; Rule on the Manner of Interpreting Sacred Scripture etc.," (April 8, 1546), in Tanner, *Decrees of the Ecumenical Councils*, 2:664.

12. Ignatius of Antioch, *Epistle to the Ephesians*, 16 (emphasis mine in this citation and those following) (ANF 1:56).

13. *Martyrdom of Polycarp*, 2 (ANF 1:39).

Similarly, in the *Letter to Diognetus* (ca. 130) we read,

> Then shalt thou condemn the deceit and error of the world . . . when thou shalt fear what is truly death, which is reserved for those who shall be condemned to the *eternal fire* . . . . Then shalt thou admire those who for righteousness' sake endure the fire that is but for a moment, and shalt count them happy when thou shalt know [the nature of] that fire.[14]

Among the post-Apostolic Fathers, Saint Justin Martyr (d. 165) connects temporal sinful acts with the eternal duration of their punishment in his *First Apology*:

> We hold this view . . . that each man goes to *everlasting punishment or salvation* according to the value of his actions. For if all men knew this, no one would choose wickedness even for a little, knowing that he goes to the *everlasting punishment of fire*; but would by all means restrain himself, and adorn himself with virtue, that he might obtain the good gifts of God, and escape the punishments.[15]

In his magnum opus, *Against Heresies*, Saint Irenaeus of Lyons (d. 202) writes:

> Thus, also the punishment of those who do not believe the Word of God, and despise His advent, and are turned away backwards, is increased; being not merely temporal, but rendered also *eternal*. For to whomsoever the Lord shall say, Depart from me, you cursed, into *everlasting fire*, (Matthew 25:41) these shall be damned *for ever*; and to whomsoever He shall say, Come, you blessed of my Father, inherit the kingdom prepared for you for eternity, (Matthew 25:34) these do receive the kingdom for ever.[16]

In his *Apology*, Tertullian (d. 220) develops the doctrinal insight that the bodies of the damned would have to be preserved incorruptible so that they may undergo perpetual physical torments by means of an undying fire:

14. *The Epistle to Diognetus*, 10 (ANF 1:29).
15. Justin Martyr, *First Apology*, 12 (ANF 1:166).
16. Irenaeus of Lyons, *Against Heresies*, 4.28.2 (ANF 1:501).

> But the profane, and all who are not true worshippers of God, in like manner shall be consigned to the punishment of *everlasting fire*—that fire which, from its very nature indeed, directly ministers to their incorruptibility . . . . For it does not consume what it scorches, but while it burns it repairs . . . . A notable proof this of the fire eternal! a notable example of the endless judgment which still supplies punishment with fuel! The mountains burn, and last.[17]

Saint Hippolytus (d. 235) provides an extended meditation on the unending pains of hell and, as with the passages of Scripture and writings of the other Fathers, forcefully lays out a motive for conversion to Christ and a life of righteousness:

> To the lovers of iniquity shall be given *eternal punishment*. And the fire which is *unquenchable and without end* awaits these latter, and a certain fiery worm which dieth not, and which does not waste the body, but continues bursting forth from the body with unending pain. No sleep will give them rest; no night will soothe them; no death will deliver them from punishment; no voice of interceding friends will profit them. For neither are the righteous seen by them any longer, nor are they worthy of remembrance.[18]

Saint Ephraem the Syrian (d. 373) explicitly says that the pains of hell will never have an end: "The judgment of the sinner will be . . . most severe and there will be *no end to his torment*, nor will he have a moment's rest . . . because it will continue *forever* and it will *not be ended* at any time."[19]

In his work *On the City of God*, Saint Augustine (d. 430) refutes the universalists of his day who denied that the punishment of the wicked is eternal, writing:

17. Tertullian, *Apology*, 48 (ANF 3:54). Other early Christian writers and Fathers who reflect on the incorruptibility of those condemned to hell so that they can suffer everlasting fire include Lactantius, *The Divine Institutes*, 7.21.1; Saint Cyril of Jerusalem, *Catechetical Lectures*, 18.18; Saint Hilary of Poitiers, *Commentary on Matthew*, 5.12; Saint John Chrysostom, *Sermon on the Resurrection of the Dead*, 8.

18. Hippolytus, *Against Plato, On the Cause of the Universe*, 3 (ANF 5:222–23).

19. *Sancti Ephraem Syri: Hymni et Sermones*, ed. Thomas Lamy (Mechliniae, 1889), 3:148: "Judicium tremendum futurum esse . . . severissimum quippe de peccatore fiet judicium et tormentorum non erit finis, nec parvo instante quiescet . . . quia in aeternum durabit et nullo unquam tempore solvetur."

> They could not invalidate nor evacuate the divine sentence which the Lord predicted that He would pronounce in the judgment, saying, "Depart from me, you cursed, into everlasting fire, prepared for the devil and his angels" (Matthew 25:41). For here it is evident that the devil and his angels shall burn in everlasting fire. And there is also that declaration in the Apocalypse, "The devil their deceiver was cast into the lake of fire and brimstone, where also are the beast and the false prophet. And they shall be tormented day and night forever" (Revelation 20:10). In the former passage "everlasting" is used, in the latter "for ever;" and by these words Scripture is wont to mean nothing else than *endless duration* . . . . Then what a fond fancy is it to suppose that eternal punishment means long continued punishment, while eternal life means life without end, since Christ in the very same passage spoke of both in similar terms in one and the same sentence, "These shall go away into eternal punishment, but the righteous into life eternal" (Matthew 25:46)! If both destinies are "eternal," then we must either understand both as long-continued but at last terminating, or both as endless. For they are correlative—on the one hand, punishment eternal, on the other hand, life eternal. And to say in one and the same sense, life eternal shall be endless, punishment eternal shall come to an end, is the height of absurdity. Wherefore, as the eternal life of the saints shall be endless, so too the eternal punishment of those who are doomed to it shall have *no end*.[20]

This brief compendium shows that the eternality of hell has been taught in Scripture in the Old Testament and in the New by Christ and the apostles; and this has been passed on consistently and faithfully by the early Church Fathers. This doctrine was not elevated to the level of a universal creed in the patristic era, but this survey indicates that there was a strong consensus of the principal figures of the patristic era that the punishments in hell are eternal in the strict sense, that is, without an end.[21]

20. Saint Augustine, *On the City of God*, 21.23, in *Nicene and Post-Nicene Fathers*, First Series, ed. Philip Schaff, trans. Marcus Dods (Hendrickson Publishers, Inc., 1999), 2:468–69.

21. This brief essay mentions only a few of the more principal early Church Fathers. In addition to the authors already mentioned, see also Saint Theophilus of Antioch, *To Autolychus*, 1.14; Saint Cyprian of Carthage, *Ad Demetrianum*, 24; Saint

MAGISTERIAL TEACHING ON THE ETERNAL DURATION OF HELL

The Catholic Church holds that the successors of Peter and the apostles, namely the popes and bishops, continue to participate in and remain subordinate to the teaching office or "magisterium" of Jesus Christ himself. There are various kinds of official, magisterial teaching having varying weights of authority to which correspond different types of assent. In the fourth session of the Council of Trent, in its second decree, the council fathers express the duty of the Church to interpret Scripture and the obligation of the faithful to adhere to that interpretation and to the interpretation of a consensus of the Fathers of the Church:

> The Council further decrees, in order to restrain those of an impudent nature, that no one, relying on his own personal judgment, shall, in matters of faith and morals pertaining to the edification of Christian doctrine, twisting sacred Scripture to his own meaning, presume to interpret Scripture contrary to that sense which holy mother Church, to whom it belongs to judge of the true sense and interpretation of the holy Scriptures, has held and does hold; or who dares to interpret sacred Scripture contrary to the unanimous consent of the Fathers.[22]

We have seen strong indications of a moral unanimity among the Fathers on the eternal duration of hell's punishments.[23] The following survey will show that the magisterium has consistently affirmed the same.

The fifth-century creed *Fides Damasi*, attributed to Pope Damasus I, professes, "It is our hope that we shall receive from him eternal life, the reward of good merit, or else [we shall receive] the penalty of *eternal* punishment for sins."[24] The ancient Athanasian Creed *Quicumque* likewise says, "At his coming, all men are to rise again with their bodies and they will give an account of their own deeds;

Basil, *Regulae brevius tractatae*, 267; Saint Augustine, *Ad Orosium contra Priscillianistas et Origenistas*, 6.7.

22. Council of Trent, Session 4 in Tanner, *Decrees of the Ecumenical Councils*, 2:664 (translations are mine unless otherwise noted).

23. Many of those fathers, being bishops and popes, were themselves members of the Church's magisterium.

24. DH 72 (emphasis mine).

and those who have done good will go on to eternal life, but those who have done evil will go into *eternal* fire."[25] In his letter *Consulenti tibi* to Bishop Exsuperius of Toulouse, dated February 20, 405, Pope Innocent I ordered that when a dying person asks for and does penance, a last communion—*viaticum*—be given them "so that such men in their extremities may be freed from *eternal* ruin with the permission of our savior."[26] The Synod of Arles in 473 had the priest Lucidius make a confession of faith that included the following, "I also confess that the *eternal* fires and the flames of hell are prepared for mortal sins; for the human faults that endure to the end are deservedly followed by the divine judgment."[27] Although every example given above is an act of the authentic magisterium, none of them clearly rises to the level of a universal and solemn dogmatic definition.

In 542, the Emperor Justinian composed nine anathemas to oppose the spreading of the Origenist doctrine of universalism, especially by certain monks in Jerusalem. These anathemas were proclaimed at the Second Council of Constantinople in 543 and Cassiodorus attests to the fact that they were confirmed several years later by Pope Vigilius.[28] The ninth of these anathemas reads, "If anyone says or holds that the punishment of the demons and of impious men is temporary and that it will have an end at some time, that is to say, there will be a complete restoration of the demons or of impious men, let him be anathema."[29] From all accounts, this put an end to the controversy about the eternal nature of the punishments of hell at that time; but it is still debated whether or not—even with the pope's approval—this teaching rises to the level of a dogmatic definition.[30]

In the *Fides Pelagii*, the profession of faith of Pope Pelagius addressed to King Childebert I on February 3, 557, citing 2 Corinthians

25. DH 76.
26. DH 212.
27. DH 342.
28. Cassiodorus, *De institutionibus divinarum litterarum*, 1.
29. DH 411.
30. Mid-twentieth-century theologians and manualists reviewed the scholarly literature on the historicity of Cassiodorus's claim that Vigilius ratified these anathemas and on whether this constitutes a definition of faith. Some have held that it does not.

5:10 ("For we must all appear before the judgment seat of Christ, so that each one may receive good or evil, according to what he has done in the body"), the pope confesses that at the final judgment those who did evil in the body and who chose to remain in their sin, Christ "will hand over by a most just judgment to the punishment of the *eternal and inextinguishable* fire, so that they may burn *without end*."[31] And Pope Innocent III in his letter *Maiores Ecclesiae causas* to Archbishop Humbert of Arles (1201), writing on the effect of baptism, says, "The punishment of original sin is the deprivation of the vision of God, but the punishment of actual sin is the torment of *eternal* hell."[32]

In the Fourth Lateran Council held in 1215, the first solemn and universal creed in several hundred years was promulgated by a general ecumenical council. Universal creeds (as opposed to creeds proclaimed by local synods or individual popes) are, in essence, dogmatic definitions of the faith. For instance, the term ὁμοούσιον ("same substance") in the Nicene Creed is tantamount to a dogmatic definition of the true and full divinity of Jesus Christ, the Son of God. In its universal creed, the *Caput firmiter*, the Fourth Lateran Council professes, "All of them [viz., the living and the dead] will rise again with their own bodies which they now bear to receive according to their works, whether these have been good or evil, the ones *perpetual punishment* with the devil and the others everlasting glory with Christ."[33] Here, the doctrine on the eternal duration of the punishment of hell is promulgated by the Church's magisterium as a defined truth, that is, a dogma of divine and Catholic faith (*de fide divina et Catholica*) since this is now taught definitively, coming as it does from a general ecumenical council. This doctrine is *divine* since it is revealed in Scripture, and it is *Catholic* since it is definitively interpreted and taught by the Church. In other words, by this act, the Church definitively and infallibly interprets the use of "eternal" (and similar terms) in Scripture as to be taken in the strict sense, namely, without termination.

Since the Fourth Council of the Lateran, the Church's magisterium

31. DH 443.
32. DH 780.
33. DH 801.

has consistently reaffirmed this dogma. In a letter to the bishop of Tusculum, *Sub catholicae professione*, dated March 6, 1254, the First Council of Lyon states, "If anyone dies in mortal sin without repentance, beyond any doubt, he will be tortured *forever* by the flames of everlasting hell."[34] In its "Decree on Justification," promulgated in session 6 on January 13, 1547, the Council of Trent teaches that after baptism, guilt and eternal punishment are remitted by sacramental confession or by the earnest desire for that sacrament.[35] And in the same council, canon 5 on the sacrament of penance defines that consideration of one's sins and of "the loss of eternal happiness and the incurring of *eternal* damnation" along with the resolve of amending one's life evoke a "true and beneficial sorrow that prepares for grace."[36] This is, arguably, the most poignant official expression of the motive for evangelization prior to the Second Vatican Council.

There are several other significant affirmations of this dogma after the Council of Trent.[37] In addition to a 1955 speech of Pius XII, the Second Vatican Council and the Congregation for the Doctrine of the Faith reaffirm the dogma that hell is eternal.[38] In the Second Vatican Council's Dogmatic Constitution on the Church, §14, the necessity not only of faith in Christ and of baptism but also of entering the Church in order to be saved is affirmed as follows: "Whosoever,

34. DH 839.

35. DH 1543.

36. DH 1705.

37. For instance, a decree of the Holy Office dated August 24, 1690, condemning certain propositions taught at the Jesuit College of Pont-a-Mousson in Champagne, teaches that mortal sins break friendship with God and deserve eternal punishment (DH 2291).

38. Pius XII, "Speech of his Holiness Pio PP. XII to the Union of Italian Catholic Jurists" (February 5, 1955), where he says "before God the remission of eternal punishment is always linked to the remission of grave guilt" ["la remissione della pena eterna è sempre congiunta con la remissione della colpa grave"]: https://www.vatican.va/content/pius-xii/it/speeches/1955/documents/hf_p-xii_spe_19550205_unione-giuristi-cattolici.html.

Among the many other magisterial documents teaching the eternal duration of the punishments of hell are the Fourth Synod of Toledo held in 633–634 (DH 485), the Sixteenth Synod of Toledo in 693 (DH 574), Pope Adrian I's letter *Institutio universalis* to the Spanish bishops ca. 790 (DH 596), and the Synod of Valence in 855 (DH 630).

therefore, knowing that the Catholic Church was made necessary by God through Jesus Christ, would refuse to enter or to remain in her could not be saved."[39] And in §48, the same document teaches, "We must be constantly vigilant so that . . . we may merit to enter into the marriage feast . . . and that we may not be ordered to go into eternal fire like the wicked and slothful servant."[40,41]

In its 1979 letter on eschatology, *Recentiores episcoporum synodi*, the Congregation for the Doctrine of the Faith affirms:

> In fidelity to the New Testament and tradition, the Church believes in the happiness of the just who will one day be with Christ. She believes that there will be *eternal punishment* of the sinner, who will be deprived of the sight of God, and that this punishment will have a repercussion on the whole being of the sinner.[42]

The *Catechism of the Catholic Church*, §1035 says,

> The teaching of the Church affirms the existence of hell *and its eternity*. Immediately after death the souls of those who die in a state of mortal sin descend into hell, where they suffer the punishments of hell, "*eternal fire*." The chief punishment of hell is *eternal* separation from God, in whom alone man can possess the life and happiness for which he was created and for which he longs.[43]

Finally, among the other great monuments of tradition, in the ancient Roman Canon (Eucharistic Prayer I in the Roman rite), the priest prays: "Command that we be delivered from *eternal* damnation and counted among the flock you have chosen." And the chant sequence *Dies Irae*, sung at requiem Masses, prays: "Grant that I may not be consumed by *everlasting* flames."

39. DH 4136.
40. DH 4168.
41. Walter M. Abbott, ed., *The Documents of Vatican II* (America Press, 1966), 715.
42. DH 4657.
43. *Catechism of the Catholic Church*, revised edition (New York: Doubleday, 1995).

Universalist Objections and Problems

Commonly, universalists argue that punishment, to be just, must be corrective of the one being punished. In his *Summa contra Gentiles*, Saint Thomas Aquinas argues that a just punishment does not always have to be remedial for the one being punished, but that at least it is to be remedial for others:

> Hereby we refute the error of those who assert that the punishment of the wicked will at length have an end. This statement seems to have originated in the opinion of certain philosophers, who maintained that all punishment is remedial, and therefore terminable at some time. . . . Even if we were to grant that all punishments are intended for the amendment of morals and for no further purpose, we would not, for that reason, have to assert that all punishments are remedial and terminable. For even according to human laws, some are punished with death for the amendment not of themselves, but of others. Hence it is said: "Strike a scoffer, and the fool will be wiser" (Prov 19:25).[44]

Another common objection is that it would be unjust to be punished eternally for a temporal, finite sinful act; this would entail being punished eternally and without limit for a sin committed in time and which is finite in nature. In his *Summa Theologiae*, Aquinas provides four reasons why an eternal punishment for a mortal sin is just: 1) "one is because they sinned against an eternal good by despising eternal life"; 2) "another reason is because . . . it belongs to the great justice of the judge that those should never cease to be punished, who in this life never ceased to desire sin"; 3) the "better answer," for Aquinas, is "from the very fact that he commits a mortal sin, he places his end in a creature; and since the whole of life is directed to its end, it follows that for this very reason he directs the whole of his life to that sin, and is willing to remain in sin forever, if he could do so with impunity"; and 4) "guilt remains for ever, since it cannot be remitted

44. Thomas Aquinas, *Summa contra Gentiles* III, c. 144 (University of Notre Dame Press, 1975); see also Aquinas's *Summa Theologiae* suppl., q. 99, a. 1, ad 3.

without grace, and men cannot receive grace after death; nor should punishment cease so long as guilt remains."[45]

Another objection suggests that those who die without hearing the Gospel may have a time after death in which they can hear the good news, repent, and convert. Traditionally, Christians understand Saint Paul's statement in 2 Corinthians 5:10 to exclude this possibility: "For we must all appear before the judgment seat of Christ, so that each one may receive good or evil, according to what he has done in the body."[46] And Christ's words, "We must work the works of him who sent me, while it is day; night comes, when no one can work" (John 9:4) seem to indicate that after the *day* of this life, when it is *night*, we can no longer "work," that is, merit, demerit, or convert. On this, Saint Cyprian of Carthage says:

> When you have once departed there, there is no longer any place for repentance, and no possibility of making satisfaction. Here life is either lost or saved; here eternal safety is provided for by the worship of God and the fruits of faith. Nor let any one be restrained either by his sins or by his years from coming to obtain salvation. To him who still remains in this world no repentance is too late.[47]

Also note that Hebrews 9:27 says, "It is appointed for men to die once, and after that comes judgment."

There is some discussion among Catholic theologians on what is minimally required for salvation for those who have reached the age of reason. Though many contemporary Catholic theologians have held the opinion that implicit faith in Christ suffices for salvation, it is not clearly the case that the Church has taught this, even on the nondefinitive level. The letter of the Holy Office to the Archbishop of Boston on the case of Fr. Leonard Feeney (1948) says that an implicit desire to enter the Catholic Church may be salvific if other things obtain, namely, supernatural faith, charity, and invincible ignorance that Christ founded the Church and made it necessary for salvation

45. See Aquinas, *Summa Theologiae* suppl., q. 99, a. 1, corp.
46. See also the profession of faith of Pope Pelagius referenced above.
47. Cyprian, *Address to Demetrianus*, 25 (ANF, 5:465).

with the necessity of means.[48] But the letter does not state that implicit faith in Christ suffices for salvation. Nor is this taught definitively in any other official Church document. This means that, at the very least, Catholic theologians in good standing may hold what most of the Fathers and Doctors of the Church have held in the past, namely, that since the passion of Christ, it is necessary for persons who have reached the age of reason to come to explicit faith in Jesus Christ in order to be saved. This point was argued recently in an article co-authored by three Catholic theologians, Fr. Thomas Crean, OP, Dr. John Joy, and Dr. Alan Fimister, "Can a Person Be Justified by Implicit Faith in Christ?"[49] If their position is correct, then this lends greater urgency to evangelization; Christian charity would effectively impel believers to share Christ with as many persons as reasonably possible.

Some argue that universalism is false because it destroys human freedom and, therefore, the possibility of genuine spiritual love, Christian virtue, and the like. But this is not necessarily the case. God is the universal first cause of all created being, including the created free will of man and of all free will acts of the rational creature. Thomists call this "physical pre-motion" and stand in the Augustinian tradition in their account of the primacy of God's causality and grace and of the subordinated and created nature of human free will. God moves men to will freely. This school of thought plays a significant role in the theological discussion and debates on predestination. In this view, God could have chosen to move all humans to freely accept his grace so that universalism would be a hypothetical possibility. According to such an account, universalism is nevertheless false but *not* because it is a metaphysical impossibility, *nor* because it destroys human freedom, love, and virtue. Rather, it is false because we know by divine revelation that hell is real, that some humans are there now, and that its punishments are without end.

In the end, regardless of the viability or helpfulness of the attempts to address these concerns, it is of overriding importance—and charity,

48. Letter of the Holy Office to the Archbishop of Boston regarding the case of Fr. Leonard Feeney on the proper understanding of the dogma "Outside the Church there is no salvation," August 8, 1949.

49. In *Divinitas*, "Nova Series," 2023, no. 1 (2023): 145–69.

in fact, demands—that Christians unambiguously warn others of the real danger of eternal punishment to which we are all subject because of the Fall. The good news of the Gospel not only proclaims what Jesus Christ saves us *for*: eternal life; but it also proclaims what Jesus saves us *from*: sin and its effects, especially everlasting separation from God and unending punishment of the body in the unquenchable flames of hell. It would be a failure of charity not to warn someone of the gravest of dangers if we have the opportunity to do so. In paragraph 1036, the *Catechism of the Catholic Church* teaches: "The affirmations of Sacred Scripture and the teachings of the Church on the subject of hell are a *call to the responsibility* incumbent upon man to make use of his freedom in view of his eternal destiny. They are at the same time an urgent *call to conversion*."

The most noble motive for repentance and conversion is the love of God above all else and obedience to him. And while the perfection of charity consists in precisely this love of God more than self, an imperfect self-love that includes a healthy desire to avoid eternal punishment is the way the process of conversion ordinarily begins for us sinners. By Christ's grace and power, this self-interest will yield to loving obedience. Including the truth of the "bad news" of the eternal nature of hell's punishments is an essential preparation for people to understand and receive the good news in repentance, faith, joy, and gratitude.

2.4 Evangelization in the New Testament

Mary Healy

THE CATHOLIC CHURCH REGARDS her evangelizing mission as being rooted in Christ's Great Commission: "Go therefore and make disciples of all nations, baptizing them in the name of the Father and of the Son and of the Holy Spirit, teaching them to observe all that I have commanded you" (Matt 28:19–20).[1] This task is not merely one among a myriad of ecclesial activities but is rather the Church's very *raison d'être*. In the famous words of Pope Paul VI, "Evangelizing is in fact the grace and vocation proper to the Church, her deepest identity. She exists in order to evangelize."[2] The Church draws her understanding of this central task from Scripture, "the highest authority in matters of faith,"[3] as interpreted within her living tradition. Given that fact, it is surprising how little attention has been paid over the centuries to what the New Testament actually teaches and models in regard to evangelization.[4]

This paper explores the New Testament's understanding of evangelization in regard to its definition, the content of the message to be proclaimed, its agents, motivation, manner, and goal. Although

1. Other biblical versions of the Commission are in Mark 16:16; Luke 24:47–48; Acts 1:8. See Vatican Council II, *Ad gentes*, §1; Paul VI, *Evangelii nuntiandi*, §15; Francis, *Evangelii gaudium*, §19. Unless otherwise noted, all biblical quotations are from the ESV.

2. Paul VI, *Evangelii nuntiandi* (December 8, 1975) (United States Catholic Conference, 1976), §14.

3. John Paul II, *Ut unum sint* (May 25, 1995) (United States Catholic Conference, 1995) §79.

4. See Mary Healy and Peter Williamson, "Biblical Orientations for the New Evangelization," *Josephinum Journal of Theology* 19, no. 1 (2012): 48–69.

written from a Catholic perspective, this paper does not aim simply to present a standard Catholic approach to the topic, but rather to take a fresh look at the biblical data even where it challenges certain assumptions common among Catholics as well as other Christians.

The Definition of Evangelization

A major cause of confusion among contemporary Catholics is the ambiguous—not to say slippery—usage of the terms "evangelize" and "evangelization." On the one hand, these terms are sometimes understood in a strict sense as referring to the preaching of the kerygma, the basic message of salvation in Jesus Christ. Thus Pope Paul VI writes, "There is no true evangelization if the name, the teaching, the life, the promises, the kingdom and the mystery of Jesus of Nazareth, the Son of God are not proclaimed."[5] On the other hand, the terms are very often used more broadly to refer to preaching in general or even to the entirety of the Church's mission, including the initial proclamation of the Gospel, catechesis, the administration of the sacraments, ongoing faith formation, pastoral care, works of mercy and charity, human development, and the transformation of cultures and societies as a whole in light of the Gospel.[6]

The New Testament, however, invariably speaks of evangelization in the stricter sense. The Greek verb *evangelizō* ("proclaim" or "announce good news") was used in secular Greek for a public proclamation of good news such as a military victory or the birth of an imperial heir.[7] In the Septuagint it often denotes the joyful announcement of future messianic blessings: "How beautiful on the mountains are the feet of him who brings good news [*evangelizomenos*]" (Isa 52:7;

5. Paul VI, *Evangelii nuntiandi* (December 8, 1975) (United States Catholic Conference, 1976), §22.

6. Cf., e.g., Paul VI, *Evangelii nuntiandi*, §§17–21; John Paul II, *Redemptoris missio*, §33; Francis, *Evangelii gaudium*, §§176–258; *Instrumentum laboris* for the 2012 Synod on the New Evangelization for the Transmission of the Christian Faith, §85.

7. The Gospel of John is noteworthy for the absence of any terms based on the root *evangel-* (good news); instead, it describes the evangelizing activity of Jesus and the disciples using the forensic terms *martyria* (testimony) and *martyreō* (testify).

cf. 40:9; 60:6; 61:1). The early Christians adopted this term and the related noun *evangelion* ("good news") as the ideal expressions for the most joyful announcement ever heard, that of God's free gift of salvation in Jesus Christ.[8] To evangelize is to proclaim the good news, with the goal of leading the hearers to faith in Christ (e.g., Acts 8:4; Gal 1:16; Eph 3:8). The New Testament also uses the term *kēryssō* ("announce, preach"), related to *kēryx* ("herald") and *kērygma* ("message"), as virtually synonymous with *evangelizō*.[9]

The New Testament authors make clear that this announcement is by no means a mere communication of information. It is a high-stakes summons, calling for a decisive response on the part of every hearer. Beginning with Jesus' own preaching, the required response is included as part of the proclamation itself: "The time is fulfilled, and the kingdom of God is at hand; repent, and believe in the gospel" (Mark 1:15), or even more succinctly, "Repent, for the kingdom of heaven is at hand" (Matt 4:17; cf. 3:2). The hearer's response determines not only his earthly allegiance but also his ultimate destiny. "Whoever believes and is baptized will be saved; but whoever does not believe will be condemned" (Mark 16:16; cf. John 3:18, 36). The proclamation therefore carries a great urgency. Evangelistic speeches in Acts often conclude with an appeal like that of Peter's Pentecost sermon: "Save yourselves from this crooked generation" (Acts 2:40; cf. 13:40–41; 2 Cor 5:20).

As C. H. Dodd observed nearly a century ago, the New Testament authors maintain a clear distinction between *kērygma* ("preaching") and *didachē* ("teaching").[10] To preach (*kēryssō*) or evangelize (*evange-*

8. Cf. Acts 5:42; 8:4, 12, 35; 1 Cor 1:17; Gal 1:16; Eph 3:8. Cesclas Spicq notes that in both secular and biblical Greek *evangelizō* and its cognate nouns express the gratuitousness of the gifts announced and the resulting joy (*Theological Lexicon of the New Testament*, trans. James Ernest [Hendrickson, 1994], vol. 2, 86–87).

9. Cf. Rom 16:25; 1 Cor 1:21; 2:4, 15:14; 2 Tim 4:17; Titus 1:3. In some cases *evangelizomai* (deponent middle voice) or *keryssō* is used without any object, meaning "to preach the Gospel"; in other cases *evangelizō* or *keryssō* is used with an object such as "the Gospel," "the kingdom," or "the word."

10. C. H. Dodd, *The Apostolic Preaching and Its Developments* (Hodder and Stoughton, 1936; repr. Baker Book House, 1980), 7–8; see Raniero Cantalamessa, *Remember Jesus Christ* (The Word Among Us, 2007), 16–25. The noun *kērygma* can refer to either

lizō) is to proclaim the basic message of the Gospel, leading to conversion; to teach (*didaskō*) is to provide the instruction or catechesis that follows conversion. Preaching/evangelizing is thus normally addressed to unbelievers (cf. Rom 15:20; 1 Cor 2:1–4; 15:1–2; 2 Tim 4:17), whereas teaching is normally addressed to believers. It is the preaching that gives rise to justifying faith: "Faith comes from what is heard, and what is heard comes by the word [*rhēma*] of Christ" (Rom 10:17; cf. 1 Cor 1:21). The preaching of the Gospel is therefore salvific. It is "the gospel . . . by which you are being saved" (1 Cor 15:1–2; cf. 1:21; Rom 1:16). That is why Paul makes a strong distinction between himself as the evangelist whose preaching gave birth to a local church, and all other teachers who built upon his work. "For though you have countless guides in Christ, you do not have many fathers. For I became your father in Christ Jesus through the gospel" (1 Cor 4:15). Paul planted the seed, but Apollos watered it; Paul laid the foundation, but another built upon it (1 Cor 3:6, 10).

The *didachē*, on the other hand, is for believers, because it is communicated effectively only to those who have already made a decision of faith in Christ, sealed in baptism, and who are thus disposed to receive Christian instruction with docility. As Paul says to the Romans, "You . . . have become obedient from the heart to the standard of teaching [*didachē*] to which you were committed" (Rom 6:17). Dodd viewed *didachē* as consisting of mainly ethical instruction (what is often called parenesis). However, numerous texts show that it also included theological doctrine. For instance, new believers are given "*didachē* about washings, the laying on of hands, the resurrection of the dead, and eternal judgment" (Heb 6:2). Bishops must be able to confute those who contradict the *didachē* (Titus 1:9). Any teaching that denies Jesus Christ as having come in the flesh is false *didachē* (2 John 9–10). The *didachē*, then, comprises the entirety of Christian doctrine and ethics—"all the words of this life" (Acts 5:20).[11] While evangelization in the strict sense both presupposes and leads

the content or the act of preaching; likewise *didachē* can refer to either the content or the act of teaching.

11. See Acts 2:42; 5:28; 17:19; 16:17; 2 Tim 4:2; Titus 1:9; 2 John 9–10.

into the full *didachē*, it does not entail the explicit exposition of this doctrine.

The *kērygma* should not be confused with a summary or distillation of the *didachē*. As Cardinal Raniero Cantalamessa, the longtime preacher to the papal household, explains, the kerygma is "rousing and not formative," "occasional, not systematic," "assertive" and "authoritative" rather than "discursive" or "dialectical."[12]

> [The kerygma] has an explosive or germinative character, so to speak. It is more like the seed that becomes a tree than the ripe fruit at the top of the tree. . . . One does not obtain it by distilling or summarizing tradition, as if it were its marrow. Rather, kerygma stands apart, or better, at the beginning of everything. Everything else develops from it.[13]

There is no need for scientific proofs, philosophic debates, or apologetic arguments to establish or defend the veracity of the kerygma; indeed, it cannot be so established. As Paul asserts, "It pleased God through the folly of the preaching [*kērygma*] to save those who believe. For Jews demand signs and Greeks seek wisdom, but we preach Christ crucified, a stumbling block to Jews and folly to Gentiles, but to those who are called, both Jews and Greeks, Christ the power of God and the wisdom of God" (1 Cor 1:21–24, author's translation).

Recovering the distinction between *kērygma* and *didachē*—or, to put it in contemporary Catholic terms, between evangelization and catechesis—is crucial to the Church's mission today. To quote Cantalamessa again:

> Churches with a strong dogmatic and theological tradition (like the Catholic and other traditional Christian Churches) risk finding themselves disadvantaged if, beneath the immense heritage of doctrine, laws, and institutions, they do not rediscover that original nucleus that is able to generate faith by itself. Presenting people today, who often lack any personal knowledge of Christ, with the entire range of

12. Raniero Cantalamessa, *The Holy Spirit in the Life of Jesus*, trans. Alan Neame (Liturgical Press, 1994), 45.

13. Raniero Cantalamessa, "The Preaching Ministry," *Asbury Journal* 63, no. 1 (2008): 33–51, at 39; available at http://place.asburyseminary.edu/asburyjournal/vol63/iss1/3/.

> doctrine is like putting one of those heavy brocaded mantles worn at one time by the clergy on the shoulders of a baby.[14]

The fact that the kerygma is elementary does not, however, mean that once people have converted to Christ, it can be set aside. Believers too need to hear the nucleus of the good news again and again. Thus the New Testament letters occasionally speak of "evangelizing" or "preaching the gospel to" audiences consisting of those who already believe (Rom 1:15; 1 Thess 2:9; 2 Tim 4:2). Moreover, Paul never misses an opportunity to recite again for those who already believe the astounding facts of what God has done for us in Christ. "God shows his love for us in that while we were yet sinners Christ died for us" (Rom 5:8); "God, who is rich in mercy, out of the great love with which he loved us, even when we were dead through our trespasses, made us alive together with Christ (by grace you have been saved), and raised us up with him" (Eph 2:4–6 RSV). Pope Francis makes this point in his encyclical on evangelization:

> On the lips of the catechist the first proclamation must ring out over and over . . . . This first proclamation is called "first" not because it exists at the beginning and can then be forgotten or replaced by other more important things. It is first in a qualitative sense because it is the principal proclamation, the one which we must hear again and again in different ways, the one which we must announce one way or another throughout the process of catechesis, at every level and moment.[15]

Nevertheless, the kerygma in itself is insufficient for forming Christians. Once hearers of the message have converted and been baptized, they need in-depth doctrinal and moral teaching for their continual growth into spiritual maturity. Thus the New Testament letters contain frequent exhortations to maturity (1 Cor 2:6–16; 14:19; Eph 4:15–16; 1 Pet 2:2; 2 Pet 3:18), as well as reproaches for immaturity (1 Cor 3:1–3; Heb 5:12–14) and commendations for growth (Col 1:6; 2 Thess 1:3). Those appointed to church leadership have the solemn

14. Cantalamessa, "The Preaching Ministry," 39.

15. Francis, *Evangelii gaudium* (November 24, 2013) (United States Conference of Catholic Bishops, 2013), §126.

duty of teaching and exhorting the faithful to this end (1 Cor 4:17; 1 Tim 4:11; 2 Tim 2:2; Titus 2:1, 2; Jas 3:1).

The Content of the Message

The Gospel, like the words of the biblical prophets, is not a message from human beings but from God. It is "the gospel of God" (Mark 1:14), "the word of God . . . which is at work in you believers" (1 Thess 2:13). It therefore has a divine energy, which even in the face of fierce opposition enables it to continue to "speed on and triumph" (2 Thess 3:1 RSV).

The content of the Gospel preached by Jesus is summed up succinctly in the Synoptics as a statement of fact and a consequent imperative (Matt 4:17; Mark 1:15). The fact is the inbreaking of God's kingdom into history in the person of Jesus, fulfilling God's promises of salvation as foretold in Scripture. The imperative is the personal response of faith and conversion that such an event demands. The proclamation carries divine authority. It "is not submitted to the scrutiny of its hearers, but requires the 'obedience of faith' (Rom 1:5)."[16]

> The proclamation of the arrival of the kingdom was a shattering event in human history. Jesus was not just another wise teacher who made his appearance and left his sayings as a source of inspiration for future disciples. The kingdom he proclaimed was not, and therefore is not, merely another alternative lifestyle that you can accept or reject on the basis of personal preference, personality configuration, convenience, or cultural heritage. The central message of the kingdom cuts completely through such superficialities and speaks to man about his very life.[17]

Following Jesus' paschal mystery and the outpouring of the Holy Spirit, the central content of the apostolic preaching becomes Christ himself, the crucified and risen Lord. What in Jesus' public

16. Xavier Léon-Dufour, *Dictionary of Biblical Theology* (Seabury, 1967), under "Preach," 451.

17. Michael Scanlan and Randall Cirner, *Deliverance from Evil Spirits: A Weapon for Spiritual Warfare* (Servant, 1980), 6–7.

ministry was "preaching the kingdom" becomes in the Church's ministry "preaching the Lord Jesus" (Acts 11:20) or "preaching good news about the kingdom of God and the name of Jesus Christ" (Acts 8:12; see 28:23, 31). The content of the preaching is fundamentally not a doctrine but a living person: "we preach Christ crucified" (1 Cor 1:23; cf. 2:2); "what we preach is not ourselves, but Jesus Christ as Lord" (2 Cor 4:5). Likewise, to be evangelized is not merely to hear the Gospel but to encounter the person of Christ and enter into a personal relationship with him (cf. Gal 4:8–9; Eph 3:19; Phil 3:8). The thoroughly Christocentric character of the apostolic preaching is a perennial challenge to a Church whose message sometimes tends to be more ecclesiocentric than Christocentric.

The letters of Paul provide only fragmentary information about the Gospel he preached, since they are addressed to believers and thus generally consist of *didachē* rather than *kērygma*. But in 1 Corinthians 15:1–8 Paul does cite explicitly "the gospel by which [he] evangelized" them (*to evangelion ho evangelisamēn*) and itemizes its basic content: Christ's death, burial, and resurrection in accordance with the Scriptures and his various resurrection appearances (cf. Rom 1:16; 2 Tim 2:8). In Acts, written later than Paul's letters, Luke portrays nine sermons that expound the content of the kerygma: five by Peter, three by Paul, and one by Stephen.[18] Although each is carefully tailored to its respective audience and circumstances, they share a common core. The various versions of the apostolic preaching found in Paul's letters and in Acts have different emphases, but manifest a fundamental unity in the early Church's understanding of the kerygma. Its content can be summarized in the following points:[19]

18. Acts narrates a full-scale sermon by Peter in 2:14–39, with shorter ones in 3:12–26; 4:8–12; 5:29–32; 10:34–43. Lengthy sermons by Paul are in Acts 13:16–41; 17:22–31, with a fragment in 14:15–17. Stephen's is in Acts 7:2–53. As Dodd notes, although the Petrine sermons are schematically composed by Luke decades after the fact, there is good evidence that they are based on Aramaic sources that go back to the preaching of the early Church at Jerusalem (*The Apostolic Preaching and Its Developments*, 19–21).

19. See the similar summary by Dodd in *The Apostolic Preaching and Its Developments*, 21–24.

- The time of fulfillment has come in Jesus the Messiah, whom God anointed with the Holy Spirit and attested with signs and wonders.
- Jesus was crucified for our sins in accord with the plan of God, foretold in Scripture.
- God has raised him from the dead and exalted him at his right hand as Savior and Lord of all.
- Christ will come again to judge the world in justice.
- Whoever believes in Christ receives salvation through the forgiveness of sins and the outpouring of the Holy Spirit in fulfillment of God's promises.
- The appeal: Repent, believe, and be baptized, and thus be saved.

One additional element appears only in the three sermons in Acts to Gentile audiences, who lacked the basic foundation of Jewish monotheism (Acts 10:34–43; 14:15–17; 17:22–31):

- The one transcendent God is creator of all, who rewards those who seek him. The appeal thus includes a summons to turn from idolatry.

Any proclamation of the kerygma in the twenty-first century must take into account the radically different cultural assumptions, psychological conditioning, and ways of thinking and speaking of today's audiences relative to the first-century Greco-Roman world. Nevertheless, closer attention to the content of the apostolic kerygma can bring greater sharpness, clarity, and vigor to the Church's evangelizing work today.

The Agents of Evangelization

The Gospels present Jesus as the first and model evangelist. In what is often called the "programmatic passage" of the Gospel of Luke, Jesus inaugurates his public ministry by summing up his own mission as an evangelizing mission: "The Spirit of the Lord is upon me, because he has anointed me to evangelize [*evangelisasthai*] the poor . . ." (Luke 4:18, literal translation, quoting from Isa 61:1). When the Synoptic

Gospels summarize the activities of his public ministry, they regularly do so by referring to his preaching the Gospel, teaching, and healing.[20] They also depict various interactions with individuals as evangelistic encounters, in which a person hears the good news and/or is healed by Jesus and responds by becoming a disciple.[21]

During his earthly ministry Jesus sends out the twelve apostles—and, in Luke, also seventy (or seventy-two) disciples—with the commission to share in his mission by preaching the Gospel both in word and in accompanying signs (Matt 10:5–8; Mark 6:12; Luke 9:1–2; 10:1–9). The Gospels report their successful accomplishment of this charge (Mark 6:12–13; Luke 9:6; 10:17–22). After his resurrection, as he is about to ascend into heaven, the charge becomes the risen Lord's formal mandate to the community of his disciples for all time: to proclaim the Gospel to the ends of the earth (Matt 28:19–20; Mark 16:15–18; Luke 24:46–49; Acts 1:8). The use of the plural "you" in all these texts underscores that the mission is not individual but communal, carried out not on one's independent initiative but in communion with the Church.[22]

The apostles (Greek *apostoloi*, "those sent out"), as his chosen leaders, have the primary responsibility for the mission (Mark 3:14; Acts 6:1–4). Yet the task is not for the apostles alone. Already during Jesus' public ministry, some of those who encounter Jesus go on to spread the good news to others in turn. For instance, the healed leper—despite Jesus' injunction to silence—goes out to "preach [*kēryssein*]" and "spread the word [*diaphēmizein ton logon*]" (Mark 1:45; cf. 7:36), standard terminology for evangelization. The two men healed of blindness "spread the word about him [*diaphēmisan auton*]" (Matt 9:31). The Gerasene demoniac "went away and began to proclaim [*kēryssein*] in the Decapolis how much Jesus had done for him" (Mark 5:20). The basic pattern for the growth of the Church emerges: the evangelizee becomes an evangelist.

To a degree surprising in the context of first-century Jewish culture, women too function as evangelists. Luke depicts Mary's visit to Elizabeth, immediately after the Annunciation, as the paradigmatic

20. Cf. Matt 4:23; 9:35; Mark 1:39; 2:2; Luke 8:1; 9:6; 16:16; 20:1.

21. E.g., Mark 10:46–52; Luke 5:1–10; 7:36–50; 8:1–3; John 9:1–38.

22. Cf. Acts 15:4; 16:2; 18:22; Gal 2:2, which demonstrate Paul's concern to remain in communion with the apostolic leadership.

act of evangelization: Mary, overshadowed by the Holy Spirit, goes forth to bear witness to Christ who has become present in her (Luke 1:39–56), just as the Church will do following Pentecost. After encountering the infant Jesus, Anna "spoke of him to all who were waiting for the redemption of Jerusalem" (Luke 2:38). During his public ministry, women healed by Jesus praise God and testify to his wondrous deeds (Luke 8:47; 13:13). The woman who anoints Jesus' head proclaims the Gospel nonverbally by her prophetic gesture, which Jesus declares to be an essential part of the preaching of the Gospel henceforth (Matt 26:13; Mark 14:3–9). The Samaritan woman at the well, after her encounter with Jesus, leaves her water jug to announce the Messiah to her townspeople, with the result that the entire town comes to faith in him (John 4:28–29, 39). All four Gospels report that it is women who first receive the commission to proclaim Jesus' resurrection (Matt 28:1–8; Mark 16:1–8; Luke 24:1–12; John 20:1–13), which for the early Church was the Gospel *in nucleo* (cf. Acts 4:2). This undisputed fact of early Christian tradition is all the more noteworthy since in Jewish law women were disqualified from being witnesses, being considered unreliable.

In Acts likewise, it is not only apostles but also ordinary disciples who evangelize. Luke highlights most prominently the evangelizing activity of the apostles Peter and Paul, but also devotes considerable space to the preaching of two of the seven men ordained to ministry, Stephen and Philip (Acts 6:8–8:40). After the martyrdom of Stephen, a persecution arises that results in the whole Jerusalem community being scattered throughout Judea and Samaria, "except the apostles" (Acts 8:1). It is these scattered lay Christians who begin spreading the Gospel to further regions, "as far as Phoenicia and Cyprus and Antioch," and even among Gentiles (Acts 8:4; 11:19). Both Acts and the Pauline letters demonstrate that Paul, the most celebrated evangelist of the early Church, constantly mentored, trained, and relied on his "co-workers," men and women who shared in his evangelizing mission in various ways.[23] Disciples like Priscilla and Aquila, after being

23. See Daniel J. Harrington, "Paul and Collaborative Ministry," *New Theological Review* 3 (1990): 62–71; George W. Murray, "Paul's Corporate Evangelism in the Book of Acts," *Bibliotheca Sacra* 155 (April–June 1998): 189–200.

discipled by Paul, in turn explain the message to others like Apollos (Acts 18:26).

The responsibility to evangelize thus rests upon all members of the Church. Yet Luke subtly implies that the ultimate subject of their evangelizing activity is the risen Jesus himself. At the beginning of Acts, Luke states that the content of his first volume, the Gospel, was "all that Jesus *began* to do and teach, until the day when he was taken up" (Acts 1:1–2, emphasis added). By implication, what the disciples do in his name is what *Jesus* continues to do and teach. Thus Paul can say that the risen Christ himself "proclaims light both to the [Jewish] people and to the Gentiles" (Acts 26:23), even though the Gentile mission began only after Jesus' ascension into heaven.

The risen Jesus is present to and active in his Church through the Holy Spirit. So, beginning at Pentecost, Luke presents the Holy Spirit as the initiator, guide, and driving force of the Church's mission.[24] It is only once the disciples are "baptized in the Holy Spirit" that the mission to preach the Gospel to the ends of the earth can begin (Acts 1:8). As soon as the Spirit is poured out, the disciples lose their previous timidity and immediately begin to "tell the mighty works of God," i.e., proclaim the kerygma (2:11). From that point on, the power to bear witness to Christ comes from the Spirit: "Then Peter, filled with the Holy Spirit, said to them . . ." (4:8; cf. 7:55–56; 1 Pet 1:12). The Spirit is active both in the evangelist and in the hearers, empowering the verbal testimony and convincing the hearers of its truth (5:32; cf. John 15:26; 1 Thess 1:5).

The Holy Spirit, moreover, initiates every new step in the Church's mission. The Spirit inspires Philip to evangelize an Ethiopian eunuch, whom Luke probably intends to depict as the first non-Jew to be baptized (Acts 8:26–39).[25] Later, the first *public* evangelization of Gentiles occurs when Peter, after receiving a heavenly vision, is instructed by the Spirit to enter the house of the Gentile centurion Cornelius. Before he finishes preaching to them, the Spirit falls on the gathered

24. See George Montague, *The Holy Spirit: Growth of a Biblical Tradition* (Paulist, 1976), 289–301.

25. See Craig Keener, *Acts: An Exegetical Commentary* (Baker Academic, 2013), vol. 2, 1565–71.

audience (10:9–48). The famous missionary journeys of Paul are initiated by a prophetic instruction of the Spirit to the disciples at Antioch (13:1–3). The Spirit twice prevents Paul from evangelizing where he intended to, and instead directs him by means of a vision to bring the Gospel to Europe (16:7–10). The biblical witness thus strongly affirms that the Holy Spirit is the principal agent of evangelization.[26] It is a fact easy to affirm in theory, yet all too often neglected in practice in the Church's mission today.

The Motive for Evangelizing

Jesus describes evangelizing as the very reason he has been "sent" into the world by the Father. "I must preach the good news [*evangelisasthai*] of the kingdom of God to the other cities also; for I was sent for this purpose" (Luke 4:43; cf. Mark 1:38; John 18:37). His own motivation to evangelize is thus inseparable from his identity and mission as the Messiah. He is the savior who has come "to seek and to save the lost" (Luke 19:10), to fulfill God's plan of salvation through his own suffering, death, and resurrection. He is the Suffering Servant prophesied by Isaiah, whom God has given "as a light for the nations, that my salvation may reach to the end of the earth" (Isa 49:6; cf. Luke 2:32), fulfilling the vocation of Israel to make known the one true God and his ways (cf. Isa 2:1–5; Zech 8:22). The dissemination of the Gospel, carried out by himself and later by the Church in his name, is the fulfillment of God's promise to Abraham that in him all the families of the earth would be blessed (Gen 12:3; cf. Gal 3:8, 14). Jesus thus evangelizes in obedience to the Father's will, giving each hearer the opportunity to receive his gift of salvation by responding to his word in faith (cf. Luke 19:9).

The Great Commission, in which Jesus associates the disciples with his own mission, likewise implies their obedience to God's saving will. Their fulfillment of this charge is, like his, not wooden obedience but rather a participation in God's salvific love. They are to imitate Jesus in his zeal for the lost and his joy at the restoration of

26. See Paul VI, *Evangelii nuntiandi*, §75.

sinners to the Father who loves them (Luke 15:6, 9, 32). The Gospel of John intimates that the sending of the disciples into the world to bear witness to Christ is ultimately rooted in the missions of the Son and Spirit, who are sent into the world by the Father: "As the Father has sent me, even so I am sending you" (John 20:21; cf. 14:26; 15:26; 17:18).

Arguably no New Testament figure apart from Jesus himself was more highly motivated to evangelize than Saint Paul, who cried out, "For necessity is laid upon me. Woe to me if I do not preach the gospel!" (1 Cor 9:16). Clearly Paul regarded his life's task as rooted in the commission entrusted to him by Christ on the road to Damascus (1 Cor 9:16).[27] Paul's motivation, like that of Jesus, is not merely the outward submission of a loyal soldier, but rather an obedience rooted in love. "For the love of Christ impels [*synechō*] us, since we are convinced that one died for all" (2 Cor 5:14, author's translation). The "love of Christ" in this text is probably intentionally ambiguous: it refers to both Christ's love for Paul, overwhelmingly revealed at his conversion on the road to Damascus (cf. Gal 2:20), and Paul's love for Christ who "took hold of" or captivated him (cf. Phil 3:12). The verb *synechō* can mean "hold fast, constrain, control, urge"; here it has the sense of a compelling motivation that drives Paul forward in his itinerant mission, at great personal cost to himself.

With the use of the first-person plural ("impels *us*"), Paul includes his fellow evangelists in this dynamic. Whoever proclaims the Gospel must, like him, be compelled by Christ's disinterested love and eschew any ulterior motives. Such false motives did in fact exist among some Christian preachers (cf. 2 Cor 2:17; 11:13; Phil 1:15, 17; 1 Thess 2:3). Then and now, they taint the work of evangelization and discredit the message. Jesus' and Paul's descriptions of their own motivations are an invitation to continual self-examination and purification of motives on the part of all preachers of the Gospel today.

27. Cf. Gal 2:7; cf. Eph 3:2; Col 1:25; 1 Thess 2:4; 1 Tim 1:11; Acts 26:14–16.

The Manner of Evangelizing

In his inaugural sermon as presented in Luke, Jesus insists that his proclamation of the Gospel is by the power of the Holy Spirit, who anoints him to evangelize not only in word but also in deeds of power that corroborate the truth of the verbal message (Luke 4:16–21; cf. 4:14; Matt 12:28; Acts 10:38). A large proportion of the Gospels is devoted to accounts of his healings, miracles, and casting out of demons. When the Evangelists summarize his ministry, along with his preaching and teaching they invariably mention his healings.[28] To the questioning disciples of John the Baptist, Jesus presents these miracles as the credentials that authenticate him as the promised Messiah (Matt 11:2–6; Luke 7:18–23; cf. Isa 35:5–6). These extraordinary signs are not merely an external proof but a visible manifestation of the presence of the kingdom he is announcing. They show in a powerfully convincing way that his Gospel is true: he truly is the Messiah, who is victorious over sin and every kind of evil; he has compassion on the sick and on sinners, and he has come to set people free. In the vocabulary of the Fourth Gospel, Jesus' "works" or "signs" (i.e., miracles) bear witness to him (John 5:36); they are a summons to belief, but without ever coercing it (10:38; 12:37; 14:11).

Jesus' evangelizing commission to his disciples likewise entails the proclamation of the Gospel both in words and in supernatural deeds that demonstrate the truth of the words. He instructs the Twelve, "Preach as you go, saying, 'The kingdom of heaven is at hand.' Heal the sick, raise the dead, cleanse lepers, cast out demons" (Matt 10:7–8 RSV).[29] The seventy are similarly instructed to heal the sick and announce the kingdom to them (Luke 10:8–9). In the Markan version of the Great Commission, this injunction becomes a permanent command and promise to the Church:

> "Go into all the world and preach the gospel to the whole creation.... And these signs will accompany those who believe: in my name they will cast out demons; they will speak in new tongues; they will pick

28. Matt 4:23; 8:16; 9:35; Mark 1:39; 3:7–10; Luke 6:17–19; 7:21; 8:2; 9:6, 11.
29. Cf. Mark 3:14–15; 6:12–13; Luke 9:1–2, 6; John 14:12.

> up serpents with their hands, and if they drink any deadly poison, it will not hurt them; they will lay their hands on the sick, and they will recover." . . . And they went out and preached everywhere, while the Lord worked with them and confirmed the *kērygma* by accompanying signs. (Mark 16:15–18, 20)

In Acts, Luke portrays the early Church's evangelization as inseparable from the signs and wonders by which God himself validates the spoken message and convinces the hearers of its truth. The proclamation of the Gospel with divine power is made possible by the outpouring of the Spirit at Pentecost (Luke 24:49; Acts 1:8; 2:16–19; 4:29–31).[30] As Jesus was "attested to you by God with mighty works and wonders and signs that God did through him" (2:22), so the apostolic preaching is now attested by signs and wonders (2:43; 5:12). The episode that immediately follows Pentecost is the dramatic healing of a lame man at the gate of the temple, which provides the occasion for Peter's preaching of the kerygma and the consequent rapid expansion of the Church (3:1–26; 4:4). The Samaritans evangelized by Philip believe the Gospel because of "the signs that he did," namely, healings and exorcisms (8:6–7). The rest of Acts is filled with accounts of healings, miracles, predictive prophecies, and other supernatural phenomena that drive the Church's remarkable missionary success.[31] It is not that miracles must attend every individual instance of evangelization—Luke records none, for instance, in Paul's preaching at Antioch, Thessalonica, Corinth, or Athens (Acts 9:22; 17:1–9; 18:1–11, 16–34)[32]—but they are a crucial part of the Church's evangelizing mission overall.

30. For an overview of the role of the Spirit in the proclamation of the Gospel and in conversion, see Gordon Fee, *God's Empowering Presence: The Holy Spirit in the Letters of Paul* (Hendrickson, 1994), 846–64.

31. Cf. Acts 6:8; 14:3; 15:12. Peter heals people by his shadow (5:14–17), cures the bedridden Aeneas in Lydda (9:32), and raises Tabitha from the dead (9:36–42). Paul strikes the magician Elymas with blindness (13:9), cures a lame man at Lystra (14:8–10), casts out a clairvoyant spirit at Philippi (16:16–18), heals people at a distance by means of handkerchiefs (19:11), restores Eutychus to life in Troas (20:7–12), heals a man of fever and dysentery on Malta (28:8–9), and is unharmed by a poisonous snake (28:3–6).

32. The fact that Paul implies that numerous miracles took place in Galatia (Gal 3:5), while Luke mentions only one Galatian miracle (Acts 14:8–10), serves as a caution against making an argument from silence that no miracles occurred in these other cities.

Paul's letters demonstrate that he regarded miracles as essential to his apostolic ministry. Although he was capable of eloquent arguments, he insisted on bringing people to faith not on the fragile basis of human persuasiveness but on the firm basis of divine power: "My speech and my message were not in plausible words of wisdom, but in demonstration of the Spirit and of power, that your faith might not rest in the wisdom of men but in the power of God" (1 Cor 2:4–5; cf. 1 Thess 1:5). By "demonstration of Spirit and power" he probably meant primarily the convincing power of the Holy Spirit at work in the hearts of the hearers, but also the miracles that often accompany the preaching of the kerygma. The miracles are the credentials that confirm his apostolic calling (2 Cor 12:12; cf. Rom 15:18–19), and that authenticate the Gospel for the hearers (Gal 3:2–5). The writer to the Hebrews likewise notes that God himself bears witness to the Gospel "by signs and wonders and various miracles and by gifts of the Holy Spirit distributed according to his will" (Heb 2:4).

Given the abundance and diversity of the biblical witnesses to the role of signs and wonders in evangelization, there are no grounds for assuming, as many Christians have through the ages, that such supernatural deeds are unnecessary or peripheral to the Church's mission, or that this aspect of Jesus' missionary mandate applied only to the apostolic age.

Extraordinary signs are, however, not the only nonverbal testimony to the Gospel. The fruit of the Spirit in the evangelist himself (Gal 5:22–23) also bears witness to the truth of the message. Thus Paul frequently draws attention to his own character as apostle. He and his co-workers "have renounced disgraceful, underhanded ways; we refuse to practice cunning or to tamper with God's word, but by the open statement of the truth we would commend ourselves to everyone's conscience in the sight of God" (2 Cor 4:2 RSV). He writes to the Thessalonians, "You know what kind of men we proved to be among you for your sake" and reminds them of the love, humility, patience, generosity, hard work, and total detachment from self-interest that characterized the missionaries who preached to them (1 Thess 1:5; 2:1–12). Luke reports the profound impression made on unbelievers by the disciples' courageous boldness in proclaiming Christ and their joy in the face of persecution (Acts 4:13; 16:25–30).

Even more, to preach the Gospel is to embody it in one's own life, which means to share in the suffering and ultimately the glory of Christ. It is to enter into the dynamic of Christ's own self-giving love, manifested in his life, death, and resurrection.[33] As preacher of the Gospel, Paul is an ambassador for Christ (2 Cor 5:20; Eph 6:20; Phlm 9), entrusted with a commission that is not his own (Eph 3:8). Yet precisely for that reason it demands the full engagement of his person. Paul provides several "hardship catalogs" detailing the sufferings of his itinerant ministry and persecution for the Gospel —not as an exercise in self-pity, but to illustrate the depths of his identification with the crucified and risen Lord whom he proclaims.[34] Paul and other preachers of the Gospel are afflicted and persecuted, "always carrying in the body the death of Jesus, so that the life of Jesus may also be manifested in our bodies. For we who live are always being given over to death for Jesus' sake, so that the life of Jesus also may be manifested in our mortal flesh" (2 Cor 4:10–11). As Luke shows in Acts, the ultimate conformity to Christ, and thus the most potent testimony to the Gospel, is to pay for the preaching of the Gospel with one's own shed blood. Thus Paul calls Stephen a "witness" (*martys*, Acts 22:20). The final chapters of Acts narrate Paul's own passion, with a striking series of parallels to Christ's passion. Paradoxically, Paul succeeds in bringing the Gospel to the center of the Empire only by means of arrest, unjust imprisonment, persecution, and suffering patterned after that of Jesus.[35] In nearly every generation since then, the blood of martyrs has both inspired and challenged Christians to continue to proclaim the undiluted Gospel, even when it is deeply unpopular. Likewise, the abundant supernatural signs that have accompanied evangelization in every age are a challenge to the contemporary Church to rely less on ourselves and more on God, expecting that he will still today "confirm the message by accompanying signs" (cf. Mark 16:20).

33. See Thomas Stegman, *2 Corinthians*, CCSS (Baker Academic), 109–12.
34. Rom 8:35; 1 Cor 4:8–13; 2 Cor 1:3–11; 4:7–12; 6:3–10; 11:23–33; 12:10.
35. See Montague, *The Holy Spirit*, 297–301.

The Goal of Evangelization

The goal (*telos*) or final cause of evangelization is of course inseparable from its motive: the evangelist desires the salvation of his or her hearers (Acts 4:12; Rom 1:16) and the reconciliation of the world to God in Christ (2 Cor 5:18–20). Within the horizon of human history, evangelization seeks to bring about the transformation not only of individuals but of cultures and nations. Luke paints an ideal picture of such transformation in his description of the primitive Christian community at Jerusalem:

> And they devoted themselves to the apostles' teaching and the fellowship, to the breaking of bread and the prayers. And awe came upon every soul, and many wonders and signs were being done through the apostles. And all who believed were together and had all things in common. And they were selling their possessions and belongings and distributing the proceeds to all, as any had need. And day by day, attending the temple together and breaking bread in their homes, they received their food with glad and generous hearts, praising God and having favor with all the people. And the Lord added to their number day by day those who were being saved. (Acts 2:42–47)

It is the beginnings of a Christian culture, a society founded on God's word and animated by the Holy Spirit, in which the Church is being built up in knowledge and love as the members care for one another, serve the neediest among them, and worship God together. The New Testament letters likewise portray life in the Church as a life of profound fraternal communion that involves continual learning from the apostolic doctrine, prayer and celebration of the Lord's supper, providing for one another's needs, and supporting one another in joy and sorrow[36]—all of which are an essential part of the Church's evangelical witness to the world.

The preaching of the Gospel is ultimately, like every action undertaken by believers, done for the glory of God (1 Cor 10:31; 2 Cor 1:20; 4:15; cf. Rev 14:6–7). The New Testament intimates that evangelization

36. See 1 Cor 12:25–26; Gal 6:1–2; Eph 4:15–16; 5:18–20; Phil 2:3–4; Col 1:28; 1 Tim 4:13, 16; Heb 6:1.

is in fact an act of worship. Strikingly, Paul employs cultic terminology to describe his preaching of the Gospel, taking the ministry of the Levitical priests in the Jerusalem temple as an image of his own apostolic ministry. Just as "those who serve at the altar share in the sacrificial offerings," so "the Lord commanded that those who proclaim the gospel should get their living by the gospel" (1 Cor 9:13–14). Paul has been given the grace "to be a minister [*leitourgos*] of Christ Jesus to the Gentiles performing the priestly service [*hierougeō*] of the gospel of God, so that the offering of the Gentiles may be acceptable, sanctified by the Holy Spirit" (Rom 15:16). As Albert Vanhoye comments on this text, "Paul is then viewing himself as a celebrant, one who offers."[37] And what he offers is evangelized Gentiles! Those who have come to faith in Christ and are now living holy lives, thanks to his preaching, are an acceptable offering to God. Joseph Fitzmyer notes that as a cultic minister, "Paul offers his evangelization of the Gentiles to God as a form of worship.... Paul implies that the preaching of the word of God is a liturgical act in itself."[38]

Conclusion

To sum up the conclusions of this study: for the New Testament, to evangelize is to proclaim the joyous tidings of the free gift of forgiveness of sins and salvation offered to all in Jesus Christ. It is distinct from teaching (*didachē*), which is the instructing of baptized believers in the full body of Christian doctrine. The content of the Gospel kerygma can be summed up as the Lord Jesus Christ, who was crucified for our sins and is now risen from the dead as Lord of all, who pours out his Holy Spirit and gives eternal life to all who repent and believe. All members of the Church are called to evangelize, although the apostles (and, for Catholics, their successors the bishops) have supreme responsibility for the Church's mission. Ultimately, it is the risen Lord Jesus, through the Holy Spirit, who is the primary agent of

37. Albert Vanhoye, *Old Testament Priests and the New Priest*, trans. J. Bernard Orchard (St Bede's, 1986), 269.

38. Joseph A. Fitzmyer, *Romans: A New Translation with Introduction and Commentary, AB* (Doubleday, 1993), 711.

evangelization. To evangelize is to participate in the missions of the Son and Spirit in obedience to the Father, sharing in their love and zeal to bring the lost home to God. Jesus' mandate to the Church in every age is to proclaim the Gospel as he did, in the power of the Holy Spirit, who confirms the message with accompanying signs and wonders, and who also brings the evangelist into profound conformity with Jesus in his passion, even to the point of shedding one's blood. The ultimate goal of evangelization is to participate in the reconciliation of the world to God in Christ, to the praise of the glory of God.

SECTION 3.
Fall 2024

October 2024
Convergence/Agreement Statement

Topic: Evangelization and Culture

1. We as Evangelicals and Catholics agree that we are called and feel impelled to announce the Gospel to everyone. Cf. the Great Commission in Mark 16:15: "Go into all the world and preach the gospel to all creation"; and the master's command to his servant in Jesus' parable in Luke 14:23: "Go out to the roads and country lanes and compel them to come in, so that my house may be full."[39]
2. Our witness to the Gospel is not just as individuals and families, and so we recognize the need to live Christian discipleship in distinctively Christian communities where the Christian way of life can be lived and others may be welcomed.

THE RELATIONSHIP OF EVANGELIZATION AND CULTURE

3. Among the many definitions and understandings of culture, we take as our working definition the one proposed by Cardinal Joseph Ratzinger in a 1993 address to the Doctrinal Commissions of Asia: "Culture is the historically developed common form of expression of the insights and values which characterize the life of a community."[40] As such, culture is both the location of and an instrument for evangelization.

39. All Scripture quotes are from the New International Version.

40. Cardinal Joseph Ratzinger, "Christ, Faith, and the Challenge of Cultures" (March 3, 1993), https://www.vatican.va/roman_curia/congregations/cfaith/incontri/rc_con_cfaith_19930303_hong-kong-ratzinger_en.html.

4. We agree with the words of Pope John Paul II that "culture is not the measure of the Gospel; rather, Jesus Christ is the measure of culture." We agree also with the statement of the Lausanne Covenant of 1974: "Culture must always be tested and judged by Scripture."
5. We understand culture to be based on what human nature is as described in Scripture, which speaks of men and women as created in the image and likeness of God (Gen 1:26–27).
6. We recognize that men and women are evangelized within the cultural contexts in which they live. We wish, therefore, to understand those cultures as best we can in order to be effective in our efforts and, to the degree possible, bring those cultures into alignment with the Gospel.
7. The work of evangelization requires careful discernment of what in a given culture can be maintained, what can be transformed, and what needs to be exposed/exorcized. The way in which the apostolic Church considered how to admit Gentiles, described in Acts 15, is a model of such discernment.
8. We recognize that we are living in times in which the predominant culture is becoming more directly anti-Christian, and that we are surrounded by a "culture of death." We lament that members of our communities are complicit in this culture and are shaped by it. We believe Evangelicals and Catholics can engage more effectively in the task of evangelization by working together to build up a culture that chooses life (Deut 30:19).

3.1 Evangelization and Culture: A Christian and Missionary Alliance Perspective

Dean M. Erickson

Introduction

THE TRUTH OF THE GOSPEL is perhaps the most basic, universal, and unifying thought within Christendom. That humanity was created in God's image, rebelled through sin, was offered redemption through Christ's crucifixion and resurrection is considered the foundation of the good news Christians are commissioned to share with all nations. Yet it is obvious to all but the most egocentric that the descriptor "all nations" includes significant cultural diversity in the world today. Due to these facts, evangelization and culture exist in perpetual tension between the unchanging singular truth of the Gospel and changing social constructs.

Sociologist Darrell L. Whiteman is a current expert in the field of evangelization across cultural boundaries. His missionary service in Papua New Guinea, the Solomon Islands, and Central Africa culminated in his role as professor at Asbury Theological Seminary for the past twenty-one years. He was the editor for *Missiology* journal for thirteen years, and former president of the American Society of Missiology and the International Association for Mission Studies. This year he published a culmination of his life's work. In the preface he summarizes the challenge of cultural perspective on the unchanging Gospel: "Confusing the gospel with their own culture or their denomination's interpretation of the gospel is a rampant problem everywhere I've observed cross-cultural ministry."[1] He continues by issuing the challenge to this generation of Christians "to confront your ethnocentrism, to discover how much of your understanding of biblical truth has been shaped by your culture, and to adjust your lifestyle to one that is more appropriate for cross-cultural ministry where you live."[2] This challenge summarizes the topic of this paper.

Beginning with a biblical foundation that recognizes the reality of cultural perspective in the metanarrative of Scripture, the paper will progress to biblical examples that illustrate the unchanging Gospel being adapted to biblical cultural situations. The paper will then turn to several brief examples from recent and current missionary efforts to effectively frame the unchanging truth of the Gospel in diverse cultural situations. Finally, the history and current efforts of the Christian and Missionary Alliance will be examined as a case study in evangelization and culture over the last 150 years. Two brief stories of current efforts of evangelization in challenging cultural situations will conclude this work.

Biblical Foundation: A Metanarrative Approach

A passage found late in the canonical New Testament serves as a fitting opening to a survey of Scripture on evangelization and culture: "In the past God spoke to our ancestors through the prophets at many times and in various ways, but in these last days he has spoken to us by his Son, whom he appointed heir of all things, and through whom also he made the universe" (Heb 1:1–2).[3] Those past times began in the ancient world. As the descendants of Noah spread out to be fruitful, multiply, and fill the earth, some paused to build a tower as a monument to themselves rather than God. In response, God confused the languages of the people (Gen 11:1–9), which is often understood as a curse. However, the result of God's action seems less to punish

1. Darrell L. Whiteman, *Crossing Cultures with the Gospel: Anthropological Wisdom for Effective Christian Witness* (Baker Academic, 2024), xvi.

2. Whiteman, *Crossing Cultures with the Gospel*, xvi.

3. Unless otherwise noted, Scripture references are to the *NIV Study Bible* (Zondervan, 1995).

and more to facilitate the dispersion of the people to spread God's planned dominion of the earth (Gen 1:28; 9:1, 7). Explaining Genesis 1:28, the NIV Study Bible notation reads: "God blessed them . . . going forth under this divine benediction—flourishing, filling the earth with his kind . . . . Human culture, accordingly, is not anti-God . . . it is the expression of humanity's bearing the image of the Creator and sharing, as God's servant, in God's kingly rule." Likewise, the diversification of language may be seen not only as a corrective prompt from God, but as a developmental step toward cultural distinctions that will reflect the indescribable God more fully.

Just after the tower of Babel story, the Genesis genealogy leads to the call of Abram to move to a promised homeland. This cross-cultural journey through the ancient Near East ends not only with Abram living among many foreign cultures at an intersection of ancient empires, but with a call to bless Abram. While the theological focus has often been on the primacy of future Israel and theological nature of the covenant presented in Genesis 12:2–3, the final clause is significant: Walter Kaiser argues convincingly[4] that this structurally and grammatically represents a purpose clause. The two doublets in v. 2 provide a rhythmic cadence leading to the unfinished doublet of v. 3:

> I will make you into a great nation, and I will bless you;
> I will make your name great, and you will be a blessing.
> I will bless those who bless you, and whoever curses you I will curse;

The purpose of these six promises is explained in the culminating capstone, read in the disjunctive Hebrew word order: "and (they) will be blessed through you, all peoples of the earth."[5] The purpose for all these blessings was not to single out Abram and his descendants for a blessing to the exclusion of all others. The purpose was to display the blessed relationship with YHWH that would draw all peoples or clans/families of the earth. God had been calling for individuals and families through the generations since Adam and Eve, with very few

4. Walter C. Kaiser, *Toward an Old Testament Theology* (Zondervan, 1978), 13, 31–32.
5. Translation my own.

responding. He continues calling, but in the divine work of grace, he focuses on one family by offering an unconditional covenant. The result of that outpouring of blessing would be a revelation of the goodness of YHWH to all who interacted with Abram's family.

The story of Genesis proceeds with the paradigm as Pharaoh curses Abram by unwittingly taking Sarah and receiving plagues while Abram gets rich (12:10–20). There is no way to explain this inequity unless Genesis 12:2–3 is recalled. In 13:1–18 Abram blesses Lot with his choice of the fields, and in turn YHWH reminds Abram that the whole land is his. Then Genesis 14 gives the same sequence of curses and blessings when the coalition of kings takes Lot captive only to receive the cursed defeat by Abram's diminutive number of warriors. When by contrast King Melchizedek of Salem spontaneously blesses Abram, he is blessed with a tithe of Abram's spoils. While the patriarchs and their descendant nation of Israel seldom act in a way worthy of such blessings, YHWH has promised to reveal himself to all people through them, ultimately through one descendant, the promised anointed one, Jesus.

Throughout the Old Testament many from outside Israel are drawn to YHWH through Israel's imperfect witness. The Canaanite Tamar goes to extraordinary lengths to guarantee an offspring from Judah (Gen 38). The Midianite Zipporah not only marries into the family but makes an unpleasant statement of faith when she circumcises Moses' son (Exod 4:24–26). The Canaanite prostitute Rahab declares her allegiance to YHWH with the same evidence rejected by her fellow residents of Jericho (Josh 2:8–11). Ruth the Moabitess forsakes all and pledges herself to an Israelite mother-in-law, Naomi, by swearing in the name of her God, YHWH (Ruth 1:16–17). In all these cases, the promise given to Abram is offered and received by those outside of the family and nation of Israel. The point made here is that God uses his blessing of Abram and Israel so that "all peoples on earth will be blessed through you." At Mount Sinai, YHWH commissions Israel: "Although the whole earth is mine, you will be for me a kingdom of priests and a holy nation" (Exod 19:5–6). As priests, their role will be to mediate, display, and proclaim what a relationship with YHWH means. Isaiah affirms this role for Israel stating in the servant songs,

"I will also make you a light for the Gentiles, that you may bring my salvation to the ends of the earth" (Isa 49:6; see also 42:6).

Matthew opens the New Testament Gospels with an unlikely genealogy of Jesus. The surprising inclusion of women in the list is striking, as it names the three foreign women mentioned in the previous paragraph. In addition to this list, Matthew includes "Solomon, whose mother had been Uriah's wife" (Matt 1:6). The careful Bible reader will remember not only that this woman is Bathsheba, but also may recall that Uriah was one of David's trusted warriors who proved a better man drunk than David was sober (2 Sam 11:13). Aside from this being an embarrassing way for Matthew to describe David's son Solomon in this genealogy, it calls to mind the similarity with the other three mothers mentioned in the list. At least one possible reason Bathsheba is not named is to remind the reader of another "outsider"—Uriah the Hittite (2 Sam 11:3).

The opening of Matthew's Gospel becomes even more significant when we read the final words of the account. After the crucifixion and resurrection of Jesus, he commissions his disciples with these words: "All authority in heaven and on earth has been given to me. Therefore, go and make disciples of all nations . . . ." (Matt 28:18–19). The Great Commission, as it is commonly called, parallels God's plan revealed at the call of Abram, to bring the good news to all nations. This commission to bring the Gospel to all nations is repeated by Luke: "And repentance for the forgiveness of sins will be preached in his name to all nations, beginning at Jerusalem. You are witnesses of these things" (Luke 24:47–48). When Luke sends his account of the origins of the Christian movement, he includes Jesus' instructions given at his ascension: "But you will receive power when the Holy Spirit comes on you; and you will be my witnesses in Jerusalem, and in all Judea and Samaria, and to the ends of the earth" (Acts 1:8).

God's plan has been consistent from the first couple in Eden, through the call of Abram, and the commissioning of the disciples, and his plan will culminate in "a great multitude that no one could count, from every nation, tribe, people and language, standing before the throne and before the Lamb" (Rev 7:9). Neither God's particular calling of Abram nor his selection of the disciples was exclusive. The plan has always been to invite people from all nations into a blessed, life-giving relationship with God.

Biblical Examples

Within this metanarrative the intercultural nature of the blessing and commission of God's people is often obscure. One must look carefully to notice, for instance, that the Passover restrictions given by Moses include: "The same law applies both to the native-born and to the foreigner residing among you" (Exod 12:49). This assumes there will be foreigners among the Israelites and makes provision for them if they convert to the worship of YHWH alone and accept the sign of the covenant. While the prophets recognize the plan of God and its sure fulfillment of Israel as a light to the nations in apocalyptic expressions (see Isa 60:3; 66:18), Israel is not overly successful in their witness to the nations. In fact, examples in the Old Testament, while present, are outliers. After God again scatters the people through exile, a story of a witness to the nations is more visible. Exile is very different than the scattering from the tower of Babel, to be sure, but the effects of the exile strangely relate to the earlier event. Rather than rallying Israel in a single land as a nation, God scattered his people into the nations. It is true that many exiles return to Jerusalem to reestablish the temple, but many also remain among the nations, building a Jewish life in diaspora, learning diverse languages, and learning how to be a unique people of God among the peoples of the earth.

By the early first century CE, Jewish people from many nations made regular trips to Jerusalem for religious festivals. At the Pentecost festival following the resurrection of Christ, the disciples were gifted the ability to speak in the native languages of the people gathered from the nations (Acts 2). In a spectacular, temporary reprieve from Babel, the language barrier dissolved, and all heard the Gospel in their own language. After a later event, Philip was instructed to cross paths with an Ethiopian worshiper on his way home from Jerusalem to explain the Gospel from Isaiah 53. The text does not tell us what language the men spoke or in what language the prophetic text was read, but the Gospel was preached, and a convert was baptized in an individual fulfillment of the Great Commission (Acts 8:26–40).

As the Gospel spread throughout the Roman Empire, God used a man with two cultural identities to overcome the cultural barrier of Jew and Gentile. Saul of Tarsus, undoubtedly named for his Benjaminite kingly ancestor, was also called by his Greek name, Paul (Acts 13:9) as he became the apostle to the Gentiles. Paul often began his missionary work by visiting the synagogues, a product of the exile mentioned above, to explain to the Jews and God-fearing Gentiles that Jesus was the long-awaited Messiah. This seldom went smoothly, but often produced a gathering of Christians who started a church nearby. This was the case in Ephesus where Paul had a particularly fruitful ministry (Acts 19). So meaningful was his ministry in Ephesus that Paul met with the Ephesian church leaders for a tearful sendoff from nearby Miletus on his return trip to Jerusalem. It is noteworthy that Paul shared with the Ephesian leaders that he had "declared to both Jews and Greeks that they must turn to God" (Acts 20:21).

The tension between the two cultures of Jews and Greeks in the early Church was the occasion for the first Church council in Jerusalem (Acts 15), and the first official clarification of the relationship between Jews and Greeks concerning the essential truth of the Gospel and distinctive practices of Jewish Christians. Paul mentions the conflict in several of his epistles, but a thorough treatment of the matter appears in his letter to the Ephesians. Beyond the treatment in Ephesians 2:11–3:13, Andrew Walls develops the deeper cultural tensions that existed and might even have continued after Acts 15.

> The Ephesian letter is not about cultural homogeneity; cultural diversity had already been built into the church by the decision not to enforce the Torah. It is a celebration of the union of irreconcilable entities, the breaking down of the wall of partition, brought about by Christ's death (Eph 2:13–18). Believers from the different communities are different bricks being used for the construction of a single building—a temple where the One God would live (Eph 2:19–22).[6]

Before following Walls's application to what he calls "The Ephesian Moment" for the modern Christian Church, a note about Paul's own

6. Andrew F. Walls, *The Cross-Cultural Process in Christian History* (T&T Clark, 2002), 77. Walls may be overstating the case in saying the Church did not enforce "the Torah," but his point remains valid.

sensitivity in writing to this mixed-culture church may be insightful. A subtle word shift appears in chapter 3. Paul follows the rich metaphor of the diverse believers in the Ephesian church as building blocks of the temple with a transition: "For this reason I, Paul, the prisoner of Christ Jesus for the sake of you Gentiles—" (Eph 3:1). English translations use various forms to communicate the disjunctive ending to the verse. Paul interrupts his thought abruptly to explain in some detail the "administration of God's grace that was given to me for you, that is, the mystery" (Eph 3:2, 3). "This mystery is that through the Gospel the Gentiles are heirs together with Israel, members together of one body, and sharers together in the promise in Christ Jesus" (Eph 3:6). This has been the subject of 2:11–22, but the source of the interruption for more explanation is significant. Paul continues his thought from 3:1 in v. 7: "I became a servant of this gospel by the gift of God's grace given me through the working of his power." The word shift from "prisoner" (3:1) to "servant" (3:7) is most often unnoticed, but is crucial to understanding the conflict and Paul's sensitivity in writing about the conflict to his Ephesian church audience.

The reason for the interruption after v. 1 becomes clear when we examine the circumstance of Paul's imprisonment. In Acts 21, after the tearful farewell offered to Paul by the Ephesian church leaders (Acts 20:37–38), Paul heads to Jerusalem and is ultimately arrested. The charge against Paul is that he brought a Gentile past the "dividing wall of hostility" (Eph 2:14) into the temple—a most serious offense. Acts 21:29 gives the parenthetic detail that the Jewish leaders in Jerusalem "had previously seen Trophimus the Ephesian in the city with Paul and assumed that Paul had brought him into the temple." Whether Paul was guilty seems doubtful based on the parenthetic detail, but it provides an explanation for Paul's shifting abruptly in Ephesians 3:1. Paul is sensitive to the hearts of the Ephesian people and must hear as he dictates or writes these opening words to his next thought—"I'm a prisoner . . . and I just made the Ephesian church people feel guilty since it was one of their own who was responsible for my arrest." After explaining the high honor he has been given by God of revealing the mystery of the Gentile inclusion into Israel's inheritance, Paul restarts his idea with the descriptor, "I became a 'servant' of this gospel by the gift of grace given me." Not the negative-sounding "prisoner" due to the Ephesian church member, but a "servant" of this Gospel by the gift of grace.

This excursus may seem off topic, but it illustrates a sensitivity in preaching the Gospel in a particular context or culture. Paul is explaining the significance of his ministry to the Gentiles, recognizes that he may have accidently guilt-tripped them, understands that this may distract from his message, explains his circumstances as a high honor and gift from God, and returns to his original point. In the highly charged division between Jew and Gentile, Paul goes the extra mile to make sure he does not distract by offending his hearers, but sensitively explains his way back to a better expression of his role in the evangelization of the Gentiles. He further ends his message in 3:13 with words of assurance to his readers in Ephesus: "I ask you, therefore, not to be discouraged because of my sufferings for you, which are your glory." The book of Ephesians gives a rich expression of the ways culture affected a faith community's understanding of the truth. In the same way, the task of evangelization must understand the culture and anticipate the potential responses to our expression of the unchanging truth of the Gospel.

Returning to "The Ephesian Moment," Walls provides a pathway toward application with a caution: "Like the old Jerusalem Christians [of Acts 15], Western Christians had long grown used to the idea that they were the guardians of a 'standard' Christianity."[7] Considering how to distinguish the truth from the trappings of Western expressions of Christianity, Walls offers warnings against two dangers. "One lies in an instinctive desire to protect our own version of Christian faith. . . . The other . . . is the postmodern option: to decide that each of the expressions and versions is equally valid and authentic, and that we are therefore each at liberty to enjoy our own in isolation from all the others."[8] The work of evangelization in any culture demands both recognizing opportunities provided by a culture and critiques of that culture, including Western expressions of the unchanging truth of the Gospel.

7. Walls, *Cross-Cultural Process*, 78.
8. Walls, *Cross-Cultural Process*, 78–79.

Examples: The Modern Evangelical Missions Movement

Among the pioneers of the modern Evangelical missionary movement are two familiar names: Adoniram Judson and Hudson Taylor. Each is remembered for their efforts at contextualizing the unchanging Gospel into new cultural situations. Adoniram Judson

> was an American linguist and Baptist missionary in Myanmar (Burma), who translated the Bible into Burmese and wrote a now standard Burmese dictionary . . . the Judsons relocated to Rangoon in 1813; there Judson mastered the Burmese language and literature and learned Pāli, the Buddhist canonical language.[9]

Judson was ahead of his time. He discovered that the pathway to sharing the unchanging Gospel with unreached people was an understanding the culture of those people. Critical to the modern missionary movement is the fact that language acquisition is an essential sociological tool for understanding both the culture and the people.

Hudson Taylor extended this contextualization beyond language to cultural appropriations such as clothing style and the distinctive Chinese top knot hairstyle. In his biography, he explains what motivated his approach to evangelization and culture:

> And why should such a foreign aspect be given to Christianity? The Word of God does not require it; nor, I conceive, could sound reason justify it. It is not the denationalization but the Christianization of this people that we seek. We wish to see Chinese Christians raised up men and women truly Christian, but withal truly Chinese in every sense of the word. We wish to see churches of such believers presided over by pastors and officers of their own country men, worshipping God in the land of their fathers, in their own tongue, and in edifices of a thoroughly native style of architecture. . . . Let us in everything not sinful become Chinese, that we may by all means "save some."[10]

9. *Encyclopedia Britannica*, "Adoniram Judson," April 8, 2025, https://www.britannica.com/biography/Adoniram-Judson.

10. Cited in Paul Sadler, "How One Man's Haircut Transformed China," November 28, 2018, https://www.gracebc.ca/blog/2018/11/27/how-one-mans-haircut-transformed-china.

A more recent influential book in the history of Evangelical missions was *Peace Child* by Don Richardson. The book narrates Richardson's experiences as a pioneer missionary to the western half of New Guinea, now called Irian Jaya. He traveled by dugout canoe to the Sawi tribal people group to study their language and introduce them to the Gospel. Though the Sawi were highly skeptical of outsiders, Don's wife Carol showed the love of Christ through providing medical treatments for those suffering ailments in the tribe. Don showed the love of Christ by his genuine interest in the Sawi language as a means to really understanding the people and their culture. An obstacle to receiving the Gospel was quickly identified in their cultural value of violence and treachery, illustrated in their dealings with a nearby rival tribe. This explained the Sawi's odd response to the crucifixion story, when they regarded Judas as the hero of the story for betraying Jesus.

When tensions between the tribes increased toward war, a fascinating ritual emerged as a solution. The *tuwi asonai manos*, "peace through a child," involved one tribe offering an infant child to the rival tribe to establish a lasting peace. In a culture where treachery was valued, harming the peace child was strictly taboo and an act understood as reprehensible violation. Richardson had found a cultural parallel to Jesus who came as a child to bring peace between God and humanity. He later named this type of cultural connection to the universal story of the Gospel a redemptive analogy. Richardson closes his narrative by stating: "Redemptive analogies, God's keys to man's cultures, are the New Testament-approved approach to cross-cultural evangelism."[11] His connection to the New Testament aptly connects these missionary accounts with the exegetical foundation laid earlier in this study.

Example: The Christian and Missionary Alliance

The origin of the Christian and Missionary Alliance fits well in the history of modern Evangelical mission work. In 1861 Albert Benjamin Simpson sensed a call to ministry as a seventeen-year-old. Being

11. Don Richardson, *Peace Child* (G/L Regal Books, 1974), 288.

a gifted student, he was accepted into Knox College's ministerial program while attending the requisite lectures at the University of Toronto. Simpson thrived in the pulpit, which paved the way for him from student preaching to prestigious Knox Presbyterian Church in Hamilton, Ontario. After eight years, Simpson had gained some notoriety and received a call from Chestnut Street Presbyterian Church of Louisville, Kentucky. While there, he was influenced by the Holiness movement when he stumbled upon a book by William Boardman, *The Higher Christian Life*. "He realized that the same One who came in to his sinful heart to cleanse and forgive did not then leave him to battle against sin on his own. This same Savior lived within him to make him holy."[12]

The American Civil War divided the major denominations as well as the churches in Louisville. Simpson advocated for reconciliation through the Evangelical Alliance and found surprising success. The late 1800s saw a wave of mass evangelistic efforts, where prominent pastors joined gifted musicians in large settings from theaters to open air meetings. Simpson invited Daniel Whittle, a colleague of D. L. Moody, and his musical partner Phillip P. Bliss to Louisville for a month of meetings in February 1875. The revival that began was extended by Simpson and other local pastors for the rest of the year. Simpson became driven to reach the lost, and Louisville was not big enough to satisfy his longing.

In 1878 Simpson attended a prophecy conference in Watkin Glenn, New York, which shook his postmillennial roots and aligned his evangelistic zeal with a premillennial motivation. After the conference, Simpson had a dream that resembled Paul's Macedonian call, in which multitudes of Chinese people seemed to be pleading with him to come. A variety of obstacles prevented Simpson from going as a missionary to China, but his heart was distinctly turned to lost souls beyond his reach. Meanwhile, he continued to grow in prominence in the Presbyterian church and was called by the notable 13th Street Presbyterian Church in New York. His first message

12. David P. Jones, *A.B.: The Unlikely Founder of a Global Movement* (The Christian and Missionary Alliance, 2019), 59.

was appropriately from Acts 1:7–8, as his sense of burden for the lost continued to grow.

This heart for the lost was completely in sync with the original founding of his new church. 13th Street Presbyterian Church began as an abolition church and an outreach to Manhattan's poor. Eventually, as the church grew, it followed an unfortunately typical path by moving north on 13th Street to a more affluent, newer neighborhood. Though it was started as a "free church," financial pressures in the new upscale setting forced the church to follow cultural conventions and charge rent for pews. This was the new environment Simpson inherited. He strongly opposed the practice of pew rental, but the structures within the church made challenging the status quo dangerous. When he evangelized a group of Italian immigrants and brought them to church, whether renters were in attendance or not, the church leadership was outraged. When Simpson suggested the new converts be baptized, the leaders instructed their new pastor to find the new converts a church where they would feel more at home.[13]

Though disturbed by this watershed event, Simpson faithfully continued his ministry, and the church continued to grow. However, in his writings he noted "the staggering amount of money spent on construction, decorations, and furnishings for churches in America. At the same time, missions giving was literally pennies on the dollar. He marveled at the huge sum of money spent on pet food as compared with the meager investment made for world evangelization."[14] Simpson lasted only two years in this affluent ministry before he conceded, "What they wanted was a conventional parish for respectable Christians. What their young pastor wanted was a multitude of publicans and sinners."[15] Simpson moved further into the city and closer to the masses neglected by his church. He rented space and opened what he named "The Gospel Tabernacle." The name was fitting, as resources were thin and the quickly growing ministry was forced

13. Robert L. Niklaus, John S. Sawin, and Samuel J. Stoesz, *All for Jesus*, 125th Anniversary Edition (The Christian and Missionary Alliance, 2013), 50.

14. Jones, *A.B.: The Unlikely Founder of a Global Movement*, 81.

15. A. E. Thompson, *The Life of A.B. Simpson* (The Christian Alliance Publishing Co., 1920), 84.

to find larger, more economical shelter several times. The settings ranged from two stints in the Grand Opera Hall to an extended stay in an open block under a donated big-top gospel tent. "The following year, a journalist reporting on the 1883 summer meetings stated that the tent was nearly full to its capacity of 2,000 people. . . . Conversions and healings were a nightly occurrence."[16]

Motivated by these events, with his growing premillennial conviction that the lost must be reached because the end was near, Simpson began training missionaries to go to "The Regions Beyond."[17] This was the title of one of Simpson's dozens of hymns, written mostly on the themes of the deeper life and world missions. His eagerness to reach the lost caused him great frustration with the expensive educational institutions of his day, which were drifting into liberalism and were not training workers to reach the lost. He began training "God's irregulars" with two years of biblical studies, theology, and missionary methods. In 1882 this effort founded the first Evangelical Bible school in the United States, which would become Nyack College, followed five years later by D. L. Moody's Bible Institute.

Several books have been written on Simpson's life and the Christian and Missionary Alliance movement that followed. To summarize the next century in the briefest of terms, Simpson's vision sparked many church revivals and planted new churches with his missionary passion. Those churches sent missionaries throughout the world prioritizing unreached people groups in an effort to fulfill Matthew 24:14: "And this gospel of the kingdom will be preached in the whole world as a testimony to all nations, and then the end will come." Those sent were called the Missionary Alliance, and those churches that supported those missionaries were called the Christian Alliance. In 1974, with hundreds of missionaries, thousands of churches worldwide, and funds flowing, the Christian and Missionary Alliance denomination was officially organized.

C&MA, or Alliance, missions have worked faithfully to fulfill the Great Commission and follow the biblical pattern outlined in the

16. Jones, *A.B.: The Unlikely Founder of a Global Movement*, 97.
17. *Hymns of the Christian Life* (Christian Publications, 1978), 460.

early pages of this paper. Priority has been given to evangelization and to methods that emulate Judson, Taylor, and a host of others who sought to understand and value the indigenous cultures of the regions beyond. Of the many examples who illustrate the value of learning the culture of the person we evangelize: "Christian and Missionary Alliance Missionary H. Myron Bromley (1925–2016) served among the Dani in the Baliem Valley of Iran Jaya on the island of New Guinea in Indonesia for nearly forty years."[18] The Dani once described Bromley this way: "Dr. Bromley knows our language and culture better than we do."[19] This is only possible by getting outside our own cultural norms and observing the real cultural norms of the person who needs the unchanging truth of the Gospel. The significance of Bromley's influence was noted by Don Richardson in the acknowledgments of *Peace Child.*

Of particular distinction is the Alliance's commitment to training indigenous church leaders. When the Gospel is received and disciples made, leaders are trained who will carry on the work in the way that best suits the indigenous culture. This method no doubt followed from the drive to reach the ends of the earth, but this meant that missionaries were not establishing churches in order to stay and pastor them themselves. Following the Apostle Paul's example, missionaries planted churches and turned those churches over to capable leaders so the missionaries could continue to reach new harvest fields. This method dictated the structural decision to grant independence to fields when enough churches and local pastors and overseers were prepared to care for their own country's ministries. These independent Alliance fields become new members of the Alliance World Fellowship but are self-governing and self-sustaining. Some of these fields now dwarf the original C&MA in the United States in number of members and churches, and many now send missionaries cross-culturally to regions not accessible to the US-based Alliance.

Meanwhile, the C&MA has diversified its missionary efforts due to the changing culture in the United States and throughout the world.

18. Whiteman, *Crossing Cultures with the Gospel*, 27.
19. Whiteman, *Crossing Cultures with the Gospel*, 27.

Many fields where Alliance missionaries were traditionally trained in church planting are today either post-Christian or closed to traditional church planting missionaries.[20]

- CAMA (Compassion & Mercy Associates): In 1974 the Alliance realized its evangelization efforts could be more effective if it took more seriously Jesus' alarming warning of "the sheep and the goats" in the Olivet Discourse. Matthew 25:31–46 clearly indicates that evangelization extends beyond preaching the Gospel. While Evangelical missions rejected the "Social Gospel" of the late nineteenth and early twentieth centuries, they had also rejected a clear call from Jesus himself to meet the physical needs of the most desperate. CAMA Relief & Development responds to disasters globally and partners locally to restore communities and alleviate poverty.

  In recent years, the diversification has increased quickly to include:

- aXcess (Church Planting) "proclaims the gospel and multiplies networks of faith communities among the least-reached of the world."[21] This is the traditional missionary, but renewed emphasis has been placed on people groups with the least access to the Gospel.
- Marketplace Ministries (Business as Mission) "facilitates marketplace professionals who bring their expertise to a community to disciple those around them."[22]
- Envision (Short-Term Missions and Leadership Development") "identifies and develops missional leaders through short-term mission opportunities and innovative ministry strategies."[23]

20. Church and Missionary Alliance, "Alliance Missions," https://cmalliance.org/our-work/alliance-missions/ (accessed June 25, 2025).
21. Church and Missionary Alliance, "Alliance Missions."
22. Church and Missionary Alliance, "Alliance Missions."
23. Church and Missionary Alliance, "Alliance Missions."

Current Examples: Personal Interviews

To protect the efforts of these Gospel workers, their identities will remain anonymous. These interviews were conducted in 2024.

FIRST INTERVIEW

An academic colleague and friend moved to Europe to work with the C&MA through Envision several years ago. On a recent visit to Crown College, he discussed the challenges faced in the culture in which he now lives. The Envision site he opened networks ministries in his city and hosts short-term mission groups seeking both training and effective witness for Christ in a cross-cultural setting. The challenge of short-term mission groups is their expectation to go into the city and do "street evangelism." While this form of evangelization had its moment, it is no longer effective in the United States and is even less so in his current European context. He described the struggle with this illustration. Imagine the outcome if you were to tell a stranger that they are to commit their life to the Fairy Godmother. He describes the trouble in his city as the people are post-post-Christian. They have forgotten what they have forgotten. This means that the Gospel story has been reduced to fairy tale status. Trying to evangelize with a straightforward presentation of the Gospel is worse than ineffective—it is counterproductive. It actually reinforces the incredibility of the story.

A fresh approach was to create a cultural center in the heart of the city and provide social support services for the people in their immediate area. They hold English classes, children's events, and other creative opportunities that emerge as they interact with their neighbors. One of the more unique and effective methods has been to designate a portion of their storefront building as an art gallery. The people of the city appreciate art and are drawn to this space, which displays local artists' work and offers a free space to socialize, allowing them to enjoy the art while connecting with the artists and meeting new neighbors. My friend prompts discussions of the transcendentals—truth, unity (oneness), beauty, and goodness—as openings to discussing truths that seem universal, are valued by those enjoying the art, and are greater than our limited existence. Those conversations begin to open doors to talking about the felt needs humans share for these elusive qualities, which offers an opportunity to discuss personal faith and fulfillment. It seems like a long way to go to get to the Gospel, but it is the only path available in this particular culture at this moment in their history.

SECOND INTERVIEW

Two college classmates were home on furlough after ministering in Japan for more than two decades. They were visiting Crown College and offered to share about the cultural struggle they face evangelizing in Japan. After an hour-long conversation, they had barely scratched the surface of the obstacles in the way of Western missionaries sharing the unchanging truth of the Gospel in their cultural setting. A few examples will serve the purpose here.

In the Japanese language, the word for "God" is used culturally or commonly for the countless ancestral and animistic spirits people have "known" since birth. Specifying a name for God (YHWH, Jesus, etc.) simply adds to the polytheistic paradigm. Monotheism is a non-starter, and henotheism is not accepted as valid. Another example is the lack of a word for "sin" in the Japanese language, perhaps because they have never known a god who distinguishes between right and wrong. The Japanese Bible translators chose the word "criminal" as a substitute, but it is unspeakably offensive to call a person a criminal, as the descriptor is reserved for the most wretched person in an honor-based society. The word "forgiveness" is problematic since forgiveness is not a virtue in Japanese. From the days of the samurai, faithful revenge remains the virtue. To overlook evil is never seen as good. The word "grace" is never attractive to a Japanese person. To receive a gift without repaying is never acceptable. "Thank you" is insufficient; a person must respond with a similar gift. To not do so is immature at best and more likely thoughtless and rude. One will forever owe a debt that "should have" been repaid. This is *so* deeply grounded in Japanese thought that the word for "thank you" is literally "there is trouble"—i.e., you did a kindness to me and have now placed a burden on my shoulders, a debt I must repay. While this may seem an insurmountable obstacle to sharing the Gospel, it may provide an opportunity to include a facet of the truth often overlooked in modern Western Gospel presentations. Included in the grace-filled offer of salvation is a call to "take up their cross and follow me" (Matt 16:24) and to reaffirm the good news of Jesus' promise: "For my yoke is easy and my burden is light" (Matt 11:30).

Conclusion

These two interviews underscore the challenges to evangelization presented by culture in other countries. These examples may seem extreme, but similar obstacles seem to be trending in the United States as Western culture drifts further from its deep Judeo-Christian roots. It is here that the story of the founding of the Christian and Missionary Alliance helps us consider the current cultural situation. Simpson confronted his high church exclusivism, which parallels the high society culture in early twentieth-century Christianity. His premillennialism, whether it was correct or not, also confronted the Social Gospel trend that pursued evangelization as merely social reform. Rejecting both exclusivism and liberalism, Simpson put aside the comforts and securities of his prestigious position and strove to follow Jesus' example as one who came to seek and save those who were lost. It is often more challenging to evaluate one's own culture to see how the status quo obscures our vision and makes us culturally less effective in evangelization. With this in mind, the topic of evangelization and culture becomes ever more important.

3.2 To Flee the Wrath That Is to Come So That We May Have Nothing to Do But Save Souls? A Short Consideration of Evangelism in the Methodist/Wesleyan Tradition Calmly Considered

Steven Hoskins

> There is only one condition previously required of those who desire admission into these societies: "a desire to flee from the wrath to come, and to be saved from their sins." But wherever this is really fixed in the soul it will be shown by its fruits.
>
> *John Wesley, The Nature, Design, and General Rule of our United Societies, 1740*

> You have nothing to do but save souls. Therefore spend and be spent in this work. And go always, not only to those that want you, but to those that want you most. Observe: It is not your business to preach so many times, and to take care of this or that society; but to save as many souls as you can; to bring as many sinners as you possibly can to repentance, and with all your power to build them up in that holiness without which they cannot see the Lord.
>
> *John Wesley, 12 Rules for Helpers, 1744*

Introduction: Calmly Considering the History of "Evangelism" in the Wesleyan/Methodist Tradition

Any consideration of the history of Methodism/Wesleyanism (hereafter M/W) as told by its many adherents broadly considered (if one includes the African and African-American denominations committed to a whosoeverwill doctrine the number is roughly, at the time of this paper, twenty-five million) will show that it has, on the one hand, either been (or at least spawned) the greatest (now three centuries long) revival movement in the history of Protestantism, if not the history of Christianity, that has, at the same time, done an excellent job in providing a pattern of discipleship for its members or, on the other hand, has been the most outstanding and productive example of a Christian discipleship movement that has been able to support that work through innovative, exciting, and downright provocative evangelistic efforts through the exhortations of fiery preachers of the Gospel to the lost. The obvious overconfidence of these chroniclers, on both sides, leads observers outside of the M/W self-confession (roughly two billion Christians) at least bemused over such a conundrum within its ranks, if not downright confused as to how to understand and collaborate with them. Any way forward in our ecumenical discussions together, deserves an explanation of sorts as to the internal conundrum of M/W, and so the purpose of this paper.

Truth be told, M/W rose in the eighteenth century through the ministrations of the Wesley brothers, John and Charles, and their friends, as one of several notable Enlightenment-driven attempts to remedy Protestant failings at the task of world evangelization (e.g. Pietist movements in general, Moravian attempts in particular) and to deal with the Christian dogma or claim of the "scandal of particularity" regarding the lordship of Jesus Christ over all of humanity.[1] Like many of these movements, for movements they were, M/W was an in-house Anglican criticism of a Protestant state church's shortcomings. While the Protestant Reformation and the churches it spawned were ripe with a plethora of wonderful ideas, visions, and accomplishments,[2] it had simply failed in any attempts to inspire any hopes for world mission. M/W grew as a corrective inspiration for the broader Reformation church of which it was a part (never forget that Wesley was never formally a "Methodist" and that he lived and died as an Anglican clergyman who saw himself as the leader of a "society"

1. Leon Hynson, "World Evangelization: A Wesleyan Proposal," *The Asbury Seminarian* 37, no. 3 (1982): 18–38, at, 18.

2. Brad Gregory, *The Unintended Reformation* (Belknap Press, 2015).

within the Anglican Church, like the Society for the Preservation of Christian Knowledge, the Society for the Reformation of Manners, the Society for the Propagation of the Gospel, and the Society for the Propagation of the Gospel in Foreign Parts, all of which he more or less belonged to during his long life, 1703–1791). The desire of M/W was to "perfect" the Anglican Church in all of its doings—theological, pastoral, devotional, pietistic, proclamatory—by providing opportunities both for conversion and gospel outreach to the masses through field preaching (a contested term that needs some explaining); published sermons on topics arresting and convicting; a wide series of published books, tracts, testimonies, and the like providing argumentative presentations on topics pointed at Anglican theology and its unwillingness to see the workings of God beyond the confines of stated doctrines and church administrative structures, ranging from the rule of bishops, state positions on issues like slavery, and the care of the poor; and by providing a "method" for making and helping disciples whose sole desire was to "flee the wrath that is to come" and do nothing but save souls so that they might make it to heaven.

To address these shortcomings within Anglicanism, M/W under the leadership of John Wesley presented its case in pithy, short, easy to communicate and understand presentations in grand Protestant fashion. God's workings in the life of any believer followed a pattern of graces—prevenient, convicting, saving, and sanctifying grace—which reached out in various and sundry ways to those who were "stupid" (Wesley's eighteenth-century word) or unaware of God's working in their lives, bringing them to a moment of awakening conviction of their need for God's grace (and need to reach their designed purpose as a creature created in the image of God), to a vitalized experience in which they were born again and knew by God's witness that they were a child of God, and then were ushered into the holy life and a boundless life of being continually sanctified or renewed in the image of God. This Wesley likened to a threefold state of human existence—natural (stupid), legal (convicted and aware of God), and evangelical or spiritual (awakened to God and saved and loving God, or sanctified).[3] He also likened the "process" to

3. John Wesley, *The Spirit of Bondage and Adoption*, Sermon 9.

someone entering a house. They first realized they were on a porch (awakening) and then walked through the door of the abode (salvation) and then into the roomy fullness of the house (the holy life).[4] At this point one could go on to tell the story of how John Wesley gave his lifelong efforts—enough to fill over thirty-two self-compiled volumes before his death—to writing and preaching sermons, testimonies, gospel tracts, and rules for the Methodist societies; compiling a "Christian Library" of necessary reading for disciples that contained over one hundred titles; and producing letters, newspapers, and scribblings that amount to well over five thousand pages,[5] to explain these ideals in as complete an accounting as he could, as any responsible, Oxford-educated, Anglican clergyman organizer of a movement would. Add to that the many thousands of hymns and gospel songs and the hymnals and gospel song books in which they appear, all written to accompany the M/W theological catalogue noted above, and one gets a sense of the power and appeal that has led to so much M/W self-reflection about the nature of what Wesley himself called the "Evangelical Revival" within Anglicanism (which quickly spread around the world—Methodists were active in at least ten countries stretching from the Caribbean region to Norway by the time of Wesley's death).

To add a bit of necessary detail, one must consider John Wesley's self-understanding of the work of his Methodist Societies and their many, often lay, preachers. Wesley self-consciously saw the work of his movement as evangelists doing what was necessary to sanctify a church that was derelict in its duty to the citizens of the English realm.[6] "Evangelist" (title) and the "work of evangelists" were Wesley's self-chosen descriptions of the work of the Methodist laborers.

4. John Wesley, "The Principles of a Methodist Farther Explained," VI.4, in *The Bicentennial Works of John Wesley*, ed. Randy Maddox and Richard Heitzenrater (Abingdon, 1991–), 9:227.

5. Most of this is now being collected into the thirty-six-volume *The Works of John Wesley, Bicentennial Edition* (Abingdon Press, 1991–, ed. Randy Maddox and Richard Heitzenrater) with annotations and notes. The print version will soon be released on its own website hosted by Candler School of Divinity, Emory University, Atlanta, GA.

6. See Jonathan Clark, *English Society, 1688–1832* (Oxford University Press, 1985), for an excellent history of the work of Methodists and their rehabilitation efforts inside the established church.

He never used the term "evangelism" to describe their work and never once published a sermon on the Great Commission (Matt 28:16–20). However, it is clear from Wesley's writings and reflections on the movement that preaching was the paramount way in which evangelists did their work, whether in the field, the class, or society meeting, often with required attendance at daily exhortations, and in one-on-one attempts at conversion.[7] One could go on. Any attempt in determining whether John Wesley and the Evangelical Revival was a legitimate form of "evangelism" would force the hand of the historian into a long consideration of Wesley and his eighteenth-century context and the theological and practical resources he used in the work, and then become more prophetic than necessary in the determination. Suffice it to say that Wesley, and the M/W movement that arose in his wake and continues today, offers the opportunity for a serious consideration of what evangelism is (how it has been stated and understood), what it does (including the consideration of what is allowable in evangelistic efforts), and how it should proceed.

So much and so good as to intentions and a brief description of M/W history in its formative century. For the purposes of our discussion and to continue in the spirit of brevity, what emerged in the history of M/W as it spread worldwide (now in over 160 nations around the world) throughout the nineteenth and twentieth centuries was a powerful worldwide movement, divided in its opinion as to whether M/W was primarily an evangelistic outreach movement to the unsaved that resulted in churches whose job it was to be revival centers to keep the fervor going, or primarily a discipling machine of an organized church/denomination guided by that mission that also did evangelism with a multiplicity of options, including dialogue with other religions, about how to best accomplish the evangelistic task.

The first option is easily caricatured by explaining the National Holiness Association (1867–1997) and the several denominations and evangelistic associations that it spawned and cooperated with.

7. Abel Stevens, *History of the Religious Movement of the Eighteenth Century, Called Methodism, Considered in Its Different Denominational Forms, and Its Relations to British and American Protestantism* (Carlton & Porter; A. Heylin, 1858–1861) notes in several places where and how Wesley and his evangelists did their work.

Formed in camp meetings after the end of the American Civil War, what was originally intended to be a series of meetings inviting Christians into the depths of the sanctified life became a series of revival networks, churches, and schools that took it as their task to present barn-burning sermons in which hearers were invited to consider their only two options with the Almighty: Holiness or Hell? Short- and long-term meetings and short- and long-winded evangelists were converted in the fires of those revivals and continued to press the method and ethos in the churches, camp meetings, and street preaching revivals to the masses to make their case.

On the other hand, the second option for the M/W crowd quickly disabused itself of such notions in favor of ecclesial respectability, with calm Chatauqua-style outdoor summer services in which plans of discipleship mingled with the enjoyment of status through various worldly entertainments (e.g. quartet singers, golf outings, and wine tastings).[8] By the time of the founding of the United Methodist Church in 1968, such calm considerations included a manual on how to have easy, substantive, and rich conversations within the confines of polite American society[9] and outside the rarefied air of established Christianity in small-group settings where one shared the M/W experience with members of other religions.[10] Many churches, my own

8. For an account of this movement in the history of the Methodist Church, now the United Methodist Church, see Russell Richey, *Methodism in the American Forest* (Oxford University Press, 2017).

9. Robert Coleman, *The Master Plan of Evangelism* (Abingdon Press, 1963). Coleman taught evangelism at Asbury Theological Seminary, a Methodist school, for over three decades. The purpose of his book was to "explore the strategies that Jesus Christ used to mobilize and train disciples."

10. See, e.g., the work of E. Stanley Jones. Jones's seventy-year career as a missionary was spent traveling the world presenting the Gospel in small group, round-table discussions without the trappings of Western civilization, and listening and encouraging people of faith from non-Christian religions to share their faith stories. He was an inspiration to Franklin Roosevelt, Mahatma Ghandi, and Martin Luther King, Jr., was twice nominated for the Nobel Peace Prize, and was a frequent lecturer at Asbury Theological Seminary. His work established the E. Stanley Jones Foundation, headquartered in the United Methodist Church, which pays the salaries for professors of Evangelism at thirteen denominationally approved United Methodist Seminaries. The Foundation's website can be viewed at www.estanleyjonesfoundation.com.

Church of the Nazarene included, are a mixture of the two. However, one could clearly tell which side one's particular church had chosen. The sermons and the approaches to the conversion of non-Christians or the unchurched were obvious even to the outside observer.

Possibilities of Convergence for Ecumenical Consideration

Beginning with the work of Albert Outler (d. 1989, Methodist observer at Vatican II) and Frank Baker (d. 1999), a renaissance has emerged within the ranks of W/M self-examination in the form of a renewed interest in W/M theological studies.[11] Important books and essays have appeared in the last generation or so on the specific topic of "Evangelism in the Wesleyan Tradition," which easily fit into the category of "specialized studies" called for in Richard Heitzenrater's "John Wesley and the Historian's Task."[12] Among these are notable works from William Abraham (*The Logic of Evangelism*, 1989), Bishop Scott Jones of the Global Methodist Church ("Elements of Wesleyan Evangelism," presented to the Oxford Institute of Methodist Theological Studies, 2002), Laceye Warner ("Towards a Wesleyan Evangelism," *Methodist History*, 2002), James Logan (*Theology and Evangelism in the Wesleyan Heritage*, 1994), Chris Bounds ("Wesleyan Eschatological Implications for the Church's Engagement with Other Religions," Oxford Institute, 2013) and Jack Jackson, the current director of the E. Stanley Jones Foundation ("Decoupling Evangelism and Coercion: Early Methodism for Twenty-First Century Mission," *Wesleyan Theological Journal*, 2009, and *Offering Christ: John Wesley's Evangelistic Vision*, 2017).

11. The Wesleyan Theological Society (which I serve as Promotional Secretary), with over fifteen hundred members internationally, is the strongest proof of this. It has given a renewed voice to W/M studies and practically created the academic discipline of Methodist/Holiness Studies. The society celebrates its sixtieth anniversary in 2025. See Jason Vickers, Steven Hoskins, and Laura Dahl, eds., *The Wesleyan Theological Tradition: Past, Present, and Future* (Baylor University Press, forthcoming 2025), which offers the best representation of that scholarship in essays from its official publication, the *Wesleyan Theological Journal*.

12. Richard Heitzenrater, *Mirror and Memory: Reflections on Early Methodism* (Kingswood Books, 1989), 211–13.

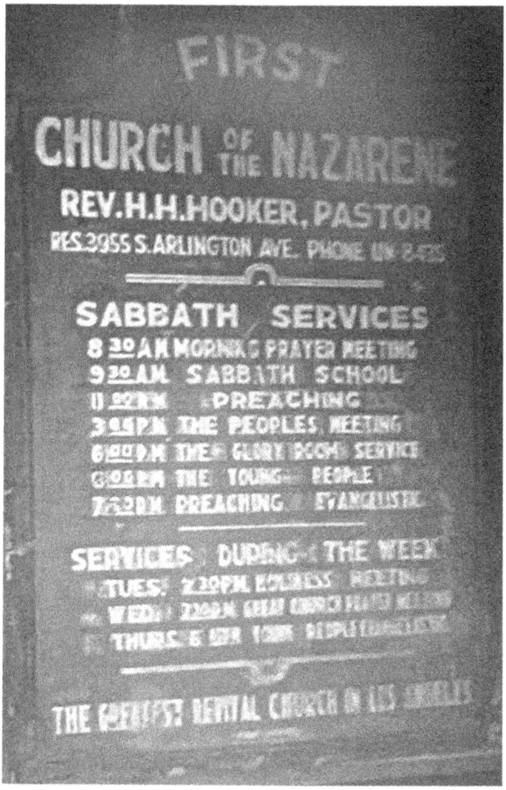

Indications of the side chosen from the history of the Church of the Nazarene

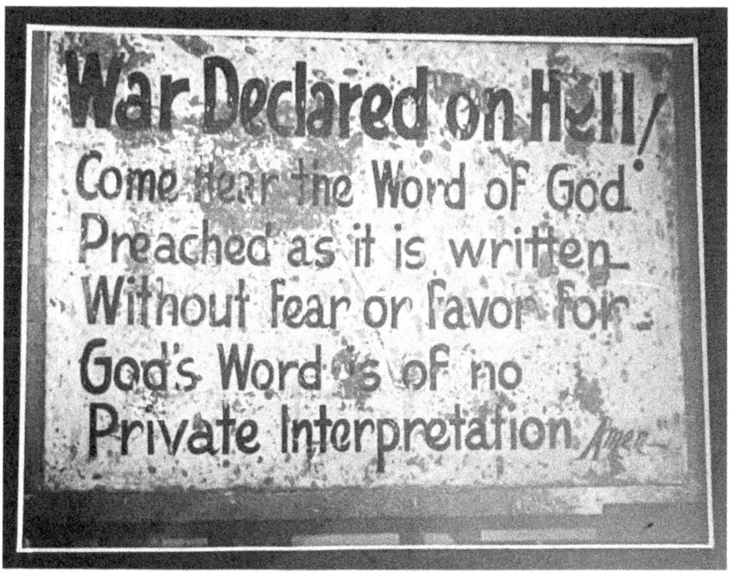

FIRST CHURCH OF THE NAZARENE
510 Woodland St. - Nashville, Tenn.
THE CHURCH WITH "A HEART INTEREST" IN HUMANITY
Office Hours: 8:00 A. M. to 4:00 P. M. - Phone 5-6226
Sunday School .... 9:30 A. M.
Morning Worship ...... 10:45 A. M.
Evangelistic Services .... 7:30 P. M.
Prayer Service Wednesday ...... 7:30 P. M.
EXODUS 20:15. THOU SHALT NOT TAKE THE FAN AWAY FROM THE CHURCH.
Opportunity is given to seek the Lord.
You could find no better Church Home.

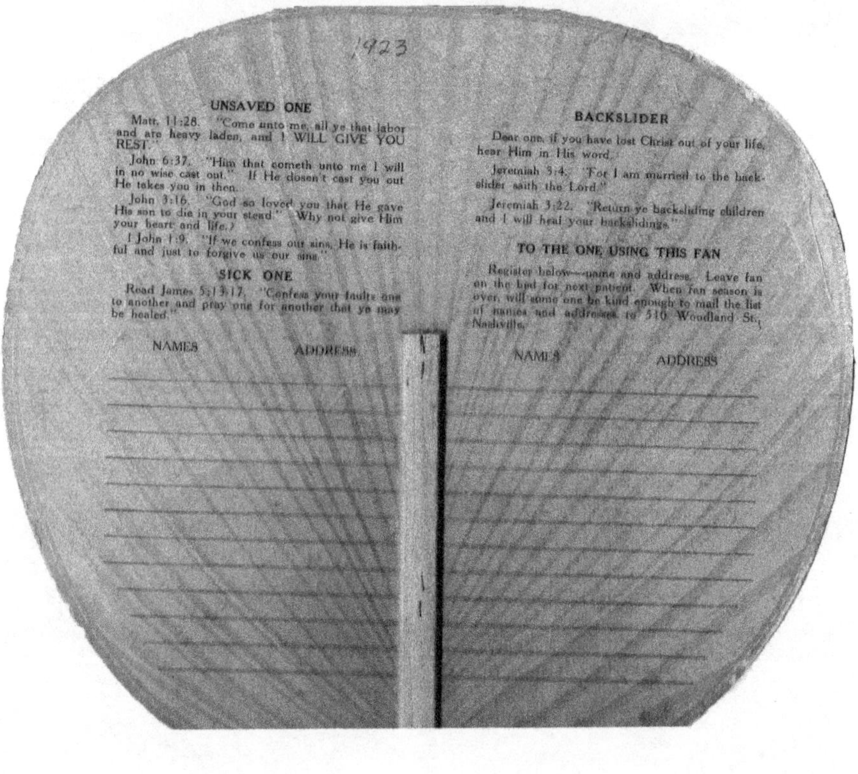
1923
UNSAVED ONE
Matt. 11:28. "Come unto me, all ye that labor and are heavy laden, and I WILL GIVE YOU REST."
John 6:37. "Him that cometh unto me I will in no wise cast out." If He dosen't cast you out He takes you in then.
John 3:16. "God so loved you that He gave His son to die in your stead." Why not give Him your heart and life.?
I John 1:9. "If we confess our sins, He is faithful and just to forgive us our sins."
SICK ONE
Read James 5:13-17. "Confess your faults one to another and pray one for another that ye may be healed."
NAMES
ADDRESS
BACKSLIDER
Dear one, if you have lost Christ out of your life, hear Him in His word.
Jeremiah 3:4. "For I am married to the backslider saith the Lord."
Jeremiah 3:22. "Return ye backsliding children and I will heal your backslidings."
TO THE ONE USING THIS FAN
Register below—name and address. Leave fan on the bed for next patient. When fan season is over, will some one be kind enough to mail the list of names and addresses to 510 Woodland St., Nashville.
NAMES
ADDRESS

What these works agree on presents a way beyond the conundrum of W/M self-understanding as noted above. They also offer some points for consideration in determining convergence in ecumenical dialogue in light of the distinctives of a renewed W/M understanding of the evangelistic task set before us today: that this dialogue is necessary first so that we might come to mutual understanding and share together in offering Christ to those that do not know him as Savior and Lord, and also so that we might move beyond any confusion caused by the evangelistic efforts of our various communions, some from within our own histories and some from the life we share as Christian churches together, as called for by Pope Benedict XVI in his ecumenical prayer service address to gathered Roman Catholics and Protestants at St. Joseph's Church, New York City, April 18, 2008.[13]

What the above writings on W/M evangelism agree on is that W/M evangelism demands the centrality of preaching in the activities of evangelism, the message of the Gospel presenting the story and claims of Christianity regarding the particular orthodoxy concerning Jesus Christ as the Second Person of the Holy Trinity and Savior and Lord of all humanity; the importance of the entirety of Christian experience through the pattern of awakening (prevenient grace), conversion (saving grace), and holiness or loving God with all of one's being (sanctifying grace); the adaptability of methods in furthering the evangelistic work of the Church; and the criterion of genuineness in evangelistic concern.[14] These together and individually are potential points of convergence for our dialogue.

Further, these W/M writings call for an understanding of evangelism that moves beyond solely considering the human means through which we present the Gospel, toward the idea that presenting the Gospel in evangelistic efforts operates under the direction of the Holy Spirit and is never coercive. As Billy Abraham noted, "The Gospel is not at our disposal to manipulate so that we can coax the modern

13. "Address of His Holiness Benedict XVI, Ecumenical Prayer Service," St. Joseph's Parish, New York, April 18, 2008, https://www.vatican.va/content/benedict-xvi/en/speeches/2008/april/documents/hf_ben-xvi_spe_20080418_incontro-ecumenico.html.

14. For an excellent summary of these see William Arnett, "The Wesleyan Conception of Evangelism," *The Asbury Seminarian* 11, no. 1 (1957): 35–43.

person into believing."[15] Instead current W/M thinking on evangelism calls for the recognition that it is the Holy Spirit who is the primary actor in eliciting any response to any evangelist's proclamation, no matter the method employed. The Methodist ethicist Brad Kallenberg states the thinking succinctly: "The human task is to dialogue with people about the story of God in Christ and let the Spirit reveal the dissonance between the hearer's life and the life of faith." This theological underpinning of every evangelistic effort deserves consideration in our dialogue. We need to find a way to remove from our words and from our acceptable methods even the slightest hint of coercion or manipulation, particularly as we evangelize those from other religious faiths. It is the hand of God that leads those who hear and obey as the Spirit leads in evangelism. Any human efforts in evangelism are really a reflection of the Holy Spirit's work. This understanding was true of Wesley, who said, "I preached to a much larger crowd.... Four or five could not bear it and went away. Some (others) would have gone away but could not; for the hand of the Lord pressed them to earth."[16] This is echoed among contemporary W/M thinkers. Albert Outler: "Evangelism is the joint operation of the Spirit and the evangelist at every step of the way—the Spirit moving in those who speak and those who hear."[17] From the current E. Stanley Jones Professor of Evangelism at Boston University: "Christian evangelism ... is premised wholly upon the faithfulness of the Spirit's witness in our lives rather than our own ability to calculate and predict how our obedience might translate into effectiveness."[18]

Another potential point of convergence may be found in a rethinking of the evangelistic task as viewed through John Wesley's patterned understanding of God's grace at work in the life of every

15. William Abraham, *The Logic of Evangelism* (Eerdmans, 1989), 205.

16. John Wesley, "Journal entry 4 July 1750," quoted in Jack Jackson, "Decoupling Evangelism and Coercion: Early Methodism for Twenty-First Century Mission," *Wesleyan Theological Journal* 47 (2009): 45–58.

17. Albert Outler, "Theory and Practice in Christian Evangelism: A Theologian's Comments," in *The Albert Outler Library*, vol. 6, *Evangelism*, ed. William Abraham (Bristol House, 1988), 21.

18. Bryan Stone, *Evangelism after Christendom: The Theology and Practice of Christian Witness* (Brazos, 2007), 12.

creature from birth to death. Jack Jackson offers a way of understanding evangelism through the W/M lens that calls for a move away from either a "conversion only" or a "discipleship only" aim or design in evangelism, to one more holistic, based on a threefold telos of the evangelistic encounter using Wesley's understanding of the states of grace (prevenient, saving, sanctifying). Jackson offers an understanding of human response to the Gospel, primarily in Christian proclamation of the Gospel through 1) awakening, 2) repentance and faith leading to conversion, and 3) the love of God leading people to sanctification.[19] This use of W/M applied theology would allow for the consideration of legitimate and acceptable evangelistic methods among us, even in our differences, by understanding that the three hoped-for ends of evangelism would allow for a more holistic understanding of evangelism and avoid a "conversion only" or "discipleship only" approach. Jackson's offering means presenting the Gospel in a way that facilitates spiritual development in and through any efforts at evangelizing anyone who does not yet know Christ as Savior.

Two other points which may emerge in ecumenical discussion aimed at finding common ground for convergence are also worth consideration. The first is the similarity between the W/M doctrine of prevenient grace and the Catholic understanding of grace and salvation as suggested by Colin Williams.[20] W/M theologian Randy Maddox notes in commenting on Williams's suggestion that W/M theology shares with Catholic doctrine that "prevenient grace is that gracious provision of God to all humankind which restores them to such a condition that they can hear, respond to, and be held accountable for God's offer of salvation in Christ."[21] This is likened to the Catholic doctrine of grace and salvation by noting that such "could only be as a result of a supernatural gift of God's grace."[22]

A second point of consideration for convergence comes from a W/M understanding following the lead of John Wesley, who believed

19. Jack Jackson, "Decoupling Evangelism and Coercion," 46.

20. Colin Williams, *John Wesley's Theology Today* (Abingdon Press, 1960), 46.

21. Randy Maddox, "Karl Rahner's Supernatural Existential: A Wesleyan Perspective," *Evangelical Journal* 5 (1987): 3–14, at 8.

22. Maddox, "Karl Rahner's Supernatural Existential," 8.

that all people will be judged (finally) by the grace afforded them, and that there may be some optimism about seeing people from other religions in eternity.[23] This in no way cancels the gravity of original sin, the brokenness of the moral image, nor the burden of cooperation with divine grace. It does posit that there is a greater potential of a "renewing power for the life of obedience which enables the manifestation of the personal and social character of the Christian hope of the eschaton in deeper and fuller ways on earth in the lives of those in other religions."[24] A similar idea is offered in the *Catechism of the Catholic Church* in the recognition that other religions, particularly monotheistic ones, have elements of truth and salvation in them.[25] This, too, may point toward a shared understanding and convergence among us.

Ecumenical Hopes for Evangelism Calmly Considered

There is certainly more that could be considered in our discussions as we ponder evangelism and our efforts in the work, that hopeful and happy task of offering Christ to a world in such desperate need of his grace and salvation. Had we but world enough and time, we could discuss acceptable methods among us and what to do with the state of Christian evangelistic proclamation in our pulpits in this age so consumed with the need for acceptance and church growth. Somewhere in our considerations for convergence we should discuss the W/M propensities for revival meetings, field preaching (considered by John Wesley as something so vile it must be submitted to, and yet it was the key to the Evangelical Revival of the eighteenth century led by the Methodist Societies), and our shared history of preaching the Gospel in street meetings, jail ministry, railroad stations, and radio

23. See Chris Bounds, "Wesleyan Eschatological Implications for the Church's Engagement with Other Religions," The Thirteenth Oxford Institute of Methodist Theological Studies (2013), 13, at https://oxford-institute.org/wp-content/uploads/2013/09/2013-5-bounds.pdf.

24. Randy Maddox, "Wesley and The Question of Truth or Salvation in Other Religions," *Wesleyan Theological Journal* 27, nos. 1–2 (2012): 7–29, at 18.

25. *Catechism of the Catholic Church*, 2nd ed. (Doubleday, 1995), §819, §837.

and television programs.[26] As we go, perhaps we also need to discuss what my people too politely refer to as "the need of the world in our day," when talking about the times in which we live, something that the great Catholic prophet-philosopher Alisdair MacIntyre reminds us of at the end of his *After Virtue*—the dark ages are already upon us.[27] MacIntyre's full quote reads:

> If my account of our moral condition is correct, we ought also to conclude that for some time now we too have reached that turning point. What matters at this stage is the construction of local forms of community within which civility and the intellectual and moral life can be sustained through the new dark ages which are already upon us.[28]

The truth of that must be somewhere, it seems to me, in our ecumenical considerations. Considering such would require that we not only contemplate what pass as acceptable methods of evangelism, but that we question our character, as well.

As to the W/M self-examination, hopefully there is the offer of a calm consideration of a better understanding of evangelism than the either-or dichotomy that so often plagues us, either "conversion only" or "discipleship only," often with well-intentioned hope of some results and success. We need to state our utter dependence upon God's grace and the workings of the Holy Spirit. We need to remind those to whom we offer Christ through evangelism of the warning that there is a need to "flee from the wrath that is to come," and we need to remind ourselves that we have "nothing to do but save souls" (even the souls of those already converted and that to the uttermost). For when W/M is "true to its heritage, Methodist evangelism has never been a quick fix . . . (but) has always been committed to a long obedience in the same direction. To be born again is not the end, but the beginning, the end is to be Christ-like. . . . Methodism is in the business of producing saints . . . who will settle for nothing less

26. Jeff Marlett, *Saving The Heartland: Catholic Missionaries in Rural America, 1920–1960* (Northern Illinois Press, 2002).

27. Alisdair MacIntyre, *After Virtue* (University of Notre Dame Press, 1981), 263.

28. MacIntyre, *After Virtue*, 263.

than a truly holy life."[29] That is the hope of any calm consideration of evangelism in ecumenical discussions and we must find ways to recognize that desire in one another. May such high and lofty ideals lead us as we pursue our points of convergence on evangelism and a better future together.

29. J. Ellsworth Kalas, "Evangelistic Ministry," *The Asbury Herald* (2007): 5.

3.3 The Evangelization of Culture: Catholic Magisterial Teaching and Assessment

Daniel A. Keating

Introduction

OUR TOPIC, EVANGELIZATION AND CULTURE, is intended to draw out the principles and practices by which we engage our culture (and all cultures) as we set out to do mission. Mission in the past generation or two has, in a sense, been dominated by an attention to the culture we live in, seeking the most effective ways to evangelize people in that culture, and at the same time, to wrestle with the question of what to invest—and what to expect—in the Christian transformation of the culture we are engaged with and living in. The Church Growth Movement is one example of this effort in the Protestant world, as is the more recent "Missional Church" movement. Sociology of religion has come to occupy an important place among those doing mission (e.g., the Pew surveys of religion and the various studies on religion and youth produced by Christian Smith), and we more and more narrowly characterize and categorize succeeding generations of people, with the aim of finding more effective ways to reach them, call them, and help them become engaged in the mission of the Gospel.

In this paper I trace the growing attention to "culture" in Catholic sources (largely magisterial teaching), and specifically to the intersection of culture and evangelization, with the goal of gaining an understanding of what is *meant* by "the evangelization of culture" or "evangelizing the culture." To conclude, I will offer my own observations and assessments about the task of evangelizing the culture today.

Historical and Ecclesial Context

Focused and sustained attention to the concept of "culture" in official Catholic writings appears first in the Vatican II Constitution on the Church in the Modern World, *Gaudium et spes*.[1] But before turning our attention to this document, I believe it is helpful to recognize that the idea of "culture," and specifically of preserving or recovering a "Christian culture," had already become a burning issue in the interwar period, beginning in the early 1930s and continuing as a significant issue through the 1960s. Among the more well-known figures who wrote specifically and in depth about the question of culture are the Catholic historian Christopher Dawson (e.g. *The Historic Reality of Christian Culture*, 1960), the Anglican poet and apologist T. S. Eliot (*Christianity and Culture: The Idea of a Christian Society*, 1940, and *Notes Toward the Definition of Culture*, 1949), the Reformed Protestant scholar H. Richard Niebuhr (*Christ and Culture*, 1951), the Catholic philosopher Jacques Maritain ("Religion and Culture," 1930; *Integral Humanism*, 1934), and the Catholic theologian Romano Guardini (*The End of the Modern World*, 1940). These authors (along with many others) characterized the crisis of the modern world specifically in terms of a crisis of *culture*, in the face of a new age emerging that was intentionally anti-Christian in its cultural features. Though their respective understandings of Christian culture and their proposed ideas for renewing Christian culture differed one from another, they shared a common concern and (often) recognized in each other allies in the effort to re-evangelize the world of their day. The point is to recognize that the idea of "culture" and its importance did not appear out of the blue in the 1960s, but had a wide, public, and ecumenical airing from leading Catholic and Protestant intellectuals in the years leading up to the Council.

1. Pope Pius XII (1939–1958), in his many encyclicals, refers to "culture" on numerous occasions in the general sense of the way of life of peoples and civilizations but does not give specific attention to the notion of culture. The one exception is found in his encyclical on mission (*Evangelii praecones*, 1951, §§58–62), in which Pius offers basic principles for what we call today the process of "inculturation."

Catholic Magisterial Teaching

GAUDIUM ET SPES (DEC. 7, 1965)

This constitution, one of the final documents promulgated at Vatican II, presents an account of the role of the Church in the modern world, and describes opportunities for dialogue with the wider society in the areas of human dignity, marriage and family, culture, economic and social life, politics, and peace among nations. Its teaching on "culture" with attention especially to evangelization can be summed up in a few headings.

First, the term "culture" is defined in its general sense to indicate "everything whereby man develops and perfects his many bodily and spiritual qualities," and this includes knowledge, labor, social life, customs, and institutions (*GS*, §53).[2] This is a general definition of culture, drawn from sociology and similar to the understandings of culture seen in the writings that preceded the Council.

Second, the Council Fathers note the vast change in modern life whereby technology and communication have united the world as never before, in a way tending toward "a more universal form of human culture" (*GS*, §54). They see in this new reality both challenges and opportunities. All this leads to a climate of great hope but also of profound anxiety. Will this more unified technological culture lead to the loss of tradition, of the qualities of the particular peoples, and even to a humanism that is cut off from God? (*GS*, §56).

Third, the Church lives in the midst of human cultures and makes use of them, each in its own way, to communicate the Gospel, but at the same time the Church is not bound to one particular culture: "Faithful to her own tradition and at the same time conscious of her universal mission, she can enter into communion with the various civilizations, to their enrichment and the enrichment of the Church herself" (*GS*, §58).[3] The Council Fathers offer this strikingly positive statement of the role of the Gospel in human culture:

2. Quotations from *Gaudium et spes* (December 7, 1965), 513–624 in *The Sixteen Documents of Vatican II* (Daughters of St. Paul, n. d.).

3. The terms "culture" and "civilization" were commonly used synonymously in the pre- and postwar writings on culture. At times, "civilization" was reckoned as human "culture" that had reached a high level of sophistication and complexity.

> The Gospel of Christ constantly renews the life and culture of fallen man, it combats and removes the errors and evils resulting from the permanent allurement of sin. It never ceases to purify and elevate the morality of peoples. By riches coming from above, it makes fruitful, as it were from within, the spiritual qualities and traditions of every people of every age. It strengthens, perfects and restores them in Christ. (*GS*, §58)

Fourth, the Council Fathers maintain that human culture has its own domain and legitimate autonomy "as long, of course, as it preserves the rights of the individual and the community, whether particular or universal" (*GS*, §59). At the same time, the Church has much to offer human culture in the task of leading it to acknowledge the full dignity of the human race.

Finally, the constitution concludes by noting the conflict that can occur between Christian faith and human cultures. The Fathers put the emphasis on *working with the culture* to attempt to bring Christian doctrine and morality into some integration with the ways of the given cultures: "May the faithful, therefore, live in very close union with the other men of their time and may they strive to understand perfectly their way of thinking and judging, as expressed in their culture" (*GS*, §62). While the Council Fathers acknowledge throughout *Gaudium et spes* both the dangers at work in contemporary culture, the fallen state of the human race, and the need for the Gospel to permeate all aspects of culture, the critique of contemporary culture is muted. The emphasis is on the opportunities for dialogue, collaboration, and the potential transformation of the culture.

POPE PAUL VI AND *EVANGELII NUNTIANDI* (DEC. 8, 1975)

Ten years later, in an encyclical aimed at recentering the Catholic Church on mission, Paul VI recalls the core teaching of *Gaudium et spes* and sharpens the need for a deep evangelization of culture:

> All this could be expressed in the following words: what matters is to evangelize man's culture and cultures (not in a purely decorative way, as it were, by applying a thin veneer, but in a vital way, in depth and right to their very roots), in the wide and rich sense which these terms have in *Gaudium et Spes*, always taking the person as one's

> starting-point and always coming back to the relationships of people among themselves and with God. (*EN*, §20)[4]

Pope Paul clarifies the distinction between the Gospel and culture but maintains that the Gospel has the capability of permeating every aspect of culture:

> The Gospel, and therefore evangelization, are certainly not identical with culture, and they are independent in regard to all cultures. . . . Though independent of cultures, the Gospel and evangelization are not necessarily incompatible with them; rather they are capable of permeating them all without becoming subject to any one of them. (*EN*, §20)

He concludes with this short statement on the Gospel and culture: "Therefore every effort must be made to ensure a full evangelization of culture, or more correctly of cultures. They have to be regenerated by an encounter with the Gospel. But this encounter will not take place if the Gospel is not proclaimed" (*EN*, 20). Pope Paul did not elaborate on the interaction of evangelization and culture, but this short contribution gave to the Catholic Church the phrase "evangelization of culture(s)." It was to become something of a battle cry in the mouth of Pope John Paul II.

THE LONG PONTIFICATE OF POPE JOHN PAUL II

Pope John Paul II made the evangelization of culture one of his watchwords. In numerous addresses throughout his long pontificate, he refers variously to "a new evangelization of culture,"[5] to the renewal of the "dialogue between faith and culture,"[6] to a "commitment to permeate today's culture with the vital sap of faith,"[7] and to

4. Quotations from Pope Paul VI, *On Evangelization in the Modern World: Evangelii nuntiandi* (December 8, 1975) (United States Catholic Conference, 1976).

5. John Paul II, "Appeal to Presidents of the Episcopal Conferences of Europe" (January 2, 1986), in *Compendium on the New Evangelization: Texts of the Pontifical and Conciliar Magisterium, 1939–2012*, Pontifical Council for the Promotion of the New Evangelization (United States Conference of Catholic Bishops, 2015), §232, p. 146.

6. John Paul II, Homily (May 11, 1986), *Compendium*, §252, p. 155.

7. John Paul II, "Address to the Bishops of Tuscany" (June 13, 1986), *Compendium*, §255, p. 157.

"a new evangelization through an authentic apostolate of culture."[8] He states that "the evangelization of cultures represents the deepest and most comprehensive way to evangelize a society,"[9] and that "rooting the Gospel in the bosom of cultures is a necessity of missionary activity."[10] Building explicitly on Paul VI's call, John Paul links the "new evangelization" with the "evangelization of culture": "A central aspect of the 'new evangelization' to which I have called the entire Church is the evangelization of culture."[11] John Paul was convinced that only a penetration and permeation of human culture with the Gospel—in every sphere—will enable the Gospel to bear fruit and reach people of today: "This discernment [of cultural trends] is a matter of some urgency if we are to be better able to understand present mentalities, to discover therein the thirst for truth and love which only Jesus can fully satisfy."[12]

Redemptoris missio

In his missionary encyclical, *Redemptoris missio* (December 7, 1990), published on the twenty-fifth anniversary of *Gaudium et spes*, John Paul explains more fully what he intends by the evangelization of culture. He emphasizes the respect that the Church grants to all cultures and invites all peoples to respond to the Gospel, "while keeping their own culture and traditions, provided that these are not contrary to the Gospel" (*RM*, §24). Missionaries must immerse themselves in the cultural milieu in which they are working. This does not mean denying one's own cultural identity, "but of understanding, appreciating, fostering and evangelizing the culture of the environment in which they are working" (*RM*, §53). He underlines with special emphasis the

8. John Paul II, "Address to the Pontifical Council for Culture" (January 13, 1989), *Compendium*, §294, p. 184.

9. John Paul II, "Address to the Latin American Episcopal Conference" (October 12, 1992), *Compendium*, §514, p. 341.

10. John Paul II, "Address to the Pontifical Council for Culture" (January 10, 1992), *Compendium*, §397, p. 258.

11. John Paul II, "Address to the Bishops of Scandinavia" (April 5, 2003), *Compendium*, §1172, p. 830.

12. John Paul II, "Address to the Pontifical Council for Culture" (January 13, 1989), *Compendium*, §294, p. 184.

need to enter into contemporary culture more deeply through modern communications media:

> Since the very evangelization of modern culture depends to a great extent on the influence of the media, it is not enough to use the media simply to spread the Christian message and the Church's authentic teaching. It is also necessary to integrate that message into the "new culture" created by modern communications. (*RM*, §37)

At the same time, John Paul recognizes that, in this process, it is the Gospel that is the measure of culture: "The new evangelization does not consist in . . . a trimming away from the Gospel everything that seems difficult for the contemporary mindset to accept. Culture is not the measure of the Gospel; rather Jesus Christ is the measure of culture and of every human activity."[13]

The Pontifical Council for Culture

To serve this goal, John Paul established the Pontifical Council for Culture[14] and gave it this assignment: "Culture is of man, by man, and for man. The vocation of the PCC, your vocation, at the turn of this century and millennium, is that of raising up a new culture of love and hope inspired by the truth that makes us free in Jesus Christ."[15]

To respond to this mandate, the Pontifical Council composed an impressive study entitled *Towards a Pastoral Approach to Culture* (*TPAC*, May 23, 1999). Here I will highlight several positions on the evangelization of culture that the document outlines. First, in the face of a potential radical relativization of culture, the Council, citing John Paul's own *Veritatis splendor* (1993, §53) proposes that

> the very progress of cultures demonstrates that there is something in man which transcends those cultures. This "something" is precisely human nature: this nature is itself the measure of culture and the

13. John Paul II, "Address to the Latin American Episcopal Conference" (October 12, 1992), *Compendium*, §507, p. 337.

14. He established it in May 1992, and it was re-established by Pope Francis in June 2022 as the Dicastery for Culture and Education.

15. John Paul II, "Address to the Pontifical Council for Culture" (January 10, 1992), *Compendium*, §397, p. 258.

> condition of ensuring that man does not become prisoner of any of his cultures, but asserts his personal dignity by living in accordance with the profound truth of his being. (*TPAC*, 2)

In other words, though cultures vary a great deal, there is a fundamental unity between them grounded in human nature as created and redeemed by God.

Second, the PCC document speaks frankly about the problem of sin, idolatry, and evil in cultures that need purification and exorcism by the Gospel:

> Marked as they are by the very tensions aimed at achieving their fulfilment and the human dynamics of their history, cultures share also in sin and, by this very fact, require the necessary discernment of Christians. (*TPAC*, 2)

> By proposing the Good News, the Church denounces the presence of sin in cultures and delivers them of it. She stigmatizes the counter-values and exorcises them. She thus provides a critical element to cultures. (*TPAC*, 5)

This is a welcome addition to the often overly positive evaluation of human culture that appears in some of the magisterial documents.

Third, though recognizing that all cultures are capable of penetration by the Gospel, and that no human culture can claim a monopoly on the Gospel, the Council document helpfully recognizes in the people of Israel a privileged culture whose life, history, and practices have been enshrined in the Scriptures: "The culture of the Bible has a unique place. It is the culture of the people of God at the heart of which he became incarnate" (*TPAC*, 3). This statement reflects the practice of the Church over the centuries of looking to the teaching and pattern of the Old Testament, without being literalistic, as a guide for how life in the Church can function.

Fourth, referencing *Evangelii nuntiandi* (§20), the document eschews a superficial enculturation or engagement with culture in favor of a deep penetration, "not in a purely decorative way, as it were, by applying a thin veneer, but in a vital way, in depth and right to their very roots" (*TPAC*, 4). This means not just a wider spread of the

Gospel, but "affecting and as it were upsetting, through the power of the Gospel, mankind's criteria of judgment, determining values, points of interest, lines of thought, sources of inspiration and models of life, which are in contrast with the Word of God and the plan of salvation" (*TPAC*, 4). Again, the emphasis on a deep and upsetting penetration of human culture is a welcome marker of what is at stake and how challenging it may be to reach this level of penetration.

Fifth, the Council study offers a useful analysis of how the evangelization of culture and the acculturation of the Gospel go hand in hand and are two sides of one coin:

> The evangelization of cultures and the inculturation of the Gospel go hand in hand, in a reciprocal relationship which presupposes constant discernment in the light of the Gospel, to facilitate the identification of values and counter-values in a given culture, so as to build on the former and vigorously combat the latter. . . . The inculturation of faith and the evangelization of culture go together as an inseparable pair, in which there is no hint of syncretism: this is the genuine meaning of inculturation. (*TPAC*, 5)

Just as the Gospel and the way of life embedded within it bring about a genuine transformation of human culture, so at the same time, the Gospel and its way of life are enabled to take on new cultural forms and expressions. The example of popular piety is offered as an example of this reciprocal process: "Popular piety is one of the best examples of genuine inculturation of faith, because it is a harmonious blend of faith and liturgy, feelings and art, and the recognition of our identity in local traditions" (*TPAC*, 28).

Finally, the PCC study points toward a cultural reality that makes our present situation in certain ways abnormal. By the use of the phrases "a coherent culture" and "a truly human culture" (*TPAC*, 11), the document recognizes that not all cultures are created equal, and that discernment is required for recognizing cultural elements that are capable of transformation by the Gospel.

All in all, *Towards a Pastoral Approach to Culture*, under the sponsorship of John Paul II, offers an illuminating and balanced perspective on the evangelization of culture called for by the Polish pope.

Bishop Robert Barron

This is perhaps the most appropriate place to include a note on the ministry of Bishop Robert Barron. Through his "Word on Fire Ministries," Barron has become perhaps the leading Catholic exponent in the United States for the evangelization of culture. As he explains this ministry, it originated from a conversation between Pope John Paul II and Cardinal George (the archbishop of Chicago) in the late 1990s. The pope asked the cardinal, "What are you doing to evangelize the culture?" Cardinal George did not know how to respond. So on returning to Chicago he contacted Fr. Barron and told him that he wanted him to evangelize the culture. And when Fr. Barron asked the cardinal what that meant, he said that they would figure that out together.[16]

For Barron, culture is "that whole array (conjuries) of practices, beliefs, convictions, and institutions by which a people finds and expresses its collective identity." To evangelize the culture is "to declare to the representatives and the practitioners of the various cultural forms that Jesus Christ is Lord, and that their work and efforts belong to Jesus and find their surest fulfillment in him."[17] Consistent with the PCC document, *Towards a Pastoral Approach to Culture*, Barron has made the transcendentals of truth, beauty, and goodness the primary means to dialogue with the culture and to function as a bridge between cultural values and the faith of the Church.

POPE BENEDICT XVI

Pope Benedict XVI spoke less frequently than his predecessor about the evangelization of culture, though he clearly recognizes the need and favors the use the phrase "the permeation of culture" by the Gospel. When addressing the Mexican bishops in the first year of his pontificate, he said: "As a missionary Church, we are all called to understand the challenges that our postmodern culture poses to the

16. Bishop Robert Barron, "To Evangelize the Culture," Salt and Light Media, October 18, 2011, YouTube video, https://www.youtube.com/watch?v=5eomgTkcpxl.

17. Barron, "To Evangelize the Culture." See also his lecture, "Evangelizing the Culture," Elmhurst University, February 9, 2012, YouTube video, https://www.youtube.com/watch?v=tlps1Svr2Fo.

new evangelization of the Continent. The Church's dialogue with the culture of our time is vital, to the Church herself and to the world."[18] Benedict counselled that "the message of salvation must be proclaimed in its integrity, so that it can succeed in permeating the roots of culture,"[19] and summed up the missionary calling of the Church today as "in a word, the entire culture of contemporary man must be permeated with the Gospel."[20]

POPE FRANCIS, *EVANGELII GAUDIUM* (NOV. 24, 2013)

To conclude this survey of magisterial teaching on the relationship between evangelization and culture, I will review what Pope Francis says about the evangelization of culture in his apostolic exhortation *Evangelii gaudium*.[21] He begins, interestingly, by speaking about the value of an "evangelized (popular) culture" in order to evangelize "contemporary secularism" (*EG*, §68). More than the sum of individual believers, an evangelized culture has for Pope Francis the resources needed to be effective when confronted by an opposing culture.

Stating that "it is imperative to evangelize cultures in order to inculturate the Gospel," and that it is important to understand "evangelization as inculturation" (*EG*, §69, §122), Francis relies on citations of previous magisterial teaching (Vatican II, John Paul II), from which he quotes extensively, to outline the importance of the evangelization of culture. Here is Francis's own description of culture:

> The concept of culture is valuable for grasping the various expressions of the Christian life present in God's people. It has to do with the lifestyle of a given society, the specific way in which its members relate to one another, to other creatures and to God. Understood in this way, culture embraces the totality of a people's life. . . . Grace

18. Benedict XVI, "Address to Mexican Bishops" (September 15, 2005), *Compendium*, §1215, p. 885.

19. Benedict XVI, "Address to the Plenary Assembly of the Pontifical Commission for Latin America" (January 20, 2007), *Compendium*, §1227, p. 896.

20. Benedict XVI, "Address to Teachers and Students of the Roman Ecclesiastical Universities" (October 27, 2007), *Compendium*, §1241, p. 914.

21. Quotations from Pope Francis, *The Joy of the Gospel: Evangelii gaudium* (November 24, 2013) (United States Conference of Catholic Bishops, 2013).

> supposes culture, and God's gift becomes flesh in the culture of those who receive it. (*EG*, §115)

At this point, Francis rehearses one of his favorite themes, that the Spirit of God who brings unity also at the same time produces diversity, and so "when properly understood, cultural diversity is not a threat to Church unity" (*EG*, §117). This brings him full circle to his original thesis, that both Catholic cultures and those cultures in which the faith is relatively new each need to inculturate the Gospel, in order to be an effective witness. He closes with a special appeal to theologians to be in dialogue with the cultures of the day in order to contribute actively to the work of evangelization: "I call on theologians to carry out this service as part of the Church's saving mission. In doing so, however, they must always remember that the Church and theology exist to evangelize, and not be content with a desk-bound theology" (*EG*, §133).

Reflections on the Evangelization of Culture

In closing, I would like to offer my own overall conclusion on the Catholic Church's teaching on evangelization and culture (and the evangelization of culture), and offer three perspectives for carrying out this task today.

My overall conclusion is that what the Catholic Church identifies as the "evangelization of culture," signaled by Pius XII as far back as 1951 and developed successively from Vatican II up to today, is at its core a thoughtful and sophisticated description of what the Church has been doing since its inception. One could argue that the issue of Jew and Gentile in the body of Christ, formally debated at the Council of Jerusalem in Acts 15, was in part a question of how the "culture" of the Jewish people should (and should not) remain part of the wider culture of the Church of the nations. Certainly, the effort of the first and second centuries in the early Church was an intensive form of "inculturation" in the Greco-Roman world, as the remarkable statement in the Letter to Diognetus (chaps. 5–6) reveals. The long engagement with Hellenistic thought and the gradual and (I believe) largely successful transformation of Hellenistic thought in the service of the Gospel also witnesses to this patient, demanding task of inculturation. The growth and development of the various liturgies in the Church, each sharing a common core but manifesting the genius of the national cultures, is evidence of the inculturation of the prayer of the Church.[22] The gradual evangelization of the tribes and peoples of Europe is perhaps the outstanding example of the evangelization of culture, yielding in the High Middle Ages what many consider the most thorough penetration of culture by the Gospel. And the missions to the Far East (India, China, Japan) and to the native peoples of the Americas give evidence of both the evangelization of culture and the inculturation of the Gospel. John Paul himself recognizes this pattern of evangelization and inculturation that goes back to the time of the first disciples:

> From the time the Gospel was first preached, the Church has known the process of encounter and engagement with cultures. Christ's mandate to his disciples to go out everywhere, "even to the ends of the earth" (Acts 1:8), in order to pass on the truth which he had revealed, led the Christian community to recognize from the first the universality of its message and the difficulties created by cultural differences.[23]

By saying this, I do not mean to simplify this long and varied history of the engagement of the Gospel with culture (which of course is always the engagement of Christian *people* with the *people* of various cultures), or to claim that this process of evangelization is simple and unvaried. On the contrary, each age is required to make use of its spiritual intelligence to perceive the ways and means of making the Gospel known and lived.

22. The *Catechism of the Catholic Church* (§1202) acknowledges this cultural variety in the liturgies of the Church: "The diverse liturgical traditions have arisen by very reason of the Church's mission. Churches of the same geographical and cultural area came to celebrate the mystery of Christ through particular expressions characterized by the culture."

23. John Paul II, *Fides et ratio* (September 14, 1998) (United States Council of Catholic Bishops, 1998), §70.

Further, I agree with those who claim that we are (and have been) living in a largely post-Christian age that is closer to the early centuries of the Church than to those periods in which a form of Christendom had been established.[24] At the same time—as also many have observed—our age is distinct from the early centuries because we are seeking to evangelize a culture that has been (and still is) actively throwing off its Christian past. This gives our task of evangelizing the culture, and evangelizing within the culture, special challenges. Here I would like to offer three perspectives on these special challenges of our time as we seek to evangelize the world we live in.

First, we need to reckon with the anti-Christian quality of the increasingly global culture just referred to. This is not just another human culture that we are seeking to evangelize; it is deeply shaped in important ways by the rejection the Gospel and the way of life entailed by the Gospel. Christopher Dawson made mention of this in the 1950s:

> Unless there is a revival or restoration of Christian culture—of the social life of the Christian community—modern civilization will become secularist in a more positive and aggressive way than it is today. And in a Godless civilization of this kind, it will be far more difficult for the individual Christian to exist and practice his religion than it has ever been before.[25]

In his study of human cultures through the ages (*The End of the Modern World*), Romano Guardini talked about the coming age as one in which there will be "the not-human man and the not-natural nature," and adds to this the coming reality of "a non-cultural culture," the contours of which he finds difficult to predict.[26] More recently, Tracey Rowland has identified the challenges posed by a "culture of death" that has set itself against the Christian Gospel: "The contemporary culture of death, as Pope Saint John Paul II called

24. See James Shea, *From Christendom to Apostolic Mission: Pastoral Strategies for an Apostolic Age* (University of Mary Press, 2020).

25. Christopher Dawson, *The Historic Reality of Christian Culture: A Way to the Renewal of Human Life* (Harper & Row, 1960), 41–42.

26. Romano Guardini, *The End of the Modern World* (ISI Books, 2001), 73, 88.

it . . . is not a culture groping its way towards a receptivity to divine revelation, but rather, a culture in rebellion against Christian beliefs and the very ideal of sanctity."[27]

All three writers are pointing to the reality of a coming anti-Christian and anti-human culture that we have seen sprout and grow around us at a fearful pace. In the face of this, the cultural optimism that is found in certain magisterial documents is difficult to sustain. We need to distinguish the positive prospects for evangelizing human culture from what can be salvaged and redeemed within a culture that is shaped specifically to oppose the teachings of Christ and the Church. This will require deep discernment to see what in our present evolving culture is redeemable or transformable, and what is inherently death-dealing (what John Paul II called "the culture of death").[28]

Second, I believe that acculturation is most effective, not mainly through analyzing and theorizing about a given culture and its possibilities (though this has an important role), but primarily by going about the work of evangelization on the ground and discovering by experience what in that culture can be maintained, what can be transformed, and what needs to be opposed. In other words, acculturation occurs primarily through the labors of evangelists who thoughtfully seek to evangelize a given culture (or subculture), and who then reflect on what is working well, what is effective, and what is bearing fruit (or not).

Third, I believe we need to recapture the wisdom and strategy of the early Church as we seek to evangelize the current culture, and this means building up genuine Christian community in which

27. Tracey Rowland, "Vatican II, John Paul II, and Postconciliar Theology," 245–62 in David Vincent Meconi and Carl E. Olsen, eds., *Called to be Children of God: The Catholic Theology of Human Deification* (Ignatius Press, 2016), 261.

28. For John Paul's teaching on "the culture of death," see *Evangelium vitae* (March 25, 1995). Notably, Christopher Dawson differed from Jacques Maritain precisely on the grounds of what he considered Maritain's unwarranted optimism. According to Jonathan Reyes, "Dawson's disagreements with Maritain were not theological or sociological, but practical. He believed that Maritain's assessment of the modern world was too optimistic and, therefore, that his prescriptions for the Church were not only flawed, but also dangerous." Jonathan Reyes, "Christopher Dawson and the Renewal of Christian Culture," PhD dissertation (University of Notre Dame, 2000), 237.

Christian culture can grow and thrive. In short, if we fail to build up and sustain genuine Christian community and culture, then we have no defense against the power of the surrounding culture and no place to bring converts to "come and see" a distinctively Christian way of life. This was the strategy recommended by Christopher Dawson; this is what Joseph Ratzinger predicted would be the near future of the Church in our time;[29] this is the kind of strategy recommended by Alisdair MacIntyre at the end of his study *After Virtue*, Rod Dreher's so-called "Benedict Option" that has aroused such controversy. There is not—and cannot be—one model for what this should look like. But if we are to be successful in evangelizing the present culture—and effectively evangelizing "in" the present culture—we need to be living a hospitable and distinctively Christian way of life that will enable those seeking refuge and life to "come and see."

29. In a radio broadcast in 1969, Joseph Ratzinger spoke about the future of the Church in the following terms: "Let us go a step farther. From the crisis of today the Church of tomorrow will emerge—a Church that has lost much. She will become small and will have to start afresh more or less from the beginning. She will no longer be able to inhabit many of the edifices she built in prosperity. As the number of her adherents diminishes, so it will lose many of her social privileges. In contrast to an earlier age, it will be seen much more as a voluntary society, entered only by free decision. As a small society, it will make much bigger demands on the initiative of her individual members." Cited in Tod Worner, "When Father Joseph Ratzinger Predicted the Future of the Church," *Aleteia*, June 13, 2016, https://aleteia.org/2016/06/13/when-cardinal-joseph-ratzinger-predicted-the-future-of-the-church.

3.4 The Modern Origins of "Culture" and the Task of Evangelization

William B. Stevenson

In a now-famous essay published only a year before his death,[1] Cardinal Avery Dulles, SJ offered a series of brief but revealing reflections on the idea of culture. They merit our attention, not only by reason of the fact that they are the mature fruit of Dulles's own extensive thinking on the matter,[2] but also because they amount to a fair summary of the seemingly endless number and kinds of ecclesiastical pronouncements on the meaning of culture. He first describes the idea of culture in its most general sense:

> In its broadest meaning, this idea embraces everything that human beings do to refashion themselves and the world in which they live. Culture is the realm of reason, freedom, and creativity; it is a carrier of truth, beauty, and goodness. Spiritual in its source and finality, culture takes root in the physical world: it becomes incarnate, so to speak, in visible and palpable symbols, which express and communicate interior attitudes.[3]

But insofar as culture is a distinctly human phenomenon, it is necessarily social in nature:

> [Culture] is used to designate the world in which people share through their insertion into communities. In its full extent, culture includes

1. Cardinal Avery Dulles, "The Evangelization of Culture and the Catholic University," *Journal of Law, Philosophy and Culture* 1, no. 1 (2007): 1–11.

2. For a thoughtful summary account of Dulles's understanding of the relationship between faith and culture, see Patrick W. Carey, "Avery Dulles, SJ: On American Culture," *American Catholic Studies* 122, no. 2 (2011): 95–112.

3. Dulles, "The Evangelization of Culture," 1.

> all the customs and institutions that serve to make life more human. In a more specialized sense, it refers to the exceptional achievements of thought, art, and literature by which people express their loftiest spiritual experiences and insights. Different ethnic and social entities develop their own distinctive cultures, which must be respected both in education and in the ministry of the Church.[4]

The social dimension of culture, moreover, has a historical aspect that expresses itself in the form of tradition. Tradition serves as a kind of collective memory or living self-presence of a culture and is the condition for its development. But the health or goodness of a culture is not coextensive with the robustness of its traditions:

> Every culture carries with it a particular set of traditions, values, and convictions. Different cultures embody the ethnic and historical traits of particular peoples. Not all cultures are equally good; none can claim to be perfect. Because human beings are subject to sin and error, culture can be distorted or perverse. It can glorify evils such as cannibalism, infant sacrifice, and temple prostitution. Rudimentary cultures need to be strengthened and enriched; decadent cultures need to be purified and regenerated; advanced cultures need to be perfected and harnessed to address the needs and problems of particular times and places.[5]

In other words, the criteria by which any culture may correctly be understood transcend the limits of culture as such. In this way Cardinal Dulles indicates the principal way in which a Catholic understanding of culture distinguishes itself from the relativism that dominates contemporary culture-talk, both within the academy and without. More specifically, it is only by the norms of nature, particularly as these are illumined by grace, that we can begin to know the true measure of a culture and to evaluate its worth.

These remarks on the nature of culture will strike the contemporary Catholic ear as being wholly uncontroversial, even unremarkable, reflecting as they do the main lines of Catholic teaching about culture as it is expressed in such prominent documents as *Gaudium et*

4. Dulles, "The Evangelization of Culture," 1–2.
5. Dulles, "The Evangelization of Culture," 2.

spes, *Evangelii nuntiandi*, *Ex corde ecclesiae*, and *Veritatis splendor*—to say nothing of so many lesser ecclesiastical documents and occasional papal addresses. But the very familiarity of this way of speaking is liable to make us insensible to its relative novelty and the sea change in thinking about human things that such speech discloses. To take but one example, culture is said to have something to do with "creativity." Yet until the nineteenth century the verb "to create" only ever had God as its subject, as it belonged to him alone to bring things into being out of nothing by his own knowledge and will. Human beings, on the other hand, by virtue of their createdness, were said to "make" artifacts in imitation of the natural order. The change in our way of speaking about "creation" and "creating" represents far more than a shift in linguistic fashion, for all important changes in language are always traceable to profound changes in thought, and in this case the person most responsible for both is Friedrich Nietzsche. Nietzsche understood that inasmuch as "making" takes nature as its norm, it appeared to limit in advance the possibilities for human greatness.[6] "Creativity," on the other hand, takes the will alone as its determining principle.[7] In this way, the Nietzschean creator is most godlike, as his work is subject to no other criteria than the "authenticity" of his own will. One needn't be a scholar or an artist to see how this difference has worked itself out in the art and music of the last 150 years. The philistine and the honest aesthete alike know and feel the natural superiority of even the simplest diatonic music to the most sophisticated twelve-tone compositions of the Second Viennese School. The thinkers of classical antiquity understood that the beauty of a work of art is always proportionate to the natural order of which it is an imitation, but the fact itself is simply perceptible to any sensitive human being.

6. That is, nature as it was conceived by the thinkers of classical antiquity and their medieval heirs. Contrary to a popular misapprehension, Nietzsche does not dispense with the idea of a normative nature but rather understands it to be identical to the will to power "and nothing else." Cf. *Beyond Good and Evil*, 36 (author's translation).

7. There is no word in ancient Greek for "create." The Septuagint translates the Hebrew בָּרָא of Gen 1:1 with the Greek ἐποίησεν, "he made." Interestingly, the English noun "creativity" does not gain real currency until the 1950s.

Behind and before the emergence of "creativity" is the equally radical and in some ways more consequential appearance of the notion of "culture" as a way of naming and thinking about the distinctively human things, especially what is highest and best in them. Until the eighteenth century *cultura* primarily meant agriculture, the cultivation of the soil and its products. It is true that Cicero, in the *Tusculan Disputations*, speaks of a *cultura animi*, but he means something quite specific by it, namely, the cultivation of the soul by philosophy.[8] The cultivation of which he speaks consists in a humane education that brings to perfection the natural potential of the soul and is rooted in a teleological conception of nature. The modern notion of "culture," on the other hand, was formed in the context of the first comprehensive philosophical critique of the principles and aspirations of Enlightenment rationality and the commercial society to which it gave birth. That critique is found in the work of Jean-Jacques Rousseau, who was "the first modern critic of modernity and one of the truly seminal writers of the entire modern period. With Rousseau, modernity reached its first great crisis."[9] In an essay entitled, "Commerce and Culture," Allan Bloom neatly summarizes the problem to which Rousseau addressed himself:

> Modern science had appeared to have shown that nature is soulless, that the beautiful cosmos, imitated by the fine arts, is a product of groundless imagination. Correspondingly, the modern science of man denied that man is the being naturally directed to virtue and knowledge and asserted instead that, akin to all the other beings, his sole concern is his preservation. Thus nature, the permanent ground of all things, the source of being, provides no support for man's humanity. Rousseau's powerful rhetoric was directed against the practical consequence of this theoretical understanding—commercial society and

8. "Ut ager quamvis fertilis sine cultura fructuosus esse non potest, sic sine doctrina animus. Ita est utraque res sine altera debilis. Cultura autem animi philosophia est: haec extrahit vitia radicitus et praeparat animos ad satus accipiendos eaque mandat iis et, ut ita dicam, serit, quae adulta fructus uberrimos ferant." Marcus Tullius Cicero, *Tusculan Disputations*, 2.5, LCL 141 (Harvard University Press, 1927).

9. Ernest L. Fortin, "Thoughts on Modernity," 145–57 in *Human Rights, Virtue, and the Common Good*, vol. 3 of *Ernest Fortin: Collected Essays*, ed. Brian Benestad (Rowman & Littlefield, 1996), 151.

> its typical atom, the *bourgeois*. Commercial society, politics stripped of imaginary goals, is dedicated to the unabashed pursuit of well-being. Its very success is vouchsafed by purifying itself of the constraints of patriotism, liberality, nobility, and other grand traits, in favor of self-interest and utility. It is in response to the economic man that the cultural movement came into being, either as a corrective to liberal society or as a radical rejection of its mercenary morals and its philistinism.[10]

Modernity is coeval with a new science of nature, which is purged of formal and final causality. The natural world is no longer a cosmos—a beautifully ordered whole—in which man is naturally at home. It consists solely of matter in motion through space, coldly indifferent to the properly human.[11] Indeed, in the state of nature human life is "solitary, poor, nasty, brutish, and short," and thus the dominating passion of human beings, and the source of their sociability, is the "fear of violent death."[12] Beginning with Francis Bacon and René Descartes, an independent and metaphysically neutral science would thenceforth be dedicated to the "relief of man's estate."[13] The investigation into and the contemplation of the natural order, once sought as an end desirable for its own sake, must be subordinated to a *technē* that promises to make men "masters and possessors of nature"[14] and serve as the foundation for a universal human community.

Rousseau was the first to expose the deficiencies in this account of nature and man's place within it. He rejected the key premise of the Enlightenment, namely that the advancement of science would necessarily lead to the improvement of society and the moral progress of human beings: "Our souls have been corrupted in proportion to

10. Allan Bloom, "Commerce and Culture," 277–94 in *Giants and Dwarves: Essays 1960–1990* (Simon and Schuster, 1990), 278.

11. It is useful to consider the difference between Plato's *Timaeus*, which contains the first-ever mathematical model of the cosmos, and which invites the reader to wonder about the connection between the cosmic and the political orders, with the Pascal of the *Pensées*, who says pusillanimously, "The eternal silence of these infinite spaces terrifies me."

12. Thomas Hobbes, *Leviathan*, XIII.

13. Francis Bacon, *The Advancement of Learning*, Book I, v, 11.

14. René Descartes, *Discourse on Method*, Part 6.

the advancement of our sciences and arts toward perfection."[15] What he saw more clearly than any of his contemporaries was that the foundational principles of modern science and the view of man that underlay them gave rise to a social world in which nearly all human relationships are utilitarian or instrumental:

> One no longer dares to appear as he is; and in this perpetual constraint, the men who form this herd called society, placed in the same circumstances, will all do the same things unless stronger motives deter them. Therefore one will never know well those with whom he deals. . . . No more sincere friendships; no more real esteem; no more well-based confidence. Suspicions, offenses, fears, coldness, reserve, hate, betrayal will hide constantly under that uniform and false veil of politeness, under that much vaunted urbanity which we owe to the enlightenment of our century.[16]

The intellectual progress of early modernity had led to the corruption of morals and the destruction of civic virtue which alone ensures and safeguards all human prospering. What we might nowadays call the "rootedness" of premodern civic life had been replaced by commerce—that is, by human relationships built on the mutual recognition of enlightened self-interest. Yet despite the fact that he is often called "the father of Romanticism," Rousseau did not long for a return to the earlier teleological view of nature:

> For, although he assailed the *philosophes* on what were largely classical grounds, he himself did not push for a return to premodern thought or take seriously the possibility of such a return. In the final analysis, his love of freedom proved stronger than his concern for virtue. The position upon which he settled was, in effect, even more modern than those of his predecessors and did more than any of them to enshrine what had become, by that time a well-established and increasingly powerful tradition.[17]

15. Jean-Jacques Rousseau, *Discourse on the Arts and Sciences* (*First Discourse*), in *The First and Second Discourses*, ed. Roger Masters, trans. Roger D. Masters and Judith R. Masters (St. Martin's Press, 1964), 39.

16. Rousseau, *Discourse on the Arts and Sciences*, 38.

17. Fortin, "Thoughts on Modernity," 152.

As Richard Velkley puts it, "The essence of the effort of Rousseau and later 'culture' is to reconcile modern, metaphysically emancipated science with the attainment of wholeness, which effort gives birth to various speculative theories . . . of freedom's self-realization."[18] In other words, Rousseau's "declaration of war"[19] on the Enlightenment in fact deepened the problem of modernity inasmuch as it took for granted the opposition between nature and civilization—an opposition wholly alien to classical and premodern philosophy. For him, the ineradicable tension between nature and politics is the source both of man's incompleteness as well as his greatness. In the end, Rousseau never seriously questioned the science of nature that provided the speculative foundations for the very movement of which he was a sworn enemy. It would be left to the greatest of Rousseau's German heirs to develop an explicit notion of "culture" on the foundations first laid by him. Immanuel Kant is the first philosopher to use the word in its modern sense.

> According to Kant, Rousseau in his later works, *Emile*, *Social Contract*, and *Nouvelle Héloïse*, proposed a possible unity that harmonized the low natural demands with the high responsibilities of morality and art. This unity he called "culture." His three *Critiques* were an attempt to systematize "culture." The first finds limits to nature as revealed by science, a realm of moved matter where all causation is mechanical. The second establishes the possibility of a realm of freedom in which will and hence responsibility are conceivable. And the third founds an entirely new realm, the aesthetic, where imagination can have free play and man's longings for beauty and purposiveness can have substance. Taken together the *Critiques* provide the philosophic grounds of "culture," and takes account of all the possibilities of the soul in its richness and its depth. The announcement of a new clarity about the true articulation of the human potential promised fulfillments of a level previously unattained.[20]

The results of Kant's project were spectacular and enduring. In fact, most of the talk, academic and popular, of "postmodernity"

18. Richard Velkley, *Being after Rousseau* (University of Chicago Press, 2002), 4.
19. Fortin, "Thoughts on Modernity," 151.
20. Bloom, "Commerce and Culture," 278.

obscures the fact that we continue to inhabit much of the world created and bequeathed to us by Kant, and nowhere is this truer than in the realm of "culture."

Whereas Rousseau was content with the apparent contradiction between his acceptance of the new science of nature and his condemnation of the human insipidness which was its consequence,[21] Kant sought a through line that gave both the world of modern science and the realm of human freedom and excellence their full weight. As Pierre Hassner puts it,

> Kant's enterprise might be said to have as its point of departure the tension between science and morality, between modern physics most systematically developed by Newton and the moral conscience most purely expressed by Rousseau—between the universal determinism implied by the former and the freedom of will implied by the latter. Kant seeks to resolve the problem by radicalizing it. He seeks to preserve the two terms not by reconciling them but by giving their tension and their coexistence a theoretical basis, namely, the articulation of the opposition between nature and freedom—between the world of phenomena and the world of noumena . . . the world of phenomena is what science can know; the world of noumena is the realm opened up by morality.[22]

Again, Kant takes for granted the modern view that human beings are by nature selfish, dominated by the will to self-preservation, utterly unconcerned with virtue. But it is precisely the selfishness of man that nature exploits to bring about a recognizably human good. For example, though the human condition in the state of nature is a *bellum omnium contra omnes*,[23] yet the natural selfishness which is the

21. "It will be difficult, I feel, to adapt what I have to say to the tribunal before which I appear. How can one dare blame the sciences before one of Europe's most learned Societies, praise ignorance in a famous Academy, and reconcile contempt for study with respect for the truly learned: I have seen these contradictions, and they have not rebuffed me." Rousseau, *Discourse on the Arts and Sciences*, 34. It should be noted that Rousseau was unrebuffed because "these contradictions" were in fact tacitly reconciled along philosophical lines which he originally discovered in Plato.

22. Pierre Hassner, "Immanuel Kant," 581–621 in *History of Political Philosophy*, 3rd edition, ed. Leo Strauss and Joseph Cropsey (University of Chicago Press, 1987), 582.

23. Thomas Hobbes, *De cive* (1642), *Praefatio*.

root of universal conflict and disorder is also the motive for countermeasures that lead to peace and order. "The political order which morality requires and which in turn is to pave the way to morality or facilitate its task is not only morally neutral but is achieved by immoral means, or would at the least be impossible without the passions and vices."[24] To borrow an image from one of John Locke's early disciples, public benefit naturally arises from private vices.[25]

For Kant the root of society is "the unsocial sociability of men, that is, the propensity of men to enter into a society, which propensity is, however, linked to a constant mutual resistance which threatens to dissolve this society."[26] Hassner notes that "the decisive element in the formula is asociality: Concord is merely the desire of men; discord is the prescript of nature, imposed in order to strain and thus develop the human being."[27] In Kant's view the city is somehow "natural," but in a way that differs in every respect from what Aristotle teaches in the *Politics*:

> People often say the members of a republican state would require to be angels, because men, with their self-seeking propensities, are not fit for a constitution of so sublime a form. But now nature comes to the aid of the universal, reason-derived will which, much as we honour it, is in practice powerless. And this she does, by means of these very self-seeking propensities, so that it only depends—and so much lies within the power of man—on a good organisation of the state for their forces to be so pitted against one another, that the one may check the destructive activity of the other or neutralise its effect. And hence, from the standpoint of reason, the result will be the same as if both forces did not exist, and each individual is compelled to be, if not a morally good man, yet at least a good citizen. The problem of the formation of the state, hard as it may sound, is not insoluble, even for a race of devils, granted that they have intelligence.[28]

24. Hassner, "Immanuel Kant," 600.

25. Bernard Mandeville, *The Fable of the Bees; or, Private Vices, Publick Benefits* (1714).

26. Immanuel Kant, "Idea for a Universal History with Cosmopolitan Intent," Fourth Principle, in *Basic Writings of Kant*, ed. Allen W. Wood (Random House, 2001), 122.

27. Hassner, "Immanuel Kant," 602.

28. Immanuel Kant, *Perpetual Peace*, trans. M. Campbell Smith (George Allen & Unwin Ltd, 1903), First Supplement.

In other words, as Fr. Ernest Fortin has put it,

> The one thing needful is not moral virtue, which it is not the business of government to promote, but the right kind of laws, by which Kant means laws that will grant to everyone as much freedom as is compatible with everyone else's freedom. Differently stated, the good city does not need good citizens. In theory, it can be made up entirely of "devils," as long as they are intelligent. Never before had the realms of ethics and politics been so sharply set apart.[29]

Like Rousseau, Kant wished to restore something like the nobility of classical antiquity, but without the teleological understanding of the soul that provided its foundations. It is in this gap that culture emerges: "Only when the true ends of society have nothing to do with the sublime does 'culture' become necessary to cover over the void."[30]

The appearance of "culture," then, is part of a larger philosophical response to a novel political situation, itself the product of a philosophical revolution. It represents an attempt to overcome the modern opposition between nature and civilization. Such an opposition stands in the starkest contrast with the thought of, say, Aristotle and Aquinas, for whom political life was not only natural, but the architectonic good without which the procurement of every other human good was impossible. In this connection, Allan Bloom (himself a great translator of both Plato and Rousseau) reminds of a fact that sheds a helpful light on contemporary culture-talk:

> It is most revealing that there is no Greek word that can even remotely translate "culture," and Greece is perhaps the peak example of what is said to be "culture." Pericles, in the fullest statement about Athens which we possess, attributes Athens' greatness—the peak of the peak—to the Athenian regime, to a political order to which men were committed body and soul. Alluding to the surpassing beauties which constitute Athenian "culture" for us, he says only that "we are lovers of beauty with economy, lovers of wisdom without softness." All the statues and spectacles are for him merely the epiphenomena of the core, love of country.[31]

29. Fortin, "Thoughts on Modernity," 152.
30. Bloom, "Commerce and Culture," 280.
31. Bloom, "Commerce and Culture," 280.

Once the naturalness of political life is denied, along with the salutary passions and virtues that support it, "culture" becomes the last refuge of the higher aspirations of the soul. In the end, the creation of this semi-autonomous aesthetic realm came at the cost of severing the beautiful from the good and the true.

It is important to state here that all talk of culture in our own day necessarily proceeds in large part on the ground first marked out by Rousseau and Kant. This presents certain difficulties for the Church, particularly when she wishes to speak on the "evangelization of culture," an expression, not incidentally, that is first found in Paul VI's 1975 apostolic exhortation *Evangelii nuntiandi*.[32] At the heart of these difficulties is the effort to harmonize a modern nonteleological understanding of nature with a premodern teleological account of the whole. As a result, "culture" is used in a dizzying number of ways, so as to function as a cypher for any number of human goods. Whereas "culture" means something quite definite in Kant, it has become an idea which is mostly suggestive—in linguistic terms, a word with many connotations but lacking a determinate denotation.[33]

32. "All this could be expressed in the following words: what matters is to evangelize man's culture and cultures (not in a purely decorative way, as it were, by applying a thin veneer, but in a vital way, in depth and right to their very roots), in the wide and rich sense which these terms have in *Gaudium et Spes*, always taking the person as one's starting point and always coming back to the relationships of people among themselves and with God.

"The Gospel, and therefore evangelization, are certainly not identical with culture, and they are independent in regard to all cultures. Nevertheless, the kingdom which the Gospel proclaims is lived by men who are profoundly linked to a culture, and the building up of the kingdom cannot avoid borrowing the elements of human culture or cultures. Though independent of cultures, the Gospel and evangelization are not necessarily incompatible with them; rather they are capable of permeating them all without becoming subject to any one of them.

"The split between the Gospel and culture is without a doubt the drama of our time, just as it was of other times. Therefore every effort must be made to ensure a full evangelization of culture, or more correctly of cultures. They have to be regenerated by an encounter with the Gospel. But this encounter will not take place if the Gospel is not proclaimed." Paul VI, *Evangelii nuntiandi* (December 8, 1975) (United States Catholic Conference, 1976), §20.

33. What is to be made, for example, of the statement in the International Theological Commission's otherwise excellent document, *Faith and Inculturation* (1988), that

Whether or to what extent a nonteleological conception of human things may be brought into happy accord with a classical view of nature is a problem that lies well beyond the scope of this essay. That it *is* a problem has long been acknowledged by a wide range of philosophical authors over the last hundred years or so. Theologians, for their part, seem unaware of, or uninterested in the issue, perhaps because of its more properly philosophical character. Be that as it may, for the thoughtful Catholic the problem is a live question that carries with it the happy responsibility of reading ecclesial teaching with as much docility as thoughtful circumspection.

Given the relatively modest scale of this essay, rather than attempting a comprehensive survey of ecclesiastical statements about culture, it seems best to review a single document that most thoroughly examines the essential nature of culture and its implications for evangelization. In this respect, it would be difficult to find a more suitable piece than the 1993 address to the Doctrinal Commissions of Asia by then-Cardinal Joseph Ratzinger, which he titled "Christ, Faith, and the Challenge of Cultures."[34] While Cardinal Ratzinger's reflections reveal his deep understanding of the philosophical roots of "culture," they are particularly striking for the way in which they regard the human phenomenon of culture in the light of both the *philosophia perennis* of metaphysical realism and the supernatural revelation of God's Word.

Cardinal Ratzinger's guiding concern is how the Church is to understand the Great Commission in view of the challenges presented by the modern notion of culture or, more problematically, "cultures." For, "the challenge of cultures," as he puts it, is that it has given rise to doubts about the universality of the Christian faith, despite the fact that from the first, the followers of Jesus Christ "saw in the faith a good which did not belong to them alone, but one to which all had a claim." The intention of his address is

among the more "urgent duties" of Christians is the "defense of the right of all to a culture"? Pp. 1–21 in International Theological Commission, *Texts and Documents*, vol. 2, *1986–2007*, ed. Michael Sharkey and Thomas Weinandy (Ignatius Press, 2009), §3.

34. Cardinal Joseph Ratzinger, "Christ, Faith, and the Challenge of Cultures" (March 3, 1993), https://www.vatican.va/roman_curia/congregations/cfaith/incontri/rc_con_cfaith_19930303_hong-kong-ratzinger_en.html.

> to consider the right and capacity of Christian faith to communicate itself to other cultures, to assimilate them and to impart itself to them. Basically, this would include all questions concerning the foundation of Christian existence: Why believe anyway? Is there truth for man, truth which is accessible and belongs to everyone, or are we destined, through various symbols, ever just to catch a glimpse of a mystery which is never really unveiled to us? Is speaking about the truth of faith a presumption or duty? Even these questions cannot be confronted head-on and discussed in their entire magnitude. We have only to keep them in the back of our minds as the setting for our discussion of faith and culture.

These questions are to form the background of Ratzinger's address because in the present context they express variously the problem posed by the modern concept of culture.[35] Thus, he says the first questions must be: "What is culture? How does it stand in relation to religion and in what way can it be in contact with religious forms which were originally foreign to it?" The remainder of this essay is an attempt to summarize his answers.[36]

Ratzinger emphasizes the fact that the idea of culture as a domain independent from, or in opposition to, religion originates in modern Europe. The idea in fact involves a falsification of the historical record, for "in all known historical cultures, religion is the essential element of culture, indeed it is its determining core. It is religion which determines the structure of values and thereby forms its inner logic." Historically, culture is inextricably bound to the cult which is its origin and "determining core." Yet, if this were the only, or even the most important, thing to be said about culture, there would result

35. In addition to the notion of culture first formulated by Kant, there is the further development of Johann Gottfried Herder, who regards culture as the expression of the unique *Volksgeist* of a people or nation. "Two primary meanings of culture emerge from this period: culture as the folk-spirit having a unique identity, and culture as cultivation of inwardness or free individuality" (Velkley, *Being after Rousseau*, 13). The first meaning (i.e., Herder's) predominates in Ratzinger's address.

36. While the whole address is filled with the kind of deep insight and wisdom so characteristic of Ratzinger's/Benedict's *oeuvre*, for reasons of space this essay will treat only of the first section, "Culture—Inculturation—the Meeting of Cultures."

an even greater difficulty than the idea of its belonging essentially to the Kantian (and secular) realm of the aesthetic:

> For it is difficult to see how a culture, living and breathing the religion with which it is interwoven, can be transplanted into another religion without both of them going to ruin. If you remove from a culture its own religion which begets it, then you rob it of its heart. Should you implant in it a new heart, the Christian heart, it seems inescapable that the organism which is not ordered to it will reject the foreign body.

If culture is simply the flowering forth of the religious *cultus* that is its source, then each culture could only retain its identity and integrity within an absolute horizon that relativizes all cultures. This is the speculative conundrum that has led to doubt about the universality of the Christian faith. If this portrayal of culture is true, then it is hard to see how the "operation" described by Ratzinger could ever succeed. It is here that he finds a through line:

> The operation can only have sense if Christian faith and the other religion, together with the culture which lives from it, do not stand in utter difference to each other. It only makes sense if they are interiorly open to one another, or to put it differently, if they naturally tend to draw near and unite. Inculturation therefore presupposes the potential universality of each culture. It presumes that in all cultures the same human nature is at work.

On this account, the heart of all culture is the "universal human disposition toward the truth," that is, the unrestricted desire to know that is the distinguishing characteristic of human nature. Thus, "the sign of a high culture is its openness, its capacity to give and receive, its power to develop, to allow itself to be purified and become more conformed to the truth and to man."

It is important to notice that culture is rooted in human nature and the merits of this or that culture must be judged according to nature's norms. But before the implications of this fact can be more fully drawn, Ratzinger attempts a kind of definition. "We might say that culture is the historically developed common form of expression of the insights and values which characterize the life of a community." He highlights several elements of this definition.

First, "culture has to do with knowledge and values," or, we might rather say, with the true and the good: "It is an attempt to understand the world and man's existence in the world, but it is not an attempt of a purely theoretical kind. Rather it is ordered to the fundamental interests of human existence." The quest for right knowledge about man and his standing in the world necessarily involves the question about "the right formation of the human community," or what for classical political philosophy is the question of the best regime. But insofar as this question concerns the architectonic good, it "always contains the prior and actually foundational question of God . . . indeed, it gets to the root of the great cultures to say that they interpret the world so as to order it to the divine."

Second, because culture in this "classical sense" means an opening to the divine, it may be described as a kind of social subject

> that conserves and develops insights which exceed the capacity of the individual, insights which can be termed pre-rational and super-rational. In so doing, cultures appeal to the wisdom of the "ancients," who stood nearer to the gods; they appeal to primordial traditions which have the character of revelation, that is to say, they do not stem from men's probing and deliberating but from an original contact with the ground of all things. In other words, cultures appeal to a communication from the divine.[37]

Consequently, a culture will be in crisis to the extent that it is "no longer able to bring this super-rational heritage into a convincing connection to new, critical knowledge."[38]

Third, because his definition includes the idea of history, culture, in Ratzinger's sense, "develops through its encounter with new reality and the arrival of new insights." The varying degrees of openness of a culture, and therefore its health or decline, are bound up with

37. One thinks in this connection with the opening line of Plato's *Laws* (whose first word is θεός): "Tell me, strangers, is it a god or some human being who is supposed to be the author of your laws?" (author's translation). The first word in a Platonic dialogue is often a reference to its central concern.

38. We might say, *mutatis mutandis*, that the current crisis of liberalism is due in no small measure to grave doubts, on the part of believers and nonbelievers alike, about whether men are indeed "endowed by their Creator with certain unalienable rights."

its temporality. Even if one grants the distinction between "cosmic/static" and "historical" cultures,[39] nevertheless, "even the cosmically directed cultures point to death and rebirth, to being human as the way. As Christians we would say they contain within them an adventistic dynamic."[40] In this way, a culture is analogous to a living organism which holds itself in being by taking into itself—metabolizing—what it is not. In other words, "appropriation" is precisely what cultures do.[41]

The foregoing effort to clarify the meaning of culture provides a way of thinking about how "cultures can meet and intermingle," and thereby to understand how the transformation of a culture by the Gospel "need not be in the least a question of alienation or violation." Indeed, he says, "a successful transformation is explained by the potential universality of all cultures made concrete in a given culture's assimilation of the other and its own internal transformation . . . only appearing to die, the culture actually rises, coming fully into its own for the first time." Because of this, Ratzinger says we should not speak of inculturation at all:

> For inculturation presumes that a faith stripped of culture is transplanted into a religiously indifferent culture whereby two subjects, formerly unknown to each other, meet, and fuse. But such a notion is first of all artificial and unrealistic, for with the exception of modern technological civilization, there is no such thing as faith devoid of culture or culture devoid of faith. It is above all difficult to envision how

39. The paradigm of this distinction may be found in the contrast between Egypt and Israel.

40. On this distinction, see Theodor Haecker, *Vergil: Vater des Abendlandes* (Jakob Hegner, 1931). Ratzinger comments on the fact that Haecker placed particular emphasis on the concept of the adventistic in pre-Christian paganism.

41. There is a great (and deeply satisfying) irony in the contemporary complaint of Hindu nationalists that Western practitioners of yoga are guilty of "cultural appropriation." In fact, the fitness-oriented *asana* practice that has come to define yoga today originated, not in the *Yoga Sutras* of Patanjali, but as the result of a fascination amongst educated nineteenth-century Indians with European bodybuilding and, later, American gymnastics. Cf. Mark Singleton, *Yoga Body: The Origins of Modern Posture Practice* (Oxford University Press, 2010). The actual "appropriation" of European culture by nineteenth-century Indians is a mark of colonial India's vitality, while the parochialism of modern Hindu nationalism is a sign of its decadence.

> two organisms, foreign to each other, should all of a sudden become a viable whole in a transplantation which stunts both of them. Only if all cultures are potentially universal and open to each other can inter-culturality lead to flourishing new forms.

It is important to read this in light of orthodox Catholic ecclesiology. For inasmuch as the Church is a visible social organism, it is itself a culture.[42] Yet, as the Mystical Body of the Incarnate Word, it is not merely potentially, but actually universal. Of course, it does possess a potency to purify, elevate, and perfect the cultures which it encounters, yet it does so without change to its essential nature, which is always and everywhere whole and entire.[43] This means that the Church does not stand as one culture among others "such that one would have to choose whether to belong to this people as a cultural community or another":

> At this point, what is special and proper to a culture becomes evident. The cultural subject "People of God" differs from the classical cultures which are defined by tribe, people, or the boundaries of a common region insofar as the People of God exists in different cultures which for their part, even as far as the Christian is concerned, do not cease to be the first and unmediated culture. Even as a Christian, one remains a Frenchman, a German, an American, and Indian, etc.

Ratzinger gives us a specifically ecclesial and evangelical application of the more general truth that *gratia non tollit naturam, sed perficit.*

It is now possible to draw from Cardinal Ratzinger's remarks some concluding inferences that bear directly upon the question that underlies this essay. That question may be restated in this way: Given the fact that modern idea of "culture" is *by nature* nonteleological, is it possible to speak of it in a manner consistent with a properly

42. The idea that individual human cultures allocate a cultural body to faith which, in itself, lacks a cultural "body" is, according to Ratzinger, a form of Manichaeanism: "Simply stated, insofar as faith tells man who he is and how he should begin being human, faith creates culture."

43. The universality of the Church is not derived from its geographical extension, for catholicity is an *essential* note of the Church. The Church was already wholly catholic at Pentecost, even though it was confined geographically to Jerusalem and its environs.

Catholic, teleological conception of nature and the human things?[44] Ratzinger demonstrates one way of doing so, and therewith offers a way through the standoff between the relativism created by the absolutizing of individual cultures and the imperative of the Great Commission.

The first thing to be noticed in Cardinal Ratzinger's address is that it does not locate culture in an independent realm of the "aesthetic." He never prescinds from the political, but rather seems to regard it, in classical fashion, as the most comprehensive of the natural human goods. The existence of an aesthetic or artistic culture standing apart from politics, the noblest of the arts, and from the passions that make the political good possible, would reduce his argument to nonsense.[45] Indeed—and this is of crucial importance—what Cardinal Ratzinger calls "culture" is in nearly every respect identical to what the Greeks meant by νόμος, a word signifying both "law," in the ordinary political sense of the word, and "convention," which comprises the ways, tastes, manners, pieties, etc., of a people—the unwritten norms of a society. The unwritten νομοί are in many respects what today we mean by "culture," but it is important to see that for the Greeks these do not exist in proud independence from the laws of a city or nation. They are, on the contrary, largely determined by them, for the greatness of law lies in its educative power, as both Plato and Aristotle taught with particular clarity and depth. On this point it is hard to see how Cardinal Ratzinger differs in any significant way from either of these thinkers.

Secondly, when he speaks of the "potential universality" of a culture, he grounds the idea in a common human, i.e., rational, nature. To put it in classical terms, there is no necessary or strict separation between νόμος and λόγος, as one sometimes finds in the thought of the fifth- and fourth-century Sophists. In fact, for Ratzinger the νομοί are nobler or baser to the extent they are grounded in and oriented to the λόγος. The nobler, healthier, or, to use his term, more "open"

44. The question, stated on page 242, still stands. What follows is not an attempt to decide conclusively whether or to what extent the harmonization of two discordant views is finally successful.

45. Tellingly, in this address on culture he never once speaks of "creativity."

the culture, the more it may be disposed to the Gospel by a kind of connaturality.[46] This is a wholly Catholic conception of culture, for it affirms both the naturalness of politics and nature's openness to the initiatives of grace. The Gospel has the unique power of creating its own culture even as it purifies and perfects the cultures it evangelizes because its νόμος *is* the λόγος.

Lastly, and most remarkably, Cardinal Ratzinger's treatment of culture and the meaning of cultures exemplifies the very principle he is expounding. For in speaking of culture in the ways just outlined he rejects the artificial opposition of nature and civilization which Kant, under the influence of Rousseau, sought to overcome by formulating the concept of culture to begin with. Yet he does so, not by dispensing with the idea of culture altogether, but by endowing it with a meaning congruent with philosophical realism and Catholic doctrine. Just as *persona* or *hypostasis* came to have wholly unprecedented meanings when pressed into the service of illuminating the mysteries of the Godhead while remaining recognizably themselves, so Cardinal Ratzinger and, to a large extent, Cardinal Dulles, have baptized "culture" in ways that enable the Church to think through the evangelistic difficulties for which that now-ubiquitous idea is finally responsible.

46. Yes, he is aware of the problem of sin: "To be sure, we must acknowledge that this optimistic diagnosis is not the whole story. The potential universality of cultures again and again comes up against almost insurmountable obstacles when we try to translate it into practical universality, for it is not only a question of the dynamic force of what we share in common . . . there is also a negative factor in human existence, an alienation, which hinders knowledge and cuts men off at least partially from the truth and thereby from one another."

Contributors

Catholic Contributing Authors

DR. MARY HEALY, PHD is Professor of Scripture at Sacred Heart Major Seminary in Detroit. She is a general editor of the Catholic Commentary on Sacred Scripture and author of three of its volumes, *The Gospel of Mark*, *Hebrews*, and *Genesis*. She served on the International Pentecostal-Catholic Dialogue and is a member of the Pontifical Biblical Commission and the Dicastery for Divine Worship and the Discipline of the Sacraments.

DR. DANIEL A. KEATING, PHD is Professor of Theology at Sacred Heart Major Seminary in Detroit, where he teaches on Scripture, the Church Fathers, ecumenism, and the New Evangelization. He is the author of *The Appropriation of Divine Life in Cyril of Alexandria* (2004), *Deification and Grace* (2007), *First and Second Peter, Jude* (2011), co-author of *James, First, Second and Third John* (2017), *Ezekiel* (2024), and *The Nicene Creed: A Scriptural, Historical, and Theological Introduction* (2024).

DR. MICHAEL SIRILLA, PHD is Professor of Theology at the Franciscan University of Steubenville in Ohio. He teaches dogmatic, systematic, and moral theology on the undergraduate and graduate levels. He is the author of *The Ideal Bishop: Aquinas's Commentaries on the Pastoral Epistles* (Catholic University of America Press, 2017). In addition to contributing multiple essays for scholarly books, his articles have been published in *The Thomist*, *Anthropotes*, *Fellowship of Catholic Scholars Quarterly*, and *Biblica et Patristica Thoruniensia*.

DR. WILLIAM B. STEVENSON, PHD is Associate Professor of Dogmatic Theology at the Saint Paul Seminary School of Divinity at the University of St. Thomas in St. Paul, Minnesota. He has published articles on philosophy and theology in *The Thomist*, *New Blackfriars*, *Moreana*, and *Logos: A Journal of Catholic Thought and Culture*.

DR. CHRISTIAN D. WASHBURN, PHD is Professor of Dogmatic Theology at Saint Paul Seminary School of Divinity. His articles have been published in journals such as *The Thomist*, *Annales Historiae Conciliorum*, and *Nova et Vetera*. He recently published a translation of Saint Robert Bellarmine's two catechisms (2023 and 2025). He was appointed by the Vatican to the International Lutheran-Roman Catholic Commission on Unity. He was also appointed by the United States Conference of Catholic Bishops to the National Catholic-Reformed Dialogue, the National Catholic-Evangelical Dialogue, and the National Catholic-Lutheran Dialogue.

Evangelical Contributing Authors

DR. GREGG ALLISON, PHD is Professor of Theology at Southern Baptist Seminary, Louisville, Kentucky. Dr. Allison is the author of over ten books, served as a missionary in Italy and Switzerland, and is the Secretary of the Evangelical Theology Society. He is also a book review editor for the *Journal of the Evangelical Theological Society*.

DR. DEAN ERICKSON, PHD is the Chair of the Department of Biblical, Theological, and Ministerial Studies at Crown College in Saint Bonifacius, Minnesota. He holds a PhD from Luther Seminary, St. Paul, Minnesota and is an ordained minister in the Christian and Missionary Alliance Church.

DR. STEVEN HOSKINS, PHD is Professor of Church History at Trevecca Nazarene University, Nashville, Tennessee, where he has served on the faculty for the past thirty years. He is an ordained minister in the Church of the Nazarene and the founding President of the Wesleyan Historical Society.

DR. DENNIS JOWERS, PHD is Professor of Theology and Apologetics at Faith Evangelical College and Seminary in Tacoma, Washington. Dr. Jowers is a member of the Korean American Presbyterian Church and the author of four books and many articles on apologetics and faith.

DR. ALEX MAYFIELD, PHD is Assistant Professor of History at Asbury University in Wilmore, Kentucky. Dr. Mayfield is the Managing Editor of *Pneuma: The Journal of the Society for Pentecostal Studies* and serves as the Principal Investigator of *The China Historical Christian Database* and the Digital Architect and Technical Advisor of *The Dictionary of African Christian Biography*, both hosted at Boston University.

DR. WILLIAM URY, PHD is the National Ambassador for Holiness, The Salvation Army. Dr. Ury holds a PhD from Drew University, taught Systematic and Historical Theology for Wesley Biblical Seminary, Jackson, Mississippi, and is a Fellow at the John and Charles Wesley Center for Christian Thought and Apologetics.

Dialogue Participants

April 2023 Dialogue

EVANGELICAL PARTICIPANTS

Dr. Bruce Cromwell, The Free Methodist Church, Chair
Dr. Dennis W. Jowers, Korean-American Presbyterian Church, Co-Chair
Dr. Steven Hoskins, Church of the Nazarene, Secretary of the Dialogue
Dr. Dean Erickson, Christian and Missionary Alliance

CATHOLIC PARTICIPANTS

Bishop David Kagan, Chair
Fr. Walter Kedjierski, Co-Chair
Dr. David P. Fleischacker
Dr. Mary Healy
Dr. Daniel A. Keating
Dr. Michael G. Sirilla
Dr. William B. Stevenson
Dr. Christian D. Washburn

November 2023 Dialogue

EVANGELICAL PARTICIPANTS

Dr. Bruce Cromwell, The Free Methodist Church, Chair
Dr. Dennis W. Jowers, Korean-American Presbyterian Church, Co-Chair
Dr. Steven Hoskins, Church of the Nazarene, Secretary of the Dialogue

Dr. Gregg Allison, Southern Baptist Convention
Dr. Dean Erickson, Christian and Missionary Alliance
Rev. Duane Fischer, The Wesleyan Church
Dr. Alex Mayfield, International Pentecostal Holiness Church

CATHOLIC PARTICIPANTS

Bishop Alfred Schlert, Chair
Fr. Russ McDougall, Co-Chair
Dr. Mary Healy
Dr. Daniel A. Keating
Dr. Michael G. Sirilla
Dr. William B. Stevenson
Dr. Christian D. Washburn

November 2024 Dialogue Participants

EVANGELICAL PARTICIPANTS

Dr. Bruce Cromwell, The Free Methodist Church, Chair
Dr. Dennis W. Jowers, Korean-American Presbyterian Church, Co-Chair
Dr. Steven Hoskins, Church of the Nazarene, Secretary of the Dialogue
Dr. Gregg Allison, Southern Baptist Convention
Dr. Dean Erickson, Christian and Missionary Alliance
Dr. Bill Ury, Salvation Army

CATHOLIC PARTICIPANTS

Bishop Alfred Schlert, Chair
Fr. Russ McDougall, Co-Chair
Dr. Daniel A. Keating
Dr. Michael G. Sirilla
Dr. William B. Stevenson
Dr. Christian D. Washburn

Index of Scripture References

Index of Subjects